THE TURKISH TRANSFORMATION

THE
TURKISH TRANSFORMATION

A Study in Social and Religious Development

BY

HENRY ELISHA ALLEN, Ph.D.

DEPARTMENT OF RELIGION
LAFAYETTE COLLEGE

GREENWOOD PRESS, PUBLISHERS
NEW YORK

To

MY MOTHER AND FATHER

ACKNOWLEDGMENTS

The author wishes to express his sincere appreciation to the large number of individuals and organizations, American and European—which includes Turks—whose help has made this book possible. Particularly is he indebted to his wife, whose companionship and hard work throughout the study have been of inestimable value.

Acknowledgment is also made to the following publishers, authors and institutions for their courtesy in permitting the quotation of copyrighted material:

George Allen and Unwin, Ltd.—L. Levonian, *Moslem Mentality*.

D. Appleton-Century Co.—Halidé Edib, *Memoirs of Halidé Edib*.

A. & C. Black, Ltd.—Halil Halid, *The Diary of a Turk*.

Doubleday, Doran & Co.—Henry Morgenthau, *Ambassador Morgenthau's Story*.

Harcourt, Brace & Co.—Hans Kohn, *A History of Nationalism in the East*.

Hutchinson & Co., Ltd.—Djemal Pasha, *Memories of a Turkish Statesman*.

Methuen & Co., Ltd.—George Young, *Constantinople*.

The Oxford University Press—Sir Mohammed Iqbal, *The Reconstruction of Religious Thought in Islam;* the Royal Institute of International Affairs, *Survey of International Affairs*, ed. by A. J. Toynbee.

The Review of Religions.

The Royal Central Asian Society, *Journal.*

Charles Scribner's Sons—A. Servier, *Islam and the Psychology of the Musulman;* A. J. Toynbee and K. P. Kirkwood, *Turkey.*

University of London Press—Count L. Ostrorog, *The Angora Reform.*

TABLE OF CONTENTS

THE TURKISH TRANSFORMATION

I

PREFATORY NOTE

Religious systems and religious thought in every section of the world are today undergoing severe periods of questioning and readjustment as men learn to control the forces of nature and lose their sense of dependence upon supernatural agencies. Islam is no exception. The last thirty-five years have seen it struck unmercifully by all the forces of scientific thought, machinery, and nationalism which developed in Christendom over a period of centuries and to which Christianity had to learn to adapt itself.

To make an exhaustive study of Islam's reaction to the influences which have been loosed upon it in recent years would require several volumes and many years of careful study and travel. For Islam cannot be treated as a unit. It includes within its ranks diversified sects with beliefs as varied as those of Christendom, which includes nominally the worshipers of Abyssinia and Concord, Massachusetts. In Islam may be found the puritanical Wahhabis of the Arabian Desert and the broad-minded followers of Baha'ullah. Their reactions to innovations will be as different as are those of Abyssinians and Unitarians. "Islam" is a term which must be used very guardedly when generalizing.

Of the composite mass which goes to make up Islam, no unit today presents a more interesting or amazing picture than Turkey in its eager rush to escape from the toils of ignorance and superstition which have for so many years retarded her progress. When one remembers the centuries of bitterness and bloodshed, of jealousy and misunderstanding,

1

in the relations of Islam and Christianity, and when one realizes that Turkey, long the champion of Moslem orthodoxy and most redoubtable aggressor for the faith of Mohammed, is now making herself into a Western nation according to the very pattern of those European states which for so many years she despised and feared, he cannot deny that he is witnessing one of history's most significant phenomena. Here before our very eyes is occurring a transition of civilizations, the abandonment of practices which originated in Arabia, based upon union of religion and politics, the adoption of patterns which developed in Europe, based upon separation of religion and politics. Far-reaching consequences of this transition may be observed in government, law, education, and social structure. Religion, which but little more than a half-century ago was the test of citizenship, has been severed from the constitution. Islam, shorn of its prestige, strives to adapt itself to a new situation wherein it must confine itself to the domain of conscience.

These alterations which are going on in Anatolia are important not only as the Westernization of an oriental people but also as providing a crucial experiment for all Islam. If the religion of Mohammed is able to function effectively in a state which does not regard the Koran as the ultimate source of all legislation, then certainly we shall have visible evidence of its adaptability and enduring vitality. Other Moslem countries, however much they may berate the Turks as backsliders, must needs observe developments carefully. Sir Mohammed Iqbal points out that "among the Muslim nations of to-day, Turkey alone has shaken off its dogmatic slumber, and attained to self-consciousness." He goes on to say that "most Muslim countries to-day are mechanically repeating old values, whereas the Turk is on the way to creating new values." [1]

[1] *The Reconstruction of Religious Thought in Islam*, p. 154.

This book has been written to aid in the understanding of those new values. It is not propaganda. The writer has not been associated with any foreign institution in Turkey, and has been motivated solely by an interest awakened ten years ago during studies in the religious sciences at the University of Chicago. In collecting data for the work two trips were made to Turkey to study the situation at first hand. It is, of course, inevitable in writing a descriptive interpretation of a transition process not yet completed that the chronicle of change stop somewhere, and accurate information on the "latest" reforms is not always easy to obtain when one is not on the spot. Thus, for example, the book must go to press with some proper names as they were before the 1935 law requiring surnames was put into effect. Nevertheless, it is hoped that this volume may prove of more than transitory value for those who seek a fuller comprehension of the roots and the characteristic patterns of this extraordinary social and religious transformation.

II

HISTORICAL INTRODUCTION

Seven hundred years ago there appeared in Anatolia a small tribe of warrior nomads from the little-known fastnesses of Central Asia. Led by the dashing hero, Ertoghrul, the little band set out, as had their relatives the Magyars, to win themselves land of their own. Not many years after their arrival these newcomers from Turkestan became converted to the faith of Islam, and from their leader of the time, whose name, Osman, was the same as that of Mohammed's companion, the third caliph, the tribe became known as Ottomans. Into the disrupted society of the time, suffering as it was from the decadence and corruption of Byzantine rule and frequent strife with the Seljuks, the entrance of the Ottoman Turks, flushed with successful conquest and inspired with religious enthusiasm by their recent conversion, proved a unifying, if somewhat fearsome, force. In 1453, after two centuries of warfare and assimilation of the motley and diversified peoples who dwelt in the Balkan Peninsula and Western Asia Minor, the Ottomans captured Constantinople and became undisputed masters of the regions which had once been the nucleus of the proud Eastern Roman Empire. Conquest followed on conquest in brilliant succession until the climax was reached in the sixteenth century, when Selim's crushing campaigns and Suleiman's genius in palace and on battlefield exalted the Turkish Empire to a position of unparalleled magnificence, making Constantinople the fear of Christendom and the hope of Islam.

4

Despite the splendid organization set up by Suleiman for the organization and administration of his vast Empire, the seventeenth century found the Turkish conquerors softening under the insidious influence of Byzantium's luxurious vices, and for nearly two hundred years, with hardly a flicker of the old-time dashing brilliance to relieve the sordid gloom of a decaying dynasty, the light of the Empire waned to a point where genuine alarm was felt. The vitality which had been the heritage of the Turks from their wild nomadic life was gone. Creativity had been crushed by the weight of Islamic formalism, whose deadening hand had left religion a matter of ritual and precedent, had left law with its sanctions so deeply grounded in the past that progress was well-nigh impossible, and had made literature something Arabicized, foreign to the Turkish spirit, and limited to an exclusive, highly educated circle.

Things had reached such a pass by the latter part of the eighteenth century that even a well-intentioned sultan like Selim III, who saw that radical reforms must be instituted if Turkey's prestige was to be saved from further humiliation at the hands of her newly Westernized foes, the Russians, was unable to realize his wishes. Control of the Empire was wholly in the hands of fanatical religious leaders and the famous band of fierce and uncontrollable warriors known as the Janissaries (Yeni Cheri). These professional troops, originally recruited in large part from children of the Christian subject populations, had become so powerful as to control even the commercial life of the capital and so reactionary as to balk at any attempt to lessen their influence or modernize their methods of fighting.

It took the accession of a bold and strong-handed reformer like Mahmud II to the throne to achieve the formation of a modernized regular army which should be able to destroy the Janissaries and clear the way for the introduction of progressive innovations. After some years of failure, Mahmud, who came to the throne in 1808, succeeded in 1826 in utterly destroying the power of the Janissaries, his new regular army massacring hundreds of them through the use of modern artillery. Mahmud, who is often called the *ghiaour* sultan because of his tendency to adopt the customs and habits of the Western *ghiaours,* and his successor, Abdul-Medjid, who followed him in 1839, brought about numerous social and administrative reforms, including adoption of the fez as the national headdress to replace the turban, which symbolized conservatism, and a proclamation of new rights and equal treatment for the subject Christian populations. The Christian rights were proclaimed twice, once in 1839 and again in 1856, and were in large part attributable to the influence of Britain's great ambassador, Stratford Canning. The difficulty with the new reforms, however, lay in the fact that they were too much imposed from above and met with little co-operation from the people of Turkey. The reactionary demonstrations which greeted each attempt at Westernization at this early period showed how far the country was from being ready to throw off its oriental ways. Nevertheless the Western sympathies of the ruling house and the aristocracy of the period immediately following the 1856 proclamation, a time known as the "Tanzimat period," opened the way for a new interest in European, particularly French, literature and history, and sowed the seeds of liberal ideas which eventually produced the Young Turk movement and such reformers as Midhat Pasha of 1876, and the constitutional movement of 1908.

Reaction seemed to be again in the saddle in the reign of Abdul-Aziz. Nevertheless a group of progressive Young Turks were able to remove him and in 1876 to bring to the throne Abdul-Hamid II with promises of a constitutional rule and a new liberal régime. Despite the hopes of Midhat Pasha, who was grand vizier, Abdul-Hamid proved to be just the opposite kind of ruler from what the progressive leaders had expected and hoped for. Before many months he had suspended the Constitution and sent the Young Turk leaders into exile. Midhat was eventually done to death in his place of exile at Taif, near Mecca.

The explanation of Abdul-Hamid's behavior seems to lie in his fear of the growing influence and rapacity of the European Powers who were at that time engaged in a deadly rivalry of imperialist expansion, in which possession of Constantinople loomed as one of the greatest prizes for Russia, Britain, or whoever else was fortunate enough to fall heir to it when the long-desired demise of the Turkish Empire should take place. Abdul-Hamid, apparently motivated by fear of these Western gluttons, who were watching and seizing every opportunity to increase their influence in Turkey and be ready to bite off delectable portions, and by disgust for everything which had any connection with the hated infidels, adopted a new and desperate policy. Instead of seeking to strengthen his Empire by the adoption of new efficient methods, he turned his back definitely on the West and sought to build bulwarks against his European foes by facing toward the Orient and calling on the Moslems of the world to unite in fighting off every approach of the hated infidel. Importation of Western literature and novelties was prohibited, and a pan-Islamic movement was commenced with emphasis being placed on Abdul-Hamid's position as caliph of Islam—a position which was asserted to give him spiritual authority over all Moslems in the world. He also proved himself adroit in playing European rivalries off against each other and thus preventing any one nation from attaining too much influence in Turkish affairs.

With such a reversion to old practices, and with all liberally inclined Turks either in exile or closely watched by palace spies, the era of progress in Turkey seemed definitely to have come to an end. But there was an Achilles' heel in the form of Turkey's young army officers. Abdul-Hamid had not been so fanatical as to restore medieval methods in his army; on the contrary, he had had his military leaders trained in Western methods and had sometimes sent them to Europe for instruction in order that he might be able to fight his adversaries with their own weapons. But these young officers who had had a glimpse of the progress and ways of the West were determined that their own country should no longer remain so far behind. Secret committees were formed, of which the one at Salonika was the most important and effective, and contact was made with the exiles in Paris and elsewhere, who furnished intellectual and moral support. In 1908 the Constitutional Revolution forced Abdul-Hamid to restore the Constitution he had set aside in 1876 and to declare a new era of liberality. An attempted reactionary counter-revolution a few months later, led by fanatical Moslems and suspected to be sponsored by Abdul-Hamid's money, was promptly subdued by the army of the Young Turks and resulted only in proving the strength and popularity of the reform and in bringing about the deposition of Abdul-Hamid in favor of Mohammed V, who was a mere puppet in the hands of the new leaders.

Division of counsels among the new leaders and consequent disputes brought constitutional rule to a virtual conclusion once again in the years immediately following 1909, and power became concentrated in the hands of three strong men—Enver, Talaat, and Djemal Pashas. Seizure of outlying Turkish possessions in North Africa and Eastern Europe by enemy Powers, and the revolt and attacks of the Balkan Christian states seeking to throw off Turkish rule, caused the government to undertake a policy of Ottomanization, or Turkification, of the Empire in an effort to solidify it and prevent further defections. The chief consequence of this policy was further to embitter the remaining subject peoples whose national individualities had begun to develop, thereby bringing about further restiveness, which the World War succeeded in precipitating into successful revolutions and attainment of independence, particularly by the Arab states. Although the men in control of Turkey's destinies at this time were sympathetic toward modernization, they found their hands too full with international matters and the task of maintaining their own hold on the controls of government to achieve anything notable in the social and internal reformation of the country. Though they were not sympathetic at heart to the Moslem religion, they were not above using it where it might serve their own ends, as in the case of the proclamation of *Djihad*, or Holy War, against the Allied Powers in 1915. No strong measures were taken to curb the influence of superstitious and unenlightened religion over the people, though secular schools were opened here and there, and a legal code was drawn up which modified the extent of Koranic influence over the Turkish society. The close of the Young Turk or Unionist régime with Turkey's collapse after the World War found Turkey physically shattered, but socially little changed from the days of unquestioned religious supremacy under Abdul-Hamid.

After this brief historical summary which may serve as a background, we must proceed to our study of the movements and forces which in the last seventeen years have achieved infinitely more in the transformation of Turkey from a medieval, superstition-ridden country to a twentieth-century, westward-looking nation than the efforts of well-meaning reformers of the past hundred years.

III

PENETRATION OF THE WEST

Many writers of Christendom who hold a narrow view of Islam would agree with André Servier when he writes, "The Musulman, bound by his religion, cannot accept Western progress. The two civilizations are too different, too much opposed, ever to admit mutual interpenetration." [1] While some justification might have been found for such a statement by an observation of remote Moslem countries where primitive conditions keep alive the traditional and Koranic practices, Turkey would certainly furnish contradictory evidence, for that country, long redoubtable as a pillar of Moslem strength, is today in process of taking over many features from the West and adapting them to her own peculiar needs. Servier might insist that Turkey in so doing is no longer a part of Islamic civilization, yet Turkey has not, up to the present time, renounced Islam in favor of the alternative Christendom, and gives little evidence of an inclination to do so. It cannot be denied that penetration has taken place, at least from the civilization of the West into that of Islamic Turkey. Whether the process will later become mutual, with Turkey furnishing features to the West in return, remains to be seen. The historic contribution of Islamic Spain to Christian Europe of five hundred years ago indicates that Western Christendom has not *ipso facto* a monopoly on perfection.

[1] *Islam and the Psychology of the Musulman* (Moss-Blundell trans.), p. 252.

It will be our task in the pages which follow to examine the channels which have served to import Western notions into Turkey and the Western sources from which the notions came. After that, we may in greater detail note the effects of the Western injection on Turkish life and thought.

From the events of the nineteenth and early twentieth centuries presented in the historical introduction it is evident that interplay was taking place between Turkey and the European nations. Outside forces were pressing in on Turkey with stringent diplomatic demands and strange new practices. Here the process seems to be that of an external insistent force battering with its novelties against a surly resisting mass. But the process had another aspect, for individuals within that resisting mass were at the same time reaching out to master for themselves certain features of the alien civilization, thereby acting as conductors in the transmission of Western ways into the Turkish East. Both factors, the battering and the conducting, are important.

Of the factors which introduced Western civilization with a battering force into Turkey, it is necessary to mention only a few of the most important ones, appreciating at the same time the fact that Turkey's geographical position as the westernmost country of Asia and in a direct line between Europe and important regions of the Near and Middle East made it inevitable that she should be struck early and severely by Europe's eastward-looking imperialist expansion. Aggressive warfare carried on by nations that sought to appropriate Turkish territory caused Turkey to realize the superiority of Western war materials and methods. Diplomatic interference in the governmental affairs of the Sublime Porte kept officials unpleasantly conscious of the assertive West. Industrialists and engineers exploiting railways and natural resources impressed the Turks with the value of Western technical skill. The system of capitulations, which permitted foreigners to live in the country subject to their own laws, kept constantly under Turkey's eyes communities with customs differing from those of the Turks, daily reminders of the West. Partly as a result of the capitulations, missionary and philanthropic enterprises were given considerable freedom in the country. Manned by devoted and able workers, foreign schools, hospitals, and publication societies were powerful agencies in carrying Western ideas into Turkey.

The mere impact of Western forces, however powerful, might not have succeeded in breaking through the protective crust of Turko-Moslem civilization. Had the ranks of Turkish society held firm, a stubborn and fanatical resistance might have been offered to Western aggression; the traditional organization might have maintained itself as an intact but constantly dwindling body, ever more compressed by the pressure of outside forces. But this was not to be, for certain individuals and groups within the Turkish society showed receptive inclinations toward Western ways, and the way was opened, as through cracks in the crust, for the infiltration of new notions. The members of Turkish society who thus opened the way to Westernization were of two main types: (1) those who stayed in the country and became acquainted with new customs by reading European books and observing Westerners in their midst, and (2) those who left home to visit Europe voluntarily as travelers or involuntarily as exiles.

Included in the first type were military and naval officers, who, as we have already noticed,[2] had been trained along strictly Western lines since the time of Sultan Mahmud II; members of the governing class in Istanbul who came in contact with the European diplomatic life in the capital; and certain of the well-to-do intelligentsia. These three groups,

[2] See Historical Introduction.

corresponding to the aristocracy of other countries, filled the rôle described by E. A. Ross as that of the "social stand-pipe" [3] for the diffusion of advanced ideas in Turkey. The novels of Pierre Loti vividly depict the Europeanization of high Turkish society with its developing interest in French literature and European governesses. The memoirs of Halidé Edib, with their picture of Turkish intellectual life in the early years of the present century, reveal Turkey's leaders as well versed in European literature, particularly French.

Turks who made up the second type of conductors of Western ideas, individuals who lived in Europe for consider-able periods, may again be divided into two classes: (1) those who were out of favor with the government and had to live outside the Empire for their own safety, and (2) those who sallied forth voluntarily, some supported by their own re-sources, others, chiefly after the Revolution of 1908, sent under government auspices. The exile group, though living abroad in cities like Paris, London, and Geneva, were able by publications and secret organizations considerably to agitate Turkish society. The work of the Turkish committee in Paris was notable for its assistance to the young Turks of Salonika who were responsible for the overthrow of Abdul-Hamid's tyranny in 1908. Similar fermentation had been caused by the writers of the 1860's, whose publications, sup-pressed in Istanbul, were smuggled into the country from London. After 1908, when more enlightened forces were directing Turkey's destiny, the government hastened the adoption of Western ideas by sending students to study in Europe. An outstanding result of this foreign study was achieved in 1924, when Turks who had carried on legal studies in Switzerland, particularly Mahmud Essad, Kemal's youthful minister of justice, reshaped the Swiss Civil Code

[3] Cf. *Social Psychology*, p. 160.

for use in Turkey, supplanting the semioriental code previously in force.[4]

In describing the interaction between Turkey and the forces of alien civilization, no distinction has hitherto been made between the various divisions of Western civilization. Our attention has been centered on the channels through which Western influences were brought to play upon the Turko-Islamic society; little has been said as yet regarding the quality and strength of these influences themselves. Obviously there are wide differences between the national cultures which go to make up Western civilization, and it is only natural that some of them should have acted more strongly than others in corrosion or stimulation of the Turko-Islamic mass.

It is a simple matter for the traveler in Turkey to observe that French civilization has been of paramount importance in the Western impact upon the Turks. A large majority of the educated classes speak French as a second language, and the outsider may with reasonable facility travel through the country on the main arteries of transportation if he has a speaking knowledge of French. Certain newspapers of Istanbul publish reduced editions in French, notably *Akcham*, *Le milliett*, and *La république*. Examples could easily be multiplied. The explanation of this predominating French influence is traceable in Turkey's political, educational, and literary history. In politics one may point out the alliance of A.D. 1535 between Suleiman the Magnificent and Francis I against the Hapsburgs. The treaty consecrating this alliance paved the way for French predominance in commercial relations. Another event which served to increase the strength of French influence was Napoleon's invasion of Egypt and the eastern end of the Mediterranean in the years 1798–

4 See below, p. 79.

1801.[5] This occurrence made a great impression upon the imagination of the Turks. Educationally one need but call attention to the large number of schools carried on in the Empire by French Catholic missionaries [6] and the great lycée of Istanbul, the Galata Serai, founded early in the latter half of the nineteenth century. This institution, controlled by the Turkish government but manned by French teachers, some of whom received their salaries from the French government, has played a leading rôle in Turkey's intellectual Westernization. As a result, too, of French influence in the country, Jesuit missionaries were able to restrain the influx of American and other Protestant literature, particularly vernacular translations of the Bible, by urging the Turks to strict censorship after the authorities had shown a tendency toward freedom of the press. In these repressive tactics the French were aided by Russia, acting in defense of the Orthodox communities for which she posed as protector.[7]

Turkish literature in its style and philosophy presents a leading example of the effect of French influence. The man chiefly responsible for bringing French influences to bear on his own literature was Shinasi Effendi, who in 1859 published a Turkish translation of French poets after a period of study in France. In 1860 he founded the first unofficial Turkish newspaper with the title, *Interpreter of Circumstances*. It was the movement begun by Shinasi which served to change Turkish literary style from something formal and artificial to one which was popular and readily understandable by any reader. Halidé Edib, discussing the new tendency in her *Memoirs*, writes:

Modern Europe was furnishing a new-current of thought and was creating a new spirit in Turkish writing. The European culture

[5] Cf. Toynbee and Kirkwood, *Turkey*, p. 128.
[6] Cf. Ross *et al.*, *The Near East and American Philanthropy*, p. 163.
[7] Cf. Barton, *Daybreak in Turkey*, p. 201.

which was most influential in Turkey was decidedly French, the *poètes philosophes*. The nightingale and the eternal rose, the spring, and nature themes of literature were giving way to a wider range of subjects and a new way of looking at man and nature, while the inward change in all directions was leading writers to search for directer and clearer expression in language. Translations from the French were introducing models of French art and thought.[8]

As Shinasi Effendi published in his paper articles on modern Europe and scientific discovery, Turks were given an idea of what was occurring in the West and a standard with which to compare in a critical spirit their own customs. Shinasi's lead was followed enthusiastically by a younger generation of writers, Namik Kemal, Abdul Hak Hamid, and Zia Pasha, whose poems, dramas, stories, and satires are regarded today as classics of the new Turkish literature. Thus it came about, as H. Kohn has written, that "in Turkey as elsewhere modern nationalist sentiment arose simultaneously with the creation of a new, unaffected, and natural literary language akin to the vernacular." [9] It is then apparent what a debt Turkey owes to French culture for the rescue of her own literary individuality.

Another group of writers, including Halid Zia, Jenab Shehabbeddine, and Hussein Jahid, carried the spirit on into the twentieth century. Halidé Edib writes:

The school was fiercely attacked by the old writers for its imitation of European culture, and had been equally criticized for lack of personality. But it must have succeeded in transmitting a new message and a new life in its work, for the new age looked up to it as the intellectual representative of the day.[10]

[8] *Memoirs of Halidé Edib*, pp. 243 f.
[9] *A History of Nationalism in the East*, p. 225.
[10] *Op. cit.*, p. 262.

No less is modern Turkish drama indebted to France for much of its present tone. When the Guedik Pasha Theater was founded in 1867 by Namik Kemal, Noury, and Ahmed Midhat Beys, French plays were translated or adapted for use on its stage. Says Halidé Edib:

Ahmed Vefik Pasha's adaptation of Molière and the translations of Dumas *fils* furnished the Turkish stage with comedy and romantic drama to begin with; and Kemal himself wrote some patriotic plays which became very popular. This Europeanized school continues to the present time and has formed the origin and the basis of the Turkish stage of to-day.[11]

In the Istanbul newspaper, *Le milliett,* a dramatic critic has discussed the intimacy of the relations existing between the French and Turkish theaters. He writes:

There are few peoples who are acquainted so closely with the French stage as the Turks. When, after the Reform, the artistic movement soared anew, it was pre-eminently the French stage which attracted it. From the time of Vefik Pasha to Rechad Noury Bey, that is to say over a long period of 80 years, it is the theatrical art of France which has been the inspiration of our stage, although the English and German theater had no less merit. But a natural penchant has always pushed us toward the French. One must search for the cause of this inclination in the points of resemblance which exist in the habits of the two nations.

Even until yesterday, in speaking of the Occident, our people understood France, and for them Europe is Paris. During the years it has been from there that we have had our new painters and new economists come. France has represented in our eyes the country from which our art should imbibe its ultimate progress, so that those who went there from here thoroughly perfected themselves.

Stamboul has many times admired Sarah Bernhardt and has appreciated that artist with as much enjoyment as if her tongue were our own. Even actors and actresses who have never set foot in Turkey are well known to us by name.

[11] *Ibid.,* p. 123.

As for those who come to visit us, in no other country are they so enjoyed and applauded as in ours, so much do their sentiments, their passions and their joys resemble ours. In a word, the French and we have traits of moral resemblance as though we grew from the same stem.[12]

The significance of this influence of France over the Turkish theater may further be emphasized when one considers the importance of the stage in the Turkish program of modernization today. Speaking at a banquet in Ankara, a former minister of public instruction, Djemal Husni, is quoted as follows:

The different events which have happened in the recent history of young nations show us the important rôle played by the theatre in the formation and realization of national ideals and in the changes desired in the social life.

This moving form of literature and art, which displays itself in real life and living action, has since ancient times been a powerful element to lead men in the path of certain ideas. The theatrical representation, which gathers together before the stage individuals working in different occupations, is the most important means of extending the ideas and collective sentiments of nations, which constitute their strongest ties. The theatre fixes the state of societies at different epochs, and encourages and strengthens especially the courses which men are wished to follow and the forms which are sought to be given to the future.[13]

France has also made important contributions to recent Turkish philosophical and political thought, as one would be led to expect from the popularity of French writings. Auguste Comte had many admirers among the leaders of Turkish thought in the nineteenth century, and his influence appears strongly in the writings of Ahmed Riza, a leader of the young Turk movement long resident in Paris. In the speeches of Republican leaders today references to the French Revolution are often met with. To list all the French writers and

12 *Le milliett,* April 6, 1930.
13 *Ibid.,* April 13, 1930.

philosophers who are read and admired in Turkey would be a longer task than we can here enter upon. Mention ought specially to be made, however, of Emile Durkheim, whose sociological ideas find a following among members of the university circle.

Although France has contributed bountifully to the Westernization of Turkey, this does not mean that other Western cultures have not had their share in the a. eration of Turkey's society. Of the others, the Anglo-Saxon represented by Britain and America requires special mention. It is still impossible accurately to measure the relative sizes of cultural contributions in a cross-fertilization process of such complexity. For the present, therefore, it must suffice to point out the presence of certain transferred ideas and practices, leaving it to a later time to determine how deeply ingrained they prove to be in the Turkish matrix.

In the middle of the nineteenth century British ideas of political reform had achieved influence among the Turkish ruling class. This was in part due to the presence and personal prestige of the great British ambassador, Stratford Canning, to whom history gives credit for certain reforms, particularly those making for extension of equal rights to Christian subject populations of Turkey. Another source of Anglo-Saxon influence was a young Turkish diplomat who had been a member of the first Ottoman diplomatic mission to the Court of St. James early in the nineteenth century, one Raif Mahmud Effendi. According to Halil Halid:

This young secretary remained in England many years and devoted himself to the study of scientific subjects, more especially geography, and afterwards published a translation of an English atlas into Turkish, the first ever prepared in that language. While in England, Mahmud Effendi used to send reports to the Sublime Porte on the forms of administration and system of government in this country [England]. When Sultan

Mahmud II came to the throne, the young diplomatist was invited to Constantinople to assist in the work of reorganising the administration; but during one of the fanatical outbursts which preceded the extermination of the Janissary corps, this first modernised statesman of Turkey was accused of being a man of "broad views," and killed in a *mêlée*. The seeds of reform sown by him, however, were not entirely destroyed; and it was chiefly owing to the work of the later Turkish statesmen, who followed his example in reorganising the system of their country, that the famous *Hatti-Sherif*, or first reform charter of the Ottoman empire, was drawn up, and, with the assistance of the friendly Powers, proclaimed.[14]

Thus through these two individuals, one representing the "battering," the other the "conducting" method, British political notions were introduced into Turkey. Despite periods of disfavor when British diplomacy was eclipsed by that of other Powers, Anglo-Saxon political ideals were radiated from the palatial embassy with its commanding position on the hill of Pera, and continued to be influential as long as Istanbul was capital of the Empire. After the war, because Istanbul was too exposed to British sea-power, the Kemalists made their decision to shift the national capital inland to Ankara.

One further channel for the introduction of British notions into Turkey was the Turkish navy, whose personnel was trained according to British regimen, corresponding to the German of the army.

Although British policy in the East is still distrusted, Anglo-Saxon culture in a broader sense seems to be attaining a position of considerable importance in the new civilization which Turkey is building. Whether this means a corresponding diminution in French influence is difficult to ascertain, for statements on the subject are very frequently biased by the individual preference of the one who speaks.

[14] *The Diary of a Turk*, pp. 192 f.

Turks who themselves are acquainted with any one of the national cultures of Europe are likely to overemphasize the value and position of that culture in their own national life. Another difficulty arises on account of the great politeness of the Turk, who in talking to the foreigner still clings to the habit of saying what he thinks will please his listener. Thus a Frenchman will be told that France is closest to the Turkish heart, while an American may be told that Turkey seeks only to emulate the United States. Another element which makes judgment difficult is a geographical one, for outside cultural influence will vary from city to city according to the presence and strength of the various foreign enterprises scattered throughout the country. In Istanbul, French may be strongest because of the vogue of French schools there. In Izmir, the presence of a colony of English business folk may put Anglo-Saxon culture in the ascendance. In Adana, Teutonic culture has made a strong impression because there happen to be German factories there.

One finds today, however, unmistakable signs that Anglo-Saxon and Teutonic culture, which Turks feel to be quite similar, are making greater and greater contributions to contemporary Turkey. The new strength is partly attributable to the removal of Arabic and Persian studies from school curriculums, leaving a vacuum which was bound to be filled by English and German studies.[15] And there are indications that French popularity is giving way to other Western cultures. At the Lycée Stamboul, a government school for boys in Istanbul, I was told by a member of the faculty that the teaching of French had been discontinued by order from Ankara. He did not venture to explain the reason for the order. At Galata Serai, stronghold of French

[15] French had already won a position alongside the classical Arabic and Persian in most Turkish higher schools.

culture in Istanbul, I was told of an attempt to secure an American athletic director. From a high Turkish official in the Galata Serai, as well as from the distinguished writer, editor, and philosopher, Dr. Abdullah Djevdet Bey, whose command of French was such that he published original poems in that tongue, I heard arguments advanced in favor of English as Turkey's second language. One reason is that a study of English opens the door to the literature and culture of two great peoples, the British and the American, whereas any other language opens to only one people's civilization. Dr. Djevdet remarked that he had been influenced in favor of English through talking with a Japanese, who reported that his nation had profited tremendously as a result of having English as its second language. In Ankara, increasing interest in English was reported to me by a number of people, including three language teachers. At the language school maintained by the Society for Public Instruction the director reported an enrolment of thirty-five for English, thirty for German, and twenty for French. In the Ministry of Public Instruction, three of the high officials speak English and follow closely, through magazines and journals, American educational developments. A member of the Grand National Assembly, high in the nation's educational circles, whose only language besides his own is French, expressed himself to me as follows:

Anglo-Saxon and Teutonic cultures seem to us the most masculine in the West and best able to furnish Turkey strength in her rebuilding. French influence has long existed in Stamboul but has been of little practical value to Turkey. French culture and French literature tend to be dainty and refined. The language is pretty, and French influence can lend a people considerable charm and a polished veneer. But Turkey realizes now that it is not grace that she needs. It is science and work. As she studies the Anglo-Saxon and Teutonic cultures, she notices that they emphasize scientific method and energetic endeavor. It is strength and creative activity, rather than appreciation of the beautiful, that Turkey needs now and expects to learn from America, England, and Germany.

Important in making America's contribution to Turkey's Westernization have been colleges, schools, playgrounds, hospitals, and publication enterprises sponsored by American philanthropic and missionary organizations. The educational institutions will be discussed in more detail in a later chapter, but it should be brought out here that all such institutions have two characters in Turkish eyes. On the one hand they are means for Turkey to learn about and absorb that knowledge of Western civilization which she is so eager to acquire. On the other hand they are dangerous and insidious representatives of a spirit alien to Turkey's national self-interest. In the former guise they are most welcome to Turkey, but when they act against the national spirit, as Turks feel they do when Christian teaching is given, the institutions are looked upon with bitter hostility. American philanthropy before the war was directed in large measure toward minority Christian populations in Turkey, and while most of the American workers who continue their enterprises under the Republic are honestly seeking to give Turkey their best services, there still exists a suspicion, based on the old prejudice against Christians, that foreign institutions are designed to undermine the national foundations. American teachers, doctors, social workers, and publicists have made and can continue to make great contributions to Turkey's mentality, health, and character, but only as long as they are able to make it clear to Turkey that they are without ulterior motive and willing to play the game according to Turkish specifications.

Anglo-Saxon literature, usually in translation, has had a

rather wide following among educated Turks. Among the
most influential have been the writings of William James,
whose pragmatic philosophy I have heard praised by leading
Turks as expressing the point of view needed by Turkey to-
day. Much interest is displayed in H. G. Wells's *Outline of
History,* points of which have been discussed by Kemal
Ataturk [16] in his six-day speech. The American Bible
Society and the Publication Committee of the American
Board Mission in Turkey have done notable work in making
available to Turks and other Near Easterners translations
not only of the Old and New Testaments, but of other volumes with ethical and religious value, such as Booker T.
Washington's *Up from Slavery,* a biography of Abraham
Lincoln, and certain of Ralph Connor's books. The mission
group also sponsored for a number of years a reading-room
and library in Istanbul, where the best literature was made
available. This room, directed by a Moslem Turk, and making no pretense of religious propagandizing, was closed for
financial reasons in 1933. A notable monthly magazine,
Muhit, published jointly by American missionaries and Moslem Turks, has been able to supply the country with high-
quality periodical reading, much of which is translated from
American magazines.

One might multiply examples of other Anglo-Saxon contributions to Turkey in education, home life, and commercial
activity. Perhaps none has greater potentiality, however, than
the moving picture, for American films, with their portrayal
of American life and customs, seem to dominate the Turkish
market, and are well patronized by an eager and impression-
able public.

---

[16] The name newly adopted by Turkey's president at the beginning
of 1935. Ataturk means Father of the Turks. His name, Mustapha
Kemal, long familiar to Western readers, has officially been abandoned.

The contributions of Teutonic civilization in the process we are describing do not differ greatly from those of Anglo-Saxon except for some which have a militaristic flavor. Germany's imperialistic schemes which began toward the close of the nineteenth century had made Turkish friendship and co-operation an important part of the "Berlin to Bagdad" venture. The friendship bore fruit in a reorganization of the Turkish army along German lines and in concessions for various enterprises, chief of which was the railroad from Istanbul destined for Bagdad. Germany's influence with Turkey's military class both before and during the World War naturally caused many officers who were important in the government to look at the West through German eyes, a fact which was advantageous for the development of Turkish industry, construction, and even agriculture according to German specifications. One of Germany's most important contributions to Turkey is noticeable in medical work. Turkish hospitals are managed along German lines, frequently with German trained nurses in charge, and many of Turkey's leading doctors have taken courses in German medical centers.

A word should be said in regard to other nations which have made smaller but important contributions to the ferment. It is noticeable that Turkey is calling much upon smaller powers such as the Scandinavian countries, Belgium, and Switzerland to help her build railroads, develop industries, and master techniques. This is due, no doubt, to previous unfortunate experiences with the larger nations, whose supposedly private corporations have been mere masks of imperialistic governments. Turkey is calling, too, upon Hungary, for the Magyars are regarded by the Turks as a brother-race, and since the Magyars, once nomadic Turanians like the Turks, have learned the intricacies of Western civilization, it may be assumed that they will make good instructors for the Turks who wish to follow the same path. Hungarians are most numerous apparently in two fields in Turkey: one, that of skilled artisans; the other, that of entertainment and music. It is as yet too soon to judge the effect on Turkey's laboring class of these Magyars, men who have close racial connection with the Turks, and who have mastered the technique to which Turkey aspires. One is led to surmise that these talented brothers from Europe will serve as far better teachers and stimulators to the supposedly clumsy and lethargic Turk than the hated Greeks and Armenians with all their ability ever could have.

Turkey is eying Japan very carefully, as one would naturally expect, noting carefully the way in which Japan is handling her problems which arise from Westernization. The example of Japan's great success in mastering European ways has no doubt been a great encouragement to the reforming leaders of Turkey.

Of Russia little need be said in this connection, though it was probably the sting of defeat by a Westernized Russian army in 1774 that first led Turkey to realize the strength of the West and seriously to consider the need of remodeling her own forces along Western lines. Czarist Russia of the nineteenth and twentieth centuries played the rôle of Turkey's deadly foe too constantly to permit of friendly cultural interchange, though there seems to have been a sympathetic connection between the Russian revolutionary agitators of 1905 and the Young Turks, both of whom were eager to temper the power of their respective extreme autocracies. As for Bolshevist Russia, her contribution of large sums of money to assist the Nationalist movement in its early days undoubtedly insured the success of the movement, though the lines of its eventual reform program were vastly different from what the Bolshevists had hoped for. The influx of vast numbers of refugees, fleeing from the Red armies after the

Revolution, added to Turkey's difficulties, overfilled as she already was with starving populations, and the refugees themselves, partisans of the Russian autocratic element so long hostile to Turkey, were not the sort either to awaken Turkey's friendly sympathy or to be invited to remain as members of Turkish society. Turkey today manifests a wholesome respect for her powerful neighbor on the north, and would do nothing knowingly to offend her. Political relationships are cordial, and there is a disposition to observe Soviet methods in education, art, and planned industrialization. Collectivism, however, seems repugnant to the Turkish mentality, and Marxist teachings are definitely unwelcome in the Kemalist state, as is witnessed by the swift punishment which is meted out to those who spread communist propaganda in the country.

IV

TURKEY'S RESENTMENT AGAINST THE
RELIGIOUS INCUBUS

In the preceding chapter it appeared that Turkey's Islamic civilization was being acted upon in various ways by forces representing strong features of the West. The process of clash and penetration was described, and the individual sources of the Western injections were set forth. The next thing, then, to engage our attention will be the effect of the Western impact upon Turkish society. It has already been pointed out in an earlier chapter how the reactionary Sultan Abdul-Hamid II made an ineffective and panic-stricken attempt to protect his Islamic domain against the alien European aggression of the nineteenth century by rallying Islam to present a united front against the *ghiaours* and to exclude Western ideas and materials. The inevitable failure of this pan-Islamic movement, whose tactics call to mind the defensive methods of the ostrich burying its head in the sand, served to intensify Turkey's distress when she awoke to the inadequacy of her oriental ways in contrast to the skill and technique of the West. The comparison of her antiquated and incrusted culture with the vital and progressive features of Western civilization which had forced their way into the very heart of her society meant a violent criticism of the outworn forms which had resisted evolution and persisted so far beyond their period of usefulness. Attacks were leveled against Islam and those who had made it a stagnant and retarding influence for Turkey.

A large share of the blame and indignant vituperation has been handed to the Moslem theologians and doctors, whose ignorance and laziness, even dishonesty, are said to have changed Islam from a progressive and vital religion to one which emphasizes tradition, form, and superstition. Writers have pointed out that while Europe was busy during the Reformation in loosening the hold of a decadent clergy, the Ulema, Mollahs, and other religious leaders of Islam were hardening Islam into a set of formal practices and closing the gate on any possibility of interpretation which might lead to progressive adaptation. A writer in the *Review of Religions,* discussing the religious situation in Turkey, declares:

Even the slightest divergence from the established church was considered the highest crime; and the faithful wandered in and out of the four water-tight compartments of schools of theology completely dazed by the priest-made dogma that neither would reconcile with the early teachings of Islam nor ring true to the advancing humanity of the present age. The clergy made every effort to circumscribe the view of every Moslim and placed the right of interpretation beyond the reach of even the intelligent seeker after truth.[1]

Another writer points out:

In the first epoch of the Islamic history, both in Bagdad and Spain, there was a great tolerance of free discussion, but afterwards our scholasticism prevented thinking with reason. Since then we have slept, and it is only in these last years that we have begun to awaken.[2]

A Russian Tatar, Mohammed Fatih, was one of the first Moslems of this century to call attention to Islam's

[1] Sirdar'Ikbal Ali Shah, "The Religious Revolt of Turkey," *op. cit.,* XXVII, No. 7 (July, 1928), 23–26; see p. 24.

[2] Djelal Noury, *The Turkish Revolution,* quoted in Levonian, *Moslem Mentality,* p. 69.

great incubus of ignorant religious leaders. Writing in 1904, he said:

> In my humble opinion the precepts of the Koran can easily be brought to conform with culture and civilisation. But unhappily there are no Ulemas living in our day capable of inspiring Islam and reconciling it with civilisation. The Ulemas of to-day occupy themselves with outward forms alone; they do not understand the philosophic spirit of Islam, and cannot therefore apply their religion advantageously in practice. Our ignorant clergy expound Islam according to their own ideas, and instead of benefiting they injure us. You Europeans have strained every nerve and rescued your religion from the guidance of ignorant popes and priests, and have spread the light in your midst. Your faith is in your own hands, your conscience is free, and your minds are enlightened, whilst our religion is still dominated by priests. Until we follow your example and escape by our own efforts from the grip of the mollahs, abandoning empty formalities, our decadence is inevitable.[3]

A scathing denunciation of the corruption, worldliness, and ignorance of the theological teachers and students who posed as leaders of the Moslem religion is contained in a recent novel by Rechad Nuri. The book, entitled *Yeşil Gece* ("Green Night"), and centered around the sacrificial devotion of a young teacher to the cause of his nation and his people, describes the early life of the young man, Shahin Effendi, his earnest enthusiasm upon entering a *medresseh,* or theological school, and the disillusionment he feels after he has seen what sort of knaves they are who are posing as holy men, leaders of the Islamic faith. The same resentfully critical spirit appeared in Turkey's first ambitious moving-picture production, *Ankara Postasi* ("The Ankara Courier"), in which two *hojas* (religious teachers) were portrayed as scoundrels whose drunkenness and attempted rape of the

---

[3] Quoted in H. Kohn, *A History of Nationalism in the East,* p. 115.

heroine led to her death and that of the young hero, her lover and dispatch carrier for the patriotic nationalists.

No less than the religious leaders of the Turks are blamed their rulers, who misused their powers and kept the people in ignorance and poverty instead of helping enlighten them. The unholy alliance of secular despotism and religious obscurantism is frequently and bitterly criticized. Things might have gone better, it is felt, if religious and secular affairs had been kept separate.

Professor Abdulbaki takes this position in one of the books he has written for the religious instruction of children of the Republic:

You understand, don't you, that religious work is one thing, while secular work is another thing. But before, those who handled religious work tried to handle the secular affairs of the world also. The Sultans took the title of Caliph, the replacer of the Prophet, and began to rule as they wished to. And the Hodjas used to say "all right" to whatever the Sultans said, and they were also in the habit of saying to the nation "There is the power of seven prophets in one Sultan. . . ." Such foolish things they said! In short the affairs of the world and the affairs of religion were not separate.

About even the smallest thing, the hodjas were asked, "Is it in harmony with religion or not?" and only after consultation was it done. For instance, as we have studied in history, printing was invented in Europe. They printed their books in the printing houses, and since everybody was able to buy books cheaply, ignorance diminished. On the other hand, in our country printing was introduced very late, because permission had to be asked of the hodjas, for they had to be satisfied, and on account of that we suffered much.

During the time of which we are speaking war and peace were all made by the decisions of the hodjas. There was no one to ask concerning the desire of the nation, nor any one to think about its interests. Once the Sultan had agreed with the head

Hodja and the other hodjas, the most impossible things were
done. . . . Heads flew off, and hearths were extinguished.[4]

The sultans, or padishahs as they are frequently called,
are similarly berated by the author of a book on civics, also
used in the schools:

The Padishahs were ruling in Turkey for many years. These
men would think only of their own amusement and would
consider the nation as a group of slaves.

In Europe there had been founded well-organized states according to new principles. On the other hand, when a movement toward modern ideas started in Turkey, the conservatives,
the fanatical people would step in and say, "This modernization
is un-religious, and it is sinful." With such trifling talk they
would prevent modernization. And already all the laws of the
Government of the Padishah were based on the principles of
religion.

So it was impossible to separate worldly and religious problems. As you know, religion teaches man more about heavenly
things, although it teaches at the same time truth and good-
ness. One must not confound heavenly things with problems of
the world. As if it were not enough to crush the people under
the title of Padishah, the old Padishahs took the title of Caliph
also, in order to give themselves importance in the public eye.
These men who used to live in palaces with all kinds of amuse-
ments and pleasures were supposed to be the representatives of
the Prophet. They never thought that religion is a concept of
the conscience and that nobody has the right to interfere with
people's religious problems. The reason why men have organized
states is not to deal with heavenly problems, but it is only to
assure the living of a comfortable and joyous life in the world.[5]

The resentful attitude against the old régime is well
summed up in the statement of a Turkish small-town official:

We Turks are not really responsible for our backwardness.
We have never been taught how to live; we have only been

[4] *Religious Lessons for the Children of the Republic of Turkey:
Fifth Grade,* chap. IV.

[5] Mitat Sadullah, *Yeni Yurt Bilgisi: Fifth Grade,* pp. 38 f.

taught resignation. The Sultan's officials exploited us; the Caliph's emissaries stupefied us. We lived under the yoke of a government without morality and a religious organization without ideals.[6]

A large number of Turks, upset by the challenge of the West, would probably agree with Djelal Noury when he says, "The fault was not with religion, but with the rulers who have made it an instrument of their despotism through their servants, the clergy."[7]

However much blame and indignation may have been loosed upon the selfishness, despotism, extravagance, inefficiency, and corruption of the rulers and the clergy, there was plenty of criticism to be leveled at the governmental system which permitted the dominance of religious laws and at the quality of the religion which permitted itself to become degenerated.

In an explanatory introduction to the new civil code which Turkey adapted from that of Switzerland in 1924, the minister of justice, Mahmud Essad, laid the blame for Turkey's backwardness directly on the deadening influence of the Islamic laws which for so many years formed the basis of Turkey's government and society. He declares:

States whose laws are based on religion become incapable after a short lapse of time of satisfying the exigencies of the country and the nation. For religions express unchanging precepts. Life goes ahead, needs change rapidly. Religious laws, in the presence of life which constantly progresses, are no more than words void of sense and forms without value. Changelessness is a dogmatic religious necessity. Also the need for religions to be nothing more than a simple affair of the conscience has become one of the principles of modern civilization and one of the characteristic differences between the old civilization and the new.

[6] Quoted in A. Colrat, "Turkey To-Day," *Living Age,* July 15, 1927.
[7] Quoted in Levonian, *op. cit.,* p. 64.

Laws which derive their inspiration from religions fetter the societies in which they are applied to the primitive epochs in which they arose, and they constitute invincible factors which prevent progress. It is indubitable that our laws, which came out of the changeless precepts of religion and which ensured a permanent place to divine elements, have been the most powerful and the most effective factor which, in modern times, has enslaved the destinies of the Turkish nation to the mentalities and institutions of the Middle Ages. . . .

In the march of our evolution one notices that all progressive steps which have been attempted in the interest of the masses have been thwarted by a class of men whose interests were compromised by the projected innovations. These men have always sought to turn people aside from the path of progress in preserving among them, in the name of religion, obscure superstitions and false beliefs. Let us not forget that the Turkish people have resolved to accept without any reservation all the principles of modern civilization. The most striking proof of this appears in the Revolution itself. If in certain quarters the civilization of to-day appears irreconcilable with the needs of Turkish society, that does not indicate an aptitude lacking in the people, but in the superannuated traditions and religious institutions which have hindered their development. . . .

The conservative spirit which aspires to chain society irrevocably to the old customs and irrational empiricism is dangerous and does not make humanity advance an inch. . . .

The purpose of laws is not to maintain old customs or beliefs which have their source in religion, but rather to assure the economic and social unity of the nation.

When religion has sought to rule human societies, it has been the arbitrary instrument of sovereigns, despots, and strong men. In separating the temporal and the spiritual, modern civilization has saved the world from numerous calamities and has given to religion an imperishable throne in the consciences of believers.[8]

Of the attacks which were directed against religion itself as displayed in Turkey, it will be sufficient to quote but one example. This is a poem written some twenty-five years ago by the writer Tewfik Fikret and has had an immense in-

[8] Editions Rizzo, *Code civil turc,* pp. xii–xvi.

fluence on the thought of the Turkish youth. My Turkish friend who rendered a translation of it into English for me declared that he, as well as many other men of his acquaintance, knew it by heart, and was frequently asked to speak it to small gatherings. The poem, he declared, was never formally published until 1927, being passed along from individual to individual. Before quoting the poem it will help to understand it as well as the author if we read what Halidé Edib has to say about Tewfik Fikret. He had a passionate belief in humanity and international understanding.

[He] attacked above all else these two things: tyranny and religion. Being a man *sans peur et sans reproche,* he did not realize the social and individual value of religion, its importance in human morals and culture, its historic necessity to complete the social evolution in the early stages of human society. He saw only how men in general suffered from the tyranny and the narrow rule of the churches, how men rent each other in the name of religion all over the world, and what political use they made of creeds and of their gods. His famous attack on religion called "History" aroused a tremendous storm in religious circles, and he was mercilessly attacked by the clericals, both during his life and after his death. . . . He was as narrow and as merciless as they [the Unionists and the reactionaries] were to those who deviated from his own line in politics and in principles of every kind, and he fought them down as ferociously as did his opponents. The inflexibility and the rocky resistance of the man constituted both his force and his weakness.[9]

The poem, which is entitled *Tarihi Kadim* ("Ancient History"), represents the poet as seeing history in the form of a skeleton, who unfolds the past as a series of bloody, vicious, and tyrannical events, illustrating the rule of might. The sections of the poem which are pertinent to our purpose are quoted with no attempt at versification to correspond with the difficult Turkish.

[9] *Memoirs of Halidé Edib,* p. 264.

Heroism is fundamentally savagery. Treading on cities and destroying armies, killing and untying, breaking, dragging, pounding, burning, devastating pitilessly, wherever you pass, your heroes fill the land with death and pain, and after you there remains no sign of crops, grass, or moss. Homes are obliterated, families suffer, no place remains unshaken.

Every *ojak* [hearth] looks like a gravestone, and roofs fall on the heads of orphans. What sights to arouse the conscience! O Leader! Down with your victories! Each victory is a vision of ruins and resembles a cemetery. O you men who conquered the world, be ashamed of this victory! Down with the old throne of independence—under your reign, people are suffering. Throngs of needy men are caused by you. You are like rooks which eat blood. Every dark place is filled with you. It is enough that you have run rough-shod over opinions, and men can live comfortably without you.

History can protect you because dark nights provide shelter for brigands. Be strangled in the darkness of history! These are the best tidings for the future. Here is true liberty. No fight, no invasion, no attack, no sultanate, no brigandage, no complaint, no despotism, no cruelty. I am myself, and you are yourself, and we need no lord or creature. If we don't need God or creatures, then the pages of the old book will be torn out. Those pages are the graves of opinions. But who can tear out your opinions? Who is going to undertake this great revolution?

VOICE: The Master of the world will do it!

But *He* [God] is the cause of all these fightings.

O heaven, which sometimes hears the sounds of pleasure, sometimes a dry voice, sometimes a painful sighing or sound of comfort, sometimes an "alas," sometimes a prayer, and sometimes quiet, and sometimes rebellious winds, sometimes grievances, sometimes blasphemy, and sometimes trembling, and sometimes tinkling of bells, sometimes you hear the quiet grievances of weakness and sometimes the thanks of cruelty, sometimes laughing, sometimes sobbing, and sometimes crying.

You tell us, O heaven, if these voices are echoed to heaven and if any prayer is accepted. O God of heaven, I have listened to your name from the fathers of religion as being matchless, having power of animating, giving food, and accepting desires, being just, and knowing everything, and being present everywhere. Though your most significant quality is that of being matchless, yet see how many partners you have in this slough. They all have the quality of being matchless. They all have their commands and sovereignty. They all have their suns, moons, and stars; they all have a promised heaven; they all have a world here and one to come; they all have angels in their heaven, but they all look to swallow humanity. From the creatures they all wish submission.

I doubt everything, and I ask everyone, and all tell me that they do not know.

Who knows? Perhaps everything is imaginary, or being deceived is a necessity. Perhaps everything is true, yet I am not aware of my mistake and wish to believe that things which do not exist do exist; but my fault is in doubting. So is it harmful, because to doubt is to run toward the light, and to make truth shine is the right of wisdom. Who knows? Perhaps there is vanity, and perhaps there is heaven. But why should this body become the slave of a thousand pains because it is made by an eternal creator? Why create man from nothing and give him the quality of decadence? Who knows? Perhaps our origin is earth, yet why should we be made of mud whose pores are full of blood and tears? Is it the result of chance? This cannot be the work of a creator. The one who creates does not destroy. O Creator, doubt is your worst enemy. It has dropped from you. This is your own error.

Today stratagems, evil, and deviltry remove you from your throne and blow out the torches in your temples, and break your statues—and you fall with all your powers.

But nothing is heard of this fall. You make no stirrings in your hell. We hear no sounds of pain. But if an atom of a creature is lost, we at least hear a cry. You fall with your heaven and sky, but from nature we hear not a sigh. On the contrary, everywhere is laughing; for only dissimulation and stupidity weep after falsity.

It was inevitable that violent things should happen to Turkey's social and religious structure when its traditional stays were being so shaken by the floods of indignant criticism which broke forth when men awoke to their own helplessness, the heritage of corrupt despotism and ignorant bigotry. Islam's attempt to weather the storm and keep alive

in the midst of radically changed conditions will be the subject of a later chapter, but now we must notice what positive
and constructive steps were taken by a desperate Turkish
society under effective leadership to restore order out of a
despondent and chaotic condition and build a social structure
which would restore Turkey to a stable position in a world
which was being shaped according to the specifications of
Western civilization. The new spirit of impatience with
sentimentality and demand for actuality and material improvement is brought out in a poem by Nazim Hikmet entitled *Eski Anadolu* ("Old Anatolia"). After describing the
poverty, filth, and immorality of peasant life, he writes:

That village which smells like a rotten pickle-pot is not long-
ing for romantic life. That which its soul cries for is two bare
words: steam and electricity. If you are not blind, you will see
that the farmer with earth-colored face and sieve-like breast,
his vermin-filled head scratched with the nails of the Multezim
[tax farmer], wants to die and be buried with his daughter, wife,
and oxen. O messieurs, with your pencils in hand and reins in
your mouth, who sigh like Pierre Loti when looking at the blind,
noseless, and decrepit peasants whose glasslike bellies bubble
like yellow narghiles in their three-horsed carts—we are sick of
listening to your nonsense! Now this truth must be pounded
into our heads: that the peasant needs soil, and the soil needs
machinery!

V

THE RUSH TO WESTERNIZE UNDER KEMAL ATATURK

Turkey's subjection to the impact of the West was, as has been seen, a process which had been going on for more than a century. Yet in the years which had elapsed up to 1918 very little had actually been done to incorporate Western notions into the life of the Turkish mass. Europeans had brought their new techniques into Turkey and a relatively small number of Turkish individuals had taken over Western customs, but either to a degree so slight as to be merely superficial or to a degree so extreme that the individual was severed from the society of his Turkish compatriots. Turkey had begun to sense more and more the strength and vitality of the alien forces and had begun to find fault with certain of her own weaknesses, but, by and large, her Orient-sprung social forms had undergone but slight changes, and whatever innovations had been introduced were more in the nature of modifications of existing forms than radical alterations or substitutions of Western practices in place of the venerable customs of the Orient.

During the World War, however, and particularly in the years which immediately followed it, there came a sudden change. The spark of indignation, which had been sputtering along like a fuse, all at once seemed to touch off the explosive material; Turkish society seemed to hurl off the burden of oriental traditions and to replace it with a miscel-

39

laneous assortment of ideas and customs borrowed from the West.

In the preceding chapter there was presented a picture of Turkish society in a distraught and dissatisfied state, on the verge of undergoing a severe readjustment. The transformation was brought about under the guidance of Mustapha Kemal Pasha (now known as Kemal Ataturk) and his comrades, who established Turkey as an independent nation and set up a constitutional representative government in a new capital.

It would obviously be foolish to assert that the modernization along Western lines which proceeded at high speed with the establishment of the Ankara government was solely the result of one man's or one group's wishes. The case of Afghanistan, where reform programs were attempted and had to be much modified, indicates that the condition of the society to be reformed is fully as important as the leader who sponsors the changes.

In the Turkey over which Kemal Ataturk assumed the leadership there had grown up a dissatisfaction with the Islamic heritage, as we have already seen. Yet even with this restlessness to work on, it is doubtful whether Kemal could have accomplished his Westernization program in such short order without the concurrent action of certain other exceptional circumstances which acted as catalytic agents in speeding up the social reaction. The effect of these circumstances was to agitate still more sharply the Turkish mass, make the Turkish people realize their individuality and unity, and place them in a grateful mood so that they were malleable in the shaping hand of their new leader.

One factor of importance was the series of wars in which Turkey became engaged, in which her Empire broke more and more away from her. Of these, the one which probably embittered the Turks more than any other was the Arab revolt which broke out in the later years of the World War and opened up the Empire to attack from the hostile Allies. Turkey no doubt took as a matter of course the rebellions of subject Christian groups, but it was disillusioning for her to have her co-religionists, different though they were racially, thus betray her. Djemal Pasha, one of Turkey's leaders during the World War, wrote in his memoirs:

> Although I had never believed in the honesty of the Sherif of Mecca, I could never have conceived that in a war, upon which the fate of the Khalifate depended, he would ally himself with the states which desired to thrust the Slav yoke upon the whole Mohammedan world, and, indeed, would go so far as to sow the seeds of discord in the whole country to gratify his personal ambitions.[1]

The fact that Moslem Arabs should thus have turned against them made the Turks more than ever hostile to the Islamic features of their civilization which they associated with Arabia. It also increased the feeling among the Turks that they must face the world virtually alone, standing on their own resources.

With the close of the World War, Turkey was subjected to a series of humiliations by the countries which had been her victorious foes. The Allies, apparently believing that Turkey had come to the end of her rope and had no more strength or spirit left to offer further resistance, proceeded to partition up the country, forcing disgraceful terms on the tottering government of Sultan Vahid-ud-Din with the Treaty of Sèvres and causing the defeated Turkish armies to surrender their arms. Working hand in glove with the various Christian minorities who inhabited Anatolia, the Allies showed their apparent intention of leaving Turkey only a small section of territory in Anatolia. Agents of the British government were working in the country seeking to create

[1] *Memories of a Turkish Statesman*, p. 211.

favorable sentiment toward England and to discourage any
show of resistance on the part of patriotic Turks.

It is possible that Turkey would have suffered her defeat
and not raised a hand to protest against the partitioning of
her homeland had it not been for one act which cut Turkey's
wounded pride to the quick and stirred the nation to a
heroic struggle for independence. This was the occupation of
Izmir by Greek troops in 1919. This invasion of Turkey's
own homelands by the nation's deadliest foe was enough
to restore a heroic spirit of resistance and to unite the people in the accomplishment of a great patriotic endeavor. The
thought of their territories being violated, their homes invaded, and their religion insulted by the hated infidels was
enough to awaken a tremendous burst of hidden energy, and
the upheaval caused a favorable condition for the dissociation and reintegration of Turkish social patterns.

Even with the aggravation of these hostile acts, however,
the traditional government and Islamic customs might have
held on to their positions in Turkish life had it not been for
the apparent collusion of the sultan's government with Turkey's foes, and declarations by both the civil and the religious branches of that government that patriotic defensive
movements were treasonable and contrary to religious law.
This was enough to convince many Turks that there was
something radically wrong with their government and religious organization. One can judge the Turkish feeling from
a statement taken from one of the school civics or *Yurt
Bilgisi* ("Knowledge of the Home") books.

The co-operation of the Caliph with the enemies during the
War of Independence proved very clearly the uselessness of
those authorities. As you know, when the Greek army began to
march into the interior of Anatolia by attacking beautiful
Izmir, all the Turks had sworn not to have their country
trampled by the enemy and had begun arming themselves in

order to drive out the Greeks. The enemy marched, burning the places through which he passed. While the Turkish heroes were struggling to crush the enemy's soldiers, they saw that the real great enemy, who bore the name of Padishah and Caliph, had co-operated with the Greeks. Yes, Vahid-ud-Din, who is the most treacherous king in the world, had gathered a band named "the Army of the Caliphate" in Istanbul and unleashed it upon the heroes who were trying to save the country. However, the brave Turk defeated both enemies, and the treacherous Vahid-ud-Din fled away on an enemy boat. The Turkish nation, which had groaned for hundreds of years under the tyranny of the Padishahs, would not, after seeing this, keep those men at its head. There remained no more place for the Padishahs and their families, who had drawn their weapons against the nation at its most sorrowful hour, and who had thought only of their own ease in the midst of the most horrible calamities. The Grand National Assembly, which realized this, abolished the reign of the Sultans, and proclaimed the Turkish Republic; it saved our nation from the tyranny of the treacherous Padishahs. Children, there is no doubt that we began to live from that day on, in an atmosphere of freedom and independence which hasn't been seen in Turkish history until now.[2]

It must not be forgotten that the Turks who were fighting in defense of their homeland in defiance of the Istanbul government were given valuable and much-needed financial assistance by Bolshevist Russia, who saw thus a chance to strike at her capitalist foes, England, France, and Italy. Furthermore, the divided councils among the Allies, with France disapproving a policy which seemed sure to give Britain a commanding position in the Near East and finally making a separate peace with the Nationalist leaders at Ankara, helped the favorable outcome of the patriotic struggle. And the French and British war spirit, which had backed Allied ventures through 1918, had dwindled at home so that peoples and governments were no longer enthusiastic over the continuance of military ventures.

[2] Mitat Sadullah, *Yeni Yurt Bilgisi: Fifth Grade*, pp. 40 ff.

It was, however, due in largest part to the full blossoming of a national consciousness which had sprouted from a long-standing rivalry with the Greeks and had budded after the Constitutional Revolution of 1908 with the foundation of the Turk "Ojak" and other societies for the advancement of Turkish lore and patriotism that men and women from every stratum of Turkish society were able to band together to preserve their country and prepare it for a great metamorphosis. The devoted and heroic spirit which inspired the Turks in their struggle during the years after 1918 is powerfully expressed by the writer Rushen Echref in his tribute to the soldiers and flag of the Nationalists, written at Ankara in January, 1921. The piece is called *Bayrağimiz* ("Our Flag").

. . . These were our soldiers. They still had the assurance and bearing which their comrades in Istanbul were forced to relinquish.[3] They were not standing like those in Istanbul with their hands in their pockets and their heads bowed. They had lifted their bayonets up to heaven like fingers made of steel. They were standing as a symbol of respect made of flesh and metal for a certain object. They remembered the beginning of a small but healthy future rather than the relics of a great but decadent past. Our flag rose gradually before them, and it started to spread into heaven like a streaming red mane. Now this red object had more that the significance of a flag: it was a leader. My soul with the miracle of it regained its warmth, stirred, and straightened up. I was face to face with new hopefulness.

The flag which had received its color from the hearts of our ancestors nearly became black in our days. It seemed about to fall like a black mourning cloth after having run from victory to victory and gracing the kavuk [4] like a red rose. But in a crowd of Turkish soldiers its old significance returned, and it seemed to be gay and no longer sorrowing. The day after Inönü [5]

---

[3] By the Allied occupation.
[4] Headdress of the famous corps of Janissaries, destroyed in 1826.
[5] Battle in the Graeco-Turkish War.

it seemed to me more fresh and glorious than at the day of the battle of Mohac. It was perhaps more courageous when it flew in the winds of conquest while fighting in Europe. But then it was less substantial. It flies now with more life in the gale of independence rising from the rebellion of a band of oppressed souls.

The moment which it passed at Mohac was the end of the road leading to conquest. But at Inönü it marked the beginning of a new road when the world thought all was ended. . . .

O God! A generation of Turks condemned to hide in their trunks flags which we have carried gloriously on our heads like drops of blood would be the most unfortunate children in the world. But cannot the drop of blood which has come out of our body re-enter it again? We are not of those who keep their flags under their heads! Ever will our heads remain under our flags!

O flag,—the God of Lionlike gazis [6] and the sacred trust of our brave şehits [martyrs]. . . . You are not created of artificial imaginations. You have sprung directly from our hearts. You are the color of the life-stream which is the most sacred thing in the human body, and on you there appear traces of heaven [the white star and crescent which stand on the red field]. That is why you will not fade nor wither. You will live as free and as red above the heads of the new generation as you have lived above the heads of our ancestors! Never shall you see the last generation of Turks!

Such, then, was the highly reactive state of Turkish society, enraged at its foes and at the impedimenta of outworn Islamic incumbrances, inspired to exert itself heroically in the accomplishment of feats undreamed of. Seething as it was, there was needed only the introduction of an element of strong leadership to precipitate a new compound of social forms and attitudes. This element of leadership was furnished in the person of Kemal Ataturk. It is not possible to give here an extensive biography of this great soldier who

---

[6] Those who have fought in holy wars and not been killed.

has meant so much to Turkey during the last twelve years. Suffice it to say that he was of Macedonian origin, coming from a poor family, that he received a military education in Istanbul, that he served his country with distinction during the World War, especially in the Dardanelles defense, that he was always strongly critical of the Young Turk policy which governed the country from 1908 to 1918, and that he was the chief initiator of the movement for the defense of Anatolia contrary to the wishes of the sultan's government in 1918–19. The force of his personality, his determination, his endurance, his executive ability, but, above all, his inspiring generalship, which led Turkey's small but brave Nationalist army to victory against the invading Greeks in 1922, raised him to the highest pinnacle in the hearts of his fellow-countrymen. In the space of a few months he became the idol of Turkey, and stories of his exploits were quick to spread, painting him as a veritable superman. The country was his to do with it what he willed, and his will was sweeping reform.

Numerous are the admiring tributes paid to the Gazi ("The Victorious One"—a title bestowed on him by the Grand National Assembly), indicating the esteem in which he is held by his grateful compatriots. The fervency of some of these show that popular imagination has raised him almost to the position of a divinity, and this partially explains the willingness of the country to carry out his wishes. Hamdullah Subhi, former president of the Turk "Ojak," and generally recognized as one of Turkey's greatest orators, rendered a classic eulogy of Turkey's heroic leader when an equestrian statue of Ataturk was unveiled in Ankara in the fall of 1927. After speaking in glowing terms of Ataturk's ability, his invincibility in battle, and his unique endowment of perspicacity, Hamdullah Subhi goes on:

He is a reformer. He discovered the spiritual chains which tie the whole Moslem world in various ways to slavery. If it is necessary for the Eastern oppressed nations to find a way which leads to a strong and happy future, it is necessary to follow the road which is pointed out by this great patriot who now overlooks the city of Ankara. At one time the application of reforms which we now witness was considered madness; to speak of such reforms was considered over-optimism; and to try to carry them out was regarded as foolishness. It was the courage of this revolutionary leader which overcame all obstacles, accomplished the impossible, and overshadowed all previous reformers.

He is a leader. He applied principles which astonished us, and he showed us the best forms in military organizations, administration, politics, sociology, and art.

He is a head. He is a head that gives courage to hopeless hearts, gathers lost intellects under a common will like a flag which shows the rallying place on a battle-field, makes others confess his superiority, and helps those who are loyal to the principles which he has applied.

He is a reviving force. The ideas upon which the new era is based have been given new life by him. He is a reviving force which has been appointed by Truth to create a new world with his deep spirit and thoughts. . . .[7]

Another Turkish writer, Ahmed Rustem, less eulogistic in his characterization, has described Ataturk as a combination of Machiavelli, Frederick the Great, and Bismarck.

Of sentimentality no trace. He is a realist of the first order. In his case the soldier, the statesman, and the reformer have been carved with great strokes of the chisel in the hardest granite . . . It is this which was precisely what he had to have in order to succeed in the formidable task which he had to accomplish.[8]

Kemal Ataturk lost no time after he had reached the position of greatest influence in the new government in

[7] In *Seçme Yazilar* ("Selected Writings"), pp. 145 ff.
[8] "Moustapha Kémal Pacha," *Bibliothèque universelle et revue de Genève,* November, 1929, pp. 618–27; see p. 624.

making it plain that he intended to make Turkey a modern Western state, and so adroitly and forcefully did he manage governmental affairs and the promulgation of new laws that he drove from the country those who differed with him either in his radical Westernization program or in his dictatorial and high-handed methods of putting the program into effect.

Kemal's chief strength lies, of course, with the people who gratefully remember his services in saving Turkey from the Greek and Allied armies. As a soldier himself he enjoys great popularity among the military men of Turkey. Army officers seem notably well dressed, and are said to be well paid. Private soldiers, too, though paid practically nothing for their compulsory service, are said by people long acquainted with Turkish life to be for the most part warmly favorable to the Gazi. With the army, then, strongly back of him, and with Turkey accustomed for centuries to leadership and control by the military class, Kemal is seen to be virtually immune from the menace of any serious armed uprising. Politically Ataturk exerts great control over his nation through the People's party which he founded and which is the only party nominating candidates for election to the Grand National Assembly.[9]

Whatever one may say against Kemal's tendency to maintain himself in control of the country, it must be borne in mind that he has shared a great deal of his glory as well as his responsibilities with his present prime minister, Ismet Iuönü, a tremendously able executive, a likeable warrior and family man, whose moral character is unimpeachable. The

[9] The attempt in 1930 to set up a recognized opposition, Fethi Bey's Liberal party, was short-lived. Apparently Ataturk will not permit the nation's progress to be slowed down by bickering and needless discussion. When the country has become sufficiently enlightened to understand democracy, we may look for a relaxation of the present system of rigid, one-party control.

co-operation between these two great leaders is a most fortunate circumstance for Turkey's well-being and progress. While Kemal's inner circle of cronies has been described as a fast and hard-drinking clique whose reputation leaves room for the circulation of many spicy rumors, he has at the same time chosen for positions of responsibility many of the best brains of the country. Such departments as those of Public Instruction and of Public Hygiene and Social Assistance, of those with which I personally have come in contact, are in the hands of men who do the government credit. While naturally the supply of qualified experts in various lines is still limited, nevertheless the improvement of Turkish schools and the large number of students who are sent to Europe annually to perfect themselves in special fields indicates an early cure for the situation. Ataturk has also cut down to a minimum the number of breeding places for unprogressive ideas, having shut down the old *medressehs*, or theological schools, and outlawed the dervish and other secret orders.

In his masterful speech delivered over a period of six days to the People's party at Ankara in 1927, Kemal said many things regarding his policies past, present, and future. Among other things he declared his intention "to raise the nation to that position to which she is entitled to aspire in the civilized world and to establish the Turkish Republic forever on firm foundations." [10] By "civilized world" he of course referred to the nations which go to make up Western civilization as contrasted to backward nations of the Orient.

It may be wondered whether Turkey does not feel that she is making a great concession amounting nearly to surrender in admitting the superiority of the Western ways which originated in countries whose religion was that of the long-despised Christianity. The answer is contained in a

[10] In the German edition of the speech, *Die nationale Revolution*, II, 387.

statement by Djelal Noury, quoted in Levonian's *Moslem Mentality:*

It is a mistake to call the modern European and American civilization a Christian civilization; that is, a civilization brought about by Christianity. The Christian religion adjusted itself to the movements in Europe, and was saved out of the old static condition, so much so that to-day there is little resemblance between the religion taught by Jesus and modern Christianity. It may even be asserted that the present Christianity differs fundamentally from the original Christianity. The Europeans have built an altogether new religion during the course of the past nineteen centuries, although they have begun with the story of Jesus. Christianity in Europe, in spite of the opposition of the clergy, has assimilated the ideas and thoughts of every age. When Europe was struggling with ignorance during the Middle Ages, Christianity also was in a pitiful condition. But about four centuries later a radical purification took place in the Christian religion. A number of nations separated themselves from the Catholic Church and formed a new organization. Even the Roman Catholic Church began to change within itself. Thus we see that Christianity could not oblige its followers to be content with the old forms. Ultimately it was the new ideas that gave to Christianity a new colour. To-day, if Christ were to come to the world, he would remain a stranger among the Christians.[11]

From the foregoing quotation it is evident that Turkey disregards any religious rivalry in the steps she is taking. Since Christianity is regarded as more influenced by than influencing Western civilization, Turkey, in accepting ideas from the West, is merely profiting from a set of secular circumstances to which the Christian religion is itself indebted.

The Turks in accepting the science of the West show no parallel intention of supplanting their allegiance to Mohammed by allegiance to Jesus Christ. It is recalled by one Moslem Turkish writer that Islam was the original sponsor

[11] *Op. cit.,* pp. 57 ff.

of science, but, having forgotten it, must relearn it from
Europe. He declares:

They were our learned men who made methods of calculations and published books on heavenly phenomena. In those
great days some of our sages measured the heavens, while others
gave methods of minute calculations to the world. Still others
had gone into the field of medicine, established hospitals, and
discovered remedies for thousands of diseases. Then we were
the sole authorities. We were recognized, and our names were
mentioned throughout the whole world. But when we left aside
those sciences, gradually we lost our reputation, and our names
were forgotten, and at last we became poor and ignorant. The
sciences that we started have been perfected and advanced in
the hands of others. Not only did we not learn the new sciences,
but we also forgot the old ones. We lost our skill in craftsmanship which we inherited from our fathers and grandfathers. We
are now in a state of needing help from Europe "from thread
to needle."

The Europeans who were once our apprentices and knelt before us now have become our masters. They sell us things
which we don't know about, measuring them in drachms and
hitting us over the head. We must ourselves adopt the European
science and craftsmanship as rapidly as possible.[12]

Turkey's determination to master the ways of the West is
further encouraged by a spirit of self-confidence—sometimes
carried almost to a fault—and a keen realization from first-
hand experience that the Europeans are no supermen with
any inherent essential superiority. The prominent Turkish
journalist, Yunus Nadi, after a trip to Europe, wrote back
to his newspaper in Istanbul, *La république,* an article
entitled "The Great School"—referring to Europe. In his
concluding paragraphs he wrote as follows:

What is the distance which separates us from Europe? No
one can find that distance very long, very wide, and very great.

[12] Ourianzade Ali Vahit, *First Sermon—from the Pulpit of Hadji
Bairam Mosque,* pp. 15 f.

It is a question of disposition. In any event it is certain that the Europeans are neither stronger nor more intelligent than we. We could declare without fear of error that there exists between them and us no difference with respect to organic constitution. Why then is it necessary that they should succeed and that we others should not be able to? Still more so when we have before our eyes an excellent model in Europe herself. Those Europeans have only been able to achieve their actual progress with short steps, slow and difficult. We have then nothing to discover in the materials. What we must do is simply to learn their methods, something not at all difficult. The fact is simply that we have to learn many things from these gentlemen and that we must proceed most methodically to be able to succeed in a space of time relatively limited and settled in advance.

Method! Method! That is the greatest mystery of occidental civilization.

We may for to-day recapitulate as follows:

We must learn in Europe, work like Europe and with Europe. And the torch which we shall hold in our hand to advance on the way of civilization can be nothing else than the method applied in Europe.[13]

The climax to Turkey's adoption of Western techniques seems to have been reached with the embarkation upon an ambitious five-year industrialization plan, calling for the erection of fifteen factories in various sections of the country. Accepted on January 9, 1934, this plan, if successfully carried out in a land pre-eminently agricultural, will be an accomplishment to which the Turks may well point with pride.

[13] *Op. cit.*, October 3, 1929.

VI

TURKEY'S CHANGED STATUS IN THE
FAMILY OF NATIONS AND IN THE
MOSLEM WORLD

Turkey under the leadership of Kemal Ataturk had thrown her lot wholly on the side of Westernization. The manifestations and consequences of this decision will occupy our full attention from this point on, for the transformed Turkish nation had opened herself to a host of new influences which could not help affecting every phase of her existence. To the outside world there was probably no change so far reaching in its effect on international relations as Turkey's complete allegiance to the Western doctrine of nationalism. In the present chapter we shall notice how Turkey's status as leader of Islam was affected, and in the chapter which follows we shall see how nationalism altered the entire structure of Turkey's internal social life.

In the preceding chapter mention was made of Turkey's desertion not only by her Christian populations but by her Arab co-religionists. This fact, together with her growing impatience against the antiquated Islamic system still clung to by most of the other Moslem countries, caused Turkey more and more to center her attention on her own needs and to shun any responsibility such as she had formerly assumed for the defense and leadership of the rest of the Moslem world.

National needs and national development came to occupy Turkey's thoughts and activities, and she sought to develop into a strong, unified, and self-sufficient state similar to her

European neighbors whom she was taking for a model. A Turkish journalist and member of the Grand National Assembly, Mahmut, wrote in his newspaper, *Le milliett*, an editorial entitled "The Rule of Our Time." He begins:

The rule of our century is nationalism, the care of nationality. This rule constitutes for every people a truth and an obligation. This truth, which history confirms more each day, is vaster and fuller of meaning for Turkey. Indeed, the events which we have gone through up till now, the bitter experiences which we have known, the special situation of our country, command us to hold to this rule more firmly than any other nation. In spite of the efforts for solidarity and peace which are being established in the political world, the only truth which has value in all countries is nationalism. . . . The first condition for occupying a choice position among the civilized countries is to have a national conscience. Better than any other nation are we able to appreciate the force of the national ideal, of the national conscience, which have led Turkey in the fight for independence to liberty and safety.[1]

Turkey made up her mind that no longer should any other purpose than the wishes and welfare of the Turkish people guide her policies. No longer were Turkish lives to be sacrificed for the selfish ambitions of a ruling family, and Turkey was through with bearing the burdens of fellow-Turanians or fellow-Moslems who dwelt outside her borders. According to Kemal himself in a talk given at Eski-Shehir during the latter part of the struggle for independence:

The policy which will be followed by the New Turkey . . . will be absolutely proportioned to the capacities and needs of the country. Neither Islamic union nor Turanianism can form a doctrine, a logical policy for us. Henceforth the governmental policy of the new Turkey is to consist in living independent, relying on her sovereignty within her national frontiers.[2]

[1] Issue of May 5, 1930.
[2] Mahmut Bey, "Le Ghazi et la révolution," *Le milliett*, November 26, 1929, to February 8, 1930, instalment No. 11.

Speaking to a group of journalists from Istanbul who had come to interview him during those same days, the Gazi spoke in similar vein:

If we are to say, "Let's please the hodjas, let's please the Moslem world, let's please everybody," it will be easy to make them all happy, but it is we who will not have attained our purpose. Men inclined to compromise cannot accomplish a revolution, and besides, in the present state of misery and disorder, it is impossible to satisfy any one whatever. When the country becomes flourishing, when the nation becomes prosperous, everybody will be happy.[3]

With Turkish feeling running strongly as it was toward concentration on national ends, it is not surprising that the position of the sultan-caliphs in Istanbul, rulers whose position as heads of the Moslem world had given them an international significance, should have been subjected to great alteration in status. Since the accession of Abdul-Hamid II, the padishahs had been losing their popularity with their Turkish subjects, but the behavior of the unfortunate Mohammed VI, Vahid-ud-Din, who came to the throne in 1918, sealed the doom of the dynasty, and brought to an end Turkey's rôle as an empire, which she had played for five centuries under the leadership of scions of the house of Osman. Vahid-ud-Din had to take the blame for the Treaty of Sèvres, the abortive document which the Allies sought to force on Turkey after the World War, and which Nationalist Turkey refused to accept. Helpless in the hands of Britain and the other Allies who had occupied Istanbul on March 16, 1920, Vahid-ud-Din appeared to be playing into the hands of Turkey's enemies, and his dispatch of troops called the "Army of the Caliphate" against the budding Nationalist movement, together with a proclamation of that movement

[3] *Ibid.*, instalment No. 24.

as contrary to government and religion, was a hostile act which the Nationalists never forgot.

When, after Kemal's army had defeated the Greeks, it became necessary to draw up terms of peace, the Allies invited both the Istanbul government and that at Ankara, which had been set up following the Allied occupation of Istanbul, late in October, 1922, to a conference at Lausanne. This caused the Ankara Nationalists to decide that the time had come to end the government of the sultans once and for all. On November 1, 1922, the Ankara Parliament passed a law declaring that the government of the sultans had ceased on March 16, 1920, the date on which the Allied occupation of Istanbul had taken place. On November 4, 1922, Refet Pasha took over the administration of Istanbul in the name of the Ankara government, and on November 17 Sultan Mohammed VI, Vahid-ud-Din, fled to Malta on board the British battleship "Malaya."

Ankara was not ready yet, however, to terminate the existence of the caliphate, although they did not propose to have any member of the house of Osman exert temporal power over them. There was still too much feeling both among Moslem Turks and among Moslems outside Turkey to permit an abrupt abolition of Turkey's symbolic leadership of the religion of Islam. An Indian Caliphate Committee had been organized to express the sentiments of the seventy million Moslems of India that the caliphate should be safeguarded. Other Moslem countries had sent representatives or gifts to the triumphant Kemal to express their admiration of the way in which he had defeated the infidels, and to state their willingness to follow the Ankara government as the rightful defenders of the faith. Many among the Nationalist Turks also felt that it would be unwise to do away with an office of international significance, thereby losing a possible asset in their international dealings and at the same time

antagonizing a large number of friendly Moslems throughout the world who had become used to regarding Turkey as
Islam's rightful protagonist. Ankara decided, accordingly, to
elect another member of the house of Osman, Abdul-Medjid,
as caliph, with powers solely spiritual and dependent on the
government of the Grand National Assembly. The office presented a curious confused mixture of functions corresponding
to those of a British king and a Roman pope. This election
took place on November 18, 1922.

George Young, who was in Istanbul at the time, has written an effective and colorful description of the ceremonies
accompanying the investiture of this new caliph who was to
attempt to perform the impossible task of maintaining a
glamorous international office without offending the jealously
nationalistic government on which he depended, and uphold-
ing the dignity of a religion which that government cared
nothing for. He writes:

Let us pay a last visit to the Old Serai [the residential palace
of the sultans until last century] to attend the ceremony. As
we cross the bridge there passes us at a trot an escort of lancers,
mounted lackeys in red, and a carriage and four with postillions.
In it sits a portly person in a fez, frock-coat and green ribbon.
It is Abdul-Medjid, son of that Abdul-Aziz who cut the tangled
knot of his fortunes with a pair of scissors.[4] Abdul-Medjid is
on his way to be invested as Caliph. The carriage whirls into the
inner court of the Old Serai. On the one side are the mediaeval
kitchens with their conical chimneys, on the other, the cupolas
of the hareem, at the end of a Byzantine portico of marbles and
coloured tiles, still delightful in its dilapidation. On the pave-
ment in front of the portico stands the Golden Throne studded
with jewels, looted from Egypt by Selim, the first Ottoman
Caliph.[5] In a circle round it stand a few reporters, some sight-

[4] Sultan Abdul-Aziz, who reigned from 1861 to 1876, died under
mysterious circumstances after being deposed, apparently having committed suicide with a pair of scissors.

[5] Historians now assert that Selim's supposed acquisition of the
caliphate in 1517 was an invention of later historians.

seeing French and Italian officers, and some American ladies. No Britisher is there but myself. I venture to slip past the chamberlains through to the Bagdad Kiosk and so get a glimpse of that most sacred of ceremonies, the Investiture of a Caliph.

But what a travesty it is! Instead of the solemn ritual in the Mosque of Eyoub and a Sultan girded with the Sword of Osman [6] receiving from the Sheikh of Islam the emblems of his spiritual power, here is a delegation of Angora deputies notifying an elderly dilettante that he has been elected by a majority vote like any Labour leader. There are the sacred relics, but the Sword of Osman remains at Eyoub to show that, though Abdul-Medjid is Caliph, he is not Sultan.[7]

It was a further notable fact at this ceremony that the prayers were said in Turkish instead of Arabic,[8] indicating still further how Turkey's national individuality was supplanting the wider allegiance to an imported religious system.

Theologians argued one way or another to prove or disprove the validity of an Islamic potentate with spiritual but no temporal power. Abdul-Medjid was in a precarious position, the center of heated controversy. It seemed impossible that he could hold on to his position in the face of nationalism and practical logic. More and more did it become apparent that Turkey must follow a path which led her away from her fellow-Moslems, and the Turks did not propose to make further exertions for Islamic countries with whom she had little in common, nor to keep alive an institution which could be of no practical benefit to themselves. Djelal Noury has said in his book, *The Turkish Revolution:* "To be faithful to the past in order to be united in fate with a body of 300 millions who never make progress is to rebel against the present and the future. . . . It means to lose national existence." [9]

---

[6] The hereditary symbol of the temporal power of the sons of Osman, or Othman, founder of the Ottoman dynasty.

[7] *Constantinople,* pp. 294 f.

[8] Toynbee and Kirkwood, *Turkey,* p. 152.

[9] Quoted in Levonian, *Moslem Mentality,* p. 62.

Kemal Ataturk has discussed the question at length both in his Six-Day Speech and in his informal talks quoted by Mahmut in "Le Ghazi et la révolution." In his words he shows repeatedly his conviction that the caliphate is in every way a liability to Turkey, that a Moslem union is a historic unreality, and that all attempts to bring Moslems together will only deflect Turkey from her supreme obligation toward her own interests. Some characteristic statements on the caliphate reveal his attitude:

Let us say, Gentlemen, that there is a Caliphate extending over the Moslem world. This responsibility is held by a personage whose title is "Caliph of the Moslems." I ask what is, according to those who speak of the duties and powers of the Caliphate, the duty of this Caliph of the Moslems. Is it not to deliver the Moslem world? There exist, in the domain over which the jurisdiction of the Caliph extends, a State of Turkey, a Persia, an Afghanistan; there is the Moslem mass of seventy million Indians, Egypt, Morocco, etc. If we admit the duties of the Caliph as they are defined in the recognized treatises, we are obligated to save all these countries. And to save them it is necessary to have energy, power, money, and men. Who can say that for this purpose the Turkish state and the population of Turkey are under the orders of the Caliphate? Who can say, "Go, Gentlemen, inflict a defeat on the entire world and save the Moslem world!" I ask the nation: Does it consent to that? Can this poor nation assume such a great responsibility? . . .

Gentlemen, it is this point of view which has moved our nation for centuries. But what has come of it? She has left millions of men in all the places where she had gone. Finally she has been driven out. And to-day she has fallen into this situation. Do you know the number of children of Anatolia exterminated in the deserts of Yemen? Can you count the number of men whom we have lost to be able to preserve Syria and Irak, to keep our hold in Egypt and Africa, and to carry conquest to the very gates of Vienna? And what all this has finally resulted in, you see. . . .

Suppose for an instant that Turkey should take seriously the duty in question, that she should aim at and have good success in freeing the Moslems, uniting them on one point and governing them. Very good! But what if, after we had for example freed Egypt, the Egyptians should say to us: "We thank you very much. But we are not willing to be governed by you. Egypt is for the Egyptians. We shall allow no one to interfere with our independence and our national sovereignty. We shall remain independent. . . .

Gentlemen, you see that it is proposed to destroy this poor nation for a whim, for an illusion, in a word, for nothing. . . .

Enough of these misfortunes into which our nation has been drawn by obstinacy in not seeing real situations and following those who are mistaken! We cannot, knowing the cause, permit the same drama to be played on! [10]

Abdul-Medjid, the unhappy last caliph of Islam, was allowed to hold his anomalous office for a little more than a year. But it was clearly impossible that the Moslem world should accept enthusiastically in the midst of all its doctrinal diversity a spiritual and dogmatic chief, particularly from Turkey, a land which had never had a reputation for theological brilliance or regularity. It was plainly brought out that a caliphate was essentially based on temporal power, and when shorn of that, a caliph could have no real authority or respect. Turkey's grasp of this fact, her unwillingness to tolerate a caliph with temporal power, and her eagerness to break away from too close a connection with the rest of Islam made it inevitable that a caliph who was not sultan could not long exist. Of the theoretical tests for a caliph set up by Moslem legists—such as descent from the Koreish, the Prophet's tribe; election by a conclave of notables; nomination by a predecessor; guardianship of the holy cities, Mecca and Medina; acceptance by all Moslems unanimously; and qualifications mental and physical—it was evident that Abdul-Medjid could satisfy at best only the second and last.

[10] *Op. cit.*, instalment No. 36; cf. also Gazi Mustapha Kemal Pascha, *Die neue Turkei*, Vol. II: *Die nationale Revolution*, pp. 244 f.

It was logical, then, for the Grand National Assembly at Ankara on March 3, 1924, to adopt a law abolishing the caliphate and banishing members of the Ottoman imperial family from Turkish territories. Turkey served notice that she was through once and for all with any responsibility for leadership of the Moslem world. In his famous speech at Ankara in 1927 Ataturk said:

Gentlemen, I must frankly and categorically declare that those who busy themselves any more with the chimaera of the Caliphate and thereby lead the Moslem world astray are nothing but enemies of the world of Islam and especially of Turkey. Hopes to set up such an imposture can only be the affairs of ignoramuses and dummies.[11]

Few tears were shed for the demise of the caliphate. Congresses assembled in Mecca and Cairo to discuss what steps Moslems should take, but no unanimity of opinion manifested itself. The virus of nationalism had apparently penetrated so far into the East that most Moslems were content to let their religious affairs be guided by local conditions and decisions. There was no Moslem ruler of sufficient prestige to be regarded by all as a defender of the faithful.

To progressive Moslem opinion the end of the caliphate was regarded as beneficial to the best interests of the religion. It is felt that emphasis will be taken from the superficial and worldly features of the religion and placed on the more vital realm of ethics and conscience. A writer in the *Review of Religions* declares that "the abolition of the Khilafat, considering its nature and the depths to which it had sunk, has put an end to a terrible evil. . . . The Muslim world can be confidently expected to fare better without it." [12]

Turkey's abolition of the caliphate does not mean, how-

[11] *Op. cit.*, II, 346 f.
[12] S. Niaz, "Changes in the Muslim East," *op. cit.*, XXVIII, No. 3 (March, 1929), 81.

ever, that her influence in the Moslem world and in the
Orient is ended or even diminished. Evidence, on the other
hand, indicates that as a progressive example to the less advanced nations her leadership will count for more than it has
ever before. Turkey's consciousness of her new rôle is frequently met with. Yacoub Kadri has discussed the subject
in *Le milliett*. He says:

We have not only proved our inexhaustible vitality in destroying, after a long series of wars, the invaders; we have not only
given proof of our intellectual youth and vigor in achieving
revolutions of democracy and civilization in life; but we have
at the same time—and what is perhaps more important than
the rest—proved that we were the only vanguard of occidental
civilization in the Orient so enveloped in darkness, and in the
vastness of Asia. To-day from Syria to Egypt, from Egypt to
China, all peoples have their eyes fixed on us and strive to follow in our footsteps. . . .

For nearly four hundred years the Europeans have tried to
introduce European civilization into the heart of Asia. But from
the first Venetian voyager to the latest convoys of colonization,
all attempts made in this vein by Europeans have served only
to lead the nations, Oriental and Asiatic, to hate that civilization. One may even say that it was after these contacts that the
abyss opened between the Orient and the Occident.

Thus it is that to-day we others constitute a bridge of steel
over this abyss.[13]

When I asked Dr. Abdullah Djevdet Bey what he felt
about Turkey's present relationship with the rest of the
Moslem world, he smilingly referred me to an interview which
he had given twelve years before on the subject of pan-
Islam in Diamontopoulo's book, *Le réveil de la Turquie*.
He is quoted as saying:

The word Pan-Islamism ought . . . to express a sympathy exclusively intellectual and literary among Moslems. To attain that
ideal we must have a Turkey advanced and modernized. Constan-

[13] Issue of March 10, 1930.

tinople ought then to be a center of enlightenment to which
Moslems might come without prejudice to imbibe ideas of
science and civilization.[14]

In Yusuf Ziya's book of religious lessons, written for use in
Turkey's middle and normal schools, the author writes: "As
we are the most progressive and the most civilized of all these
Moslem countries, we should try to progress more and become good examples." [15]

Of the Moslem nations which have sought to preserve
close friendship with the new Turkey, none has shown more
enthusiasm in following Turkey's lead than Afghanistan under the rules of Amanullah, Nadir, and Mohammed Zahir.
Turkish officers have been invited to assist the Afghan army.
Afghan cadets have been sent to Turkish military schools.
Amanullah's government also sent boys and girls to Turkey's
civil schools: six boys to the primary boarding schools,
ninety-eight boys and fifteen girls to lycées. The girl students were recalled subsequently by Nadir Khan when he
came into office as a concession to the public opinion which
had revolted against the extreme steps taken by Amanullah.

When the Afghan ambassador, Gulam Nebi Khan, presented his credentials on April 6, 1930, he addressed the
following words to the Gazi:

Your Excellency! . . . Historical and social reasons have so
strengthened the fraternal relations existing between the two
countries that no force and no hand could break them. I could
even say that the two powers represent an organism of two
bodies with one soul. The history of the world in general and
that of the Orient in particular will not fail to record the success obtained in the Revolution and the path of progress by the
noble and industrious Turkish nation, coming again to life under
the guidance of Your Excellency, whose generous and courageous protection in delivering that active and valiant nation

[14] *Op. cit.*, pp. 259 f.
[15] *Islam Dini* ("The Religion of Islam"), I, 32.

from its moral and material shackles has directed it on the path of progress. The noble Afghan nation, in joyously assisting the advances realized by her Turkish brothers, appreciates them with sincerity.[16]

Turkey's abandonment of the caliphate and an assumption of solely secular relations with the rest of the world paved the way for a closer entente with Persia, whose differences with Turkey had frequently waxed bitter during the more than four hundred years that Turkey stood firm for the orthodoxy of Sunni beliefs while Persia upheld the Shiite doctrines. The sentiment is growing that Turkey and Persia should forget their religious differences and co-operate more closely in their endeavors to replace ignorant fanaticism with enlightenment. Instead of going to war, or at least having strained relations, because Turkey recognizes the first three caliphs, Abu-Bakr, Omar, and Othman, who are regarded by the Persian Shiites as impostors, or because the sons of Ali, so venerated by the Shiites, were killed by Sunnis some thirteen hundred years ago, Turkey and Persia are seeing that they have much more to gain by standing together politically and economically.[17] A Persian member of Parliament in the course of a visit to Istanbul gave an interview to *Le milliett* in which he voiced the following sentiments:

I visited Turkey for the first time in 1913. Since then there has been great change and immense advances. The Persians love the Turks with a fraternal affection and follow their activity with great interest. We all know that the savior of Turkey, the great Gazi, Mustapha Kemal Pasha, who is a man of genius,

[16] In *Le milliett,* April 8, 1930.

[17] Occasional incidents arise to disturb the peace, such as the Kurdish raids of 1930, but the friendly interchange of visits by important officials, particularly Riza Shah's visit to Ankara in June, 1934, gives evidence of the real cordiality existing between the governments. It is also of interest to note that in the fall of 1934 a commission of Turks was selected to settle a border dispute between Persia and Afghanistan.

is a guide and an example for the Orient. All Persia speaks affectionately the name of your great President.[18]

Although Turkey's leaders at the present time are in large part men of military training or experience, and although many of Turkey's past heroes have been glorious warriors, there is probably no nation in the world more sincerely eager for the preservation of peace than is the Turkish Republic. The National Pact of 1920 disavowed all ideas of "irredentism," and the government today has been doing its best to establish friendly relations with all nations. For Turkey has been totally disillusioned by her war experiences and realizes that she must have peace in order to cure the vast number of ills which have come to her as a result of war. After visiting an obscure village near Merzifun where a young man apologized for its small size, remarking that 120 men had gone away to the recent wars and never returned, I was able, though the number must have been exaggerated, to form some idea of the tremendous losses in man-power which Turkey must have suffered. Yusuf Kemal, who was the first minister of foreign affairs of the Ankara government and is still an important figure in national affairs, remarked feelingly in the course of a conversation that "untilled fields, unworked mines, disease, poverty—all have their fundamental roots in Turkey's more than ten years of constant war." Such seems to be the almost unanimous feeling of Turkish public opinion.

Ataturk himself has left no doubt as to his own feelings on the subject of war and peace. Addressing the population of Ismidt at the close of the victorious campaign against the Greeks, he said:

The wars which have continued up to to-day have brought it about, unfortunately, that our agriculture has remained back-

[18] Issue of March 30, 1930.

ward. Henceforth we shall avoid inopportune acts of this kind. We shall render our farmers more active. The nation henceforth will take up arms for only one cause: to defend from within her national frontiers, her life, her independence, her sovereignty. We shall have no more an aggressive military policy. No more shall we run after conquests. . . . We shall reduce as much as possible the duration of military service. We shall not limit military art to the handling of a gun; but we shall strive to teach our soldiers things which could allow them to be useful to their surroundings when they return to their homes and resume their work in the fields.[19]

Discoursing later on the contrast between his new policies and those of the Empire, he referred bitterly to the drain of wars of conquest on Turkey's own condition: "What happened to those armies of conquest which went into Asia, Europe, and Africa? They remained there; they died and disappeared there where they had gone. And as a result, the mother country remained empty and in ruins." [20]

One of the most notable declarations of Turkey's desire for peace in her foreign relations is contained in a speech made to the Grand National Assembly by the foreign minister, Tewfik Ruchdi Aras, at the time of the ratification of the Turco-Hellenic Treaty:

You are aware that your Minister of Foreign Affairs has never ceased to proceed along the path traced for him by your High Assembly and to work for peace with great ardor and tireless activity, and even, I may say, with love. We owe to our efforts, guided by these principles, the majority of the pacts of friendship and arbitration concluded with neighboring states as well as with other countries.

The very necessities of our great national revolution and of

[19] *Op. cit.,* instalment No. 43.

[20] *Ibid.,* instalment No. 69. In this connection it is of interest to note that the Ministry of National Defense customarily receives the largest appropriation of any department in Turkey's general budget. Yet where this amount in 1926 was 64,004,925 Turkish liras, in 1933 it was only 33,326,640.

the special geographic position of our country have always obliged us to maintain an extreme interest in the cause of peace, as much for ourselves as for the entire world. Every time that we have been invited to a meeting in any country whatever for the purpose of peace, each time that a formula of peace had to be found for participation in the meeting, to subscribe to the formula we have laid down two conditions: equal treatment for all, and exclusion of every hostile intention against any one. We were not ignorant of the fact that every peace based on an equilibrium of forces set up by groupings of powers working together by a special agreement has never been an absolute and permanent peace. . . . We knew furthermore that means of violence and compulsion do not constitute a foundation for peace, but lead definitely to war. . . .

Believing that every separate alliance brings about others, Turkey has abstained from participation in such initiatives. But she hastened to subscribe to the Kellogg Pact which required a universal entente among all the nations. . . .

The Turkish nation, solidly supporting her great President, forms a unity, and certain of her power to defend and conserve her existence, looks for her development in peace.[21]

Further evidence of Turkey's interest in world-peace is found in her entrance into the League of Nations in July, 1932. With her assumption of a seat on the League Council in the fall of 1934, a strong influence for world-stability has been added to that important body.

There are some thinkers among the Turks who see in nationalism no hindrance to a broad and humanitarian world-outlook, saying, as does Halidé Edib, that "it is after I have loved my own people and tried to understand their virtues and their faults with open-minded humility that I begin to have a better understanding of other people's sufferings and joys, and of their personality expressed in their national life." [22] There are others who have told me that they feel nationalism a cramping force and prefer to extend their

[21] *Le milliett,* June 19, 1930.
[22] *Memoirs of Halidé Edib,* p. 326.

loyalties and affections to all humanity irrespective of nationality. But the largest part of vocal public opinion reveals a
nationalism strongly self-centered, one which manifests no
ulterior designs on any other people but which recognizes
that this is a world where each nation must guard its own
rights and does not propose to be victimized by the greed of
any other nationality. Therefore Turkey's eagerness for peace
does not, much as it might like to, express itself in dis-
armament, but in the maintenance of efficient defensive
forces.

The Turkish writer and deputy, Falih Rifki, has said:

While those who hold the world under their law arm themselves more strongly each day and give their children a warlike
education, it would be senseless to lead the Turkish nation to
fix its gaze on the mirage of peace and to conduct it toward a
dangerous optimism.[23]

In no uncertain terms Abel Adam discusses the question
in his *Book of Mustafa Kemal:*

To-day we are living in the era of nationalism; we have not
yet reached the era of humanism. European civilization acts on
the principle of nationalism; we must also do likewise. No
nation recognizes the rights of other nations, or shows mercy or
runs to help others. The terrible wars in Europe show this
principle plainly. . . . Europe acts on the principle of nationalism. We see an English type which is willing to kindle the whole
world in order to light his pipe. All European Powers are like
that. We, the Turks, also shall be so. This is an exigency of the
present-day humanity; therefore it is useless to criticize it or
speak against it. Movements contrary to this principle are
simply ridiculous. The League of Nations is a pitiful example
of this sarcasm. To-day there is no humanitarian mentality in
Europe, and therefore we also cannot act on humanitarian logic.
We have nationalism and nationalistic logic only. This is the
struggle for existence, and it is the foundation of life everywhere. This is an axiom; it is self-evident.[24]

[23] *Le milliett,* September 30, 1929.
[24] Quoted in Levonian, *op. cit.,* p. 55.

VII

THE CONSTRUCTION OF A LOYAL, UNIFIED POPULATION

Turkey's decision to make of herself a nation like the states of Western Europe brought changes not only in her attitude toward the rest of the world as described in the preceding chapter but in the whole internal structure of the country. Probably no alteration was as shattering to the old order as the steps taken to concentrate and unify the population within Turkey's new frontiers.

The Turkish Empire ever since its inception had been one of the most loosely knitted conglomerations of peoples and religions ever to owe ostensible allegiance to one sovereign. Its territorial extent alone in its days of widest expanse, when it reached from the very gates of Persia as far west as Hungary and took in Arabia, North Africa, and regions north of the Black Sea, was enough to prevent the development of unity among the diverse peoples included. Differences in race, in language, and in religion all contributed elements of disharmony which made it a virtually impossible task to build up a common *esprit de corps* in the old Ottoman Empire. Comprising units, many of which had been conquered and brought into subjection against their will, the imperial government had to devote a large part of its attention to the suppression of uprisings, and as long as the various units proved subservient and prompt in fulfilling financial obligations, the sultan-caliphs were content to let each preserve its own cultural individuality. Even though the religion of Islam lent to

69

the whole an outward appearance of integration, since the ruler was chief sponsor of the religion, and the official law was based on the Koran, there were various Christian and Jewish communities which had not been compelled to adopt the religion and culture of their conquerors. As a matter of fact each distinctive religious group was allowed to organize into an autonomous, self-governing body or *millett*, whose highest governing official was an ecclesiastical dignitary who was appointed by and responsible to the sultan. This arrangement had been worked out in the fifteenth century when Mohammed II, the Conqueror, had captured Constantinople and in accordance with Islamic practice legitimatized the presence within the state of bodies immune from the laws of the state and with no sense of loyalty to the sovereign power. Even though it was possible for members of these independent *milletts* to reach positions of responsibility, dignity, and honor in the sultanic government, there were very few compulsory obligations imposed on the semi-independent communities. Military service was not required, being handled by Moslems, and even freedom to have independent schools was permitted by Turkish insouciance.

Still a third disruptive influence, in addition to territorial ungainliness and the *milletts*, was that of the capitulations. These special privileges, enjoyed by European governments, and permitting citizens of those countries to be exempt from Turkish law and subject to the laws of their own country when in Turkish territory, seem to have been continuations extended by the Turks of trading privileges originally granted to Genoese and Venetian traders by emperors of Byzantium before the Turkish conquest.[1] While these concessions were greatly widened in the sixteenth and later centuries, they seem at first apparently to have been merely a courteous

[1] See George Young, *Constantinople*, pp. 93, 107 f., etc.

continuation of an international agreement. As years wore on, however, and the Turkish government became weaker and more corrupt and the European Powers became more insistent and grasping, the capitulatory privileges more and more offered footholds for imperialistic intrigue and struck deeply into the vitals of the Empire, obstructing as much as possible any unifying Turkification.

Under such circumstances as have been described the Turkish Empire could expect nothing but added unrest, heightening rivalries among her component groups, and secession of the unassimilated racial and religious elements as soon as they developed sufficient national consciousness and military strength. The obstructions to Turkey's unification began naturally to be eliminated in this way through the revolt and establishment of separate governments of various Christian provinces, principally in the Balkans. Russia, Austria, France, England, and Italy helped the process along by appropriating contiguous territories, or seizing lands which seemed strategically or economically important. Thus by the outbreak of the World War Turkey's territories had shrunk until she had lost most of her Christian-inhabited territories in Europe, and all of North Africa. The World War and the revolt of the Arabs severed from her dominion the rest of her lands which were not primarily Turk inhabited. Turkey's acceptance of this situation, and repudiation of any desire to maintain dominion over the territories which had revolted from her rule, were contained in the Turkish National Pact, set forth at Istanbul on January 28, 1920, by the Nationalists who were shortly to set up their government at Ankara. Article 1 states:

The fate of the territories of the Ottoman Empire [2] exclusively populated by Arab majorities and finding themselves, since the

[2] On the abandoned use of the term "Ottoman," see note on p. 113 below.

conclusion of the armistice of October 30, 1918, under the occupation of enemy armies, must be regulated according to the
freely expressed will of the local populations.

The parts of the Ottoman Empire situated this side of and
beyond the line of occupation and inhabited by an Ottoman
Moslem majority whose constituent elements, united by religious
and cultural ties and by the same ideal, are animated by a
reciprocal respect for their ethnic rights and their social conditions, form a whole which permits, under any pretext whatever, no dissociation whether by fact or by right.[3]

Thus did the new leaders of Turkey make it clear that they
would not interfere with peoples who objected to their rule,
at the same time insisting that they intended to have no one
interfere with their own independent national existence.

One step, then, in Turkish national integration—that of
eliminating appendant regions with discordant aspirations—
was brought about by force of circumstances and was finally
accepted by the Turks without remorse. But there were other
disharmonizing factors in Turkey's own Anatolia as we have
seen: the capitulations and the *milletts*. These presented problems immensely more difficult to solve.

The capitulations, it was noticed, had been a source of increasing irritation to the Turks who had set their minds on
establishing an efficient and respected government. After the
outbreak of war in 1914 the Young Turks in power thought
they saw an opportunity to end the system which was such a
source of embarrassment. Accordingly, on September 9, 1914,
some weeks before Turkey actually entered the hostilities, the
government, in a unilateral declaration, announced the
termination of the capitulatory privileges, accompanied by
great rejoicing and celebration in Turkey.[4] The abolition of
the capitulations in such a fashion was not, however, recognized by the foreign governments who had enjoyed them, and

---

[3] Schlicklin, *Angora,* p. 14.
[4] Cf. Wilson, *Modern Movements among Moslems,* pp. 278 ff.

when at the conclusion of hostilities in 1918 the Allied Powers proceeded to avail themselves of the rights as if they had never been withdrawn, the Turks realized that the West intended to play the old game of interference. The Nationalists, in their Pact of January 28, 1920, voiced their opposition to any such resumption of the dangerous privileges. In article 6 they affirmed:

It is a fundamental condition of our life and continued existence that we, like every country, should enjoy complete independence and liberty in the matter of assuring the means of our development, in order that our national and economic development should be rendered possible and that it should be possible to conduct affairs in the form of a more up-to-date regular administration. For this reason we are opposed to restrictions, inimical to our development, in political, judicial, financial and other matters.[5]

It was not until 1923, however, when the Treaty of Lausanne finally terminated the war waged by Turkey in defense of her national life, that the nations of the West gave up their capitulatory privileges and granted to Turkey the right to manage her own affairs as they did themselves. Thus was brought about another step in the attainment of national unification.

The abandonment of the *millett* system, however, was a major operation on Turkey's body politic which occasioned a tremendous internal readjustment. It had become increasingly clear to the Turks that the presence within their own boundaries of groups not amenable to the laws of the government was a constant source of friction and intrigue. Although the large Jewish community had proved themselves valuable subjects, had not been involved in treasonable affairs, and had consequently been rewarded with an existence unmolested and respected on the whole, the Christian communi-

[5] Toynbee and Kirkwood, *Turkey,* p. 141.

ties, Greek and Armenian, were quite a different proposition. Unlike the Jews, who had no "protecting" governments to interfere on their behalf, the Christian populations were, with the flourishing of European imperialism, constantly ministered to by foreign Christian governments, whose anxiety over the welfare of their oppressed Christian brethren in Turkey was generally tinged with the less altruistic motive of using the minority populations as a means to attain a foothold in the territories of the Turkish Empire, whose demise these Western Powers were ghoulishly awaiting.

The menace to Turkey of these Christian *milletts*, whose consciousness of national individuality was being encouraged by the European Powers, became threatening in the nineteenth century. Reactionary protests against the measures adopted about the middle of the century to give Christian populations more rights had brought out spasmodic outbreaks, but apparently the first Turk to recognize the danger for Turkey in a powerful Armenian population whose young bloods were excited with revolutionary notions by Russian agents was the sinister sultan Abdul-Hamid II. His answer to the threat was a crude one and brought on himself and his country the reputation of being cold-blooded assassins. He sought to cure the trouble by massacring the Armenian populations, the worst slaughters occurring about the year 1895.

He was unsuccessful in accomplishing his purpose, faced as he was by the opposition of public opinion in Europe and his own country. In 1915, however, when most of the world was wrapped up in thoughts of war, the governing clique decided to rid their country once and for all of the unassimilated Armenians. Again deportations and massacres, which this time accomplished the desired result.

At the time that these harsh measures were being taken, one of the triumvirate which was controlling Turkish affairs explained the point of view of the Turks in an interview quoted by the American ambassador, Mr. Morgenthau. The speaker was Talaat Pasha:

We base our objections to the Armenians on three distinct grounds. In the first place, they have enriched themselves at the expense of the Turks. In the second place, they are determined to domineer over us and to establish a separate state. In the third place, they have openly encouraged our enemies. They have assisted the Russians in the Caucasus and our failure there is largely explained by their actions. We have therefore come to the irrevocable decision that we shall make them powerless before this war is ended.[6]

Ambassador Morgenthau, who was strongly critical of Turkish wartime policies and used every means at his disposal to protest against the Armenian deportations, quotes another statement from a government official showing the fear with which the Turks regarded the Armenians in their midst:

There are twenty-eight million people in Turkey and one million Armenians, and we do not propose to have one million disturb the peace of the rest of the population. The great trouble with the Armenians is that they are separatists. They are determined to have a kingdom of their own, and they have allowed themselves to be fooled by the Russians. Because they have relied upon the friendship of the Russians, they have helped them in this war. We are determined that they shall behave just as Turks do. . . . It is our own experience with revolutions which makes us fear the Armenians. If two hundred Turks could overturn the Government, then a few hundred bright, educated Armenians could do the same thing. We have therefore deliberately adopted the plan of scattering them so that they can do us no harm. As I told you once before, I warned the Armenian Patriarch that if the Armenians attacked us while we were engaged in a foreign war, that we Turks would hit back and that we would hit back indiscriminately.[7]

[6] *Ambassador Morgenthau's Story,* p. 337.
[7] *Ibid.,* pp. 347 f.

As a result of the deportations and bloody treatment of the Armenians, spurred on by a jealous fear for their own national well-being, the Turks had by the end of the war reduced the Armenian population within their borders to a negligible quantity. Many, of course, escaped from the country alive and were assisted in their distress by philanthropic organizations, among which the American Near East Relief performed outstanding service.

There remains to be considered what was perhaps the greatest danger of all to Turkey's successful attainment of solid and strong nationhood—the Greeks. Although they were not scattered as widely over Anatolia as were the Armenians, their location at important points along Turkey's seacoast, particularly in the neighborhoods of Istanbul, Izmir, Samsun, and Trebizond, as well as their skill in commerce and crafts, gave them a very important position in the life of Turkey. Ever since Greece had attained her independence as a separate kingdom in 1830, true Greeks had cherished the dream of restoring the old Byzantine Empire, joining Anatolia with the lands already comprising Greece to form a state whose power and glory should be reminiscent of the days when Constantinople was the queen city of the world. Thanks to the vitality of their *millett* and their wealth successfully accumulated in commercial and other enterprises, the Greek population of Turkey seemed to be in a strong position to bring their aspirations to an actuality in the parlous days which followed the World War. With Allied consent Greek troops landed in Izmir in 1919, much to the delight of the Greek residents of Turkey. The story of how the fresh and well-equipped Greek army invaded Anatolia only to be crushingly repulsed and routed by the Turks, who had been aroused to the point of desperation by this violation of their homeland, is vividly portrayed by A. J. Toynbee in his book, *The Western Question in Greece and Turkey*. So violently had the primitive hatreds and passions on both sides been aroused in the years from 1919 to 1922 that it was plainly impossible for the two peoples to continue living side by side. Since Turkey had emerged victorious, it was obvious that something would have to be done to remove the Greeks. Treatment such as that accorded the Armenians was out of the question since the Greeks were connected with a recognized nation with whom Turkey was avowedly at war. The only possible way out of the situation seemed to be an exchange of populations which would uproot all the Greek families in Turkey, many of whom had dwelt on the land for centuries, and send them to Greece, and perform a corresponding transfer of the Turkish families who had been left in Greek territory after the wave of Turkish dominion had been swept back in the various wars of the preceding hundred years. It was an extreme measure, fruitful of tremendous suffering and one not flattering to human nature which could permit hatreds to attain such a degree of bestiality. Yet to the framers of the Treaty of Lausanne it seemed the only safeguard against an outbreak of further troubles which might produce even worse sufferings. Thus by an official migration of hundreds of thousands of refugees, most of whom were forced to leave cherished homes and property to return to a strange fatherland, the national security of Turkey was assured. Nationhood, one of the novelties learned from the West, had been bought with a great price.

By the severe extirpating tactics just described Turkey had rid herself of the dangers from large disloyal populations in her midst and consequent threats against her own sovereignty in Anatolia. Yet she was not entirely freed from population worries, for in her largest city, Istanbul, thousands of Greeks, Armenians, and Jews continued to dwell: the Greeks by special exemptions from the general exchange of populations, the Armenians by good fortune in having escaped the policy of extermination elsewhere accorded their race, the Jews because their lot had not been much affected in the general unpleasantness. There were also in Istanbul and elsewhere numbers of citizens of other nations engaged in business and other enterprises. These various peoples, although they represented but a small fraction of Turkey's total population, had nevertheless to be taken into consideration in shaping Turkey's future course. According to official figures compiled in Turkey's first census in 1927, the country divides itself religiously as follows: Moslems 13,269,606; Catholics (presumably Roman), 39,511; Protestants, 6,658; Orthodox (presumably Greek), 109,905; Armenians (presumably Gregorians), 77,433; Christians (presumably Nestorians), 24,-307; Jews, 81,872; other religions, 17,494; those whose religion is not known or who have none, 2,702.[8] It thus appears that only 2.64 per cent of the total population is non-Moslem. Of the 63 *vilâyets* or states into which Turkey is divided there are only two in which the percentage of Moslems is lower than 94, six in which it is lower than 98, and 16 in which it is lower than 99. The *vilâyet* of Istanbul, which has a total population of 794,444, contains 547,126 Moslems or 68.86 per cent.

Figures for residents of foreign nationalities in Turkey for the same year (1927) show that only 0.64 per cent of the entire population are not Turkish citizens, most of whom are from European countries.[9] In the same connection it is interesting to note that 3.23 per cent of the population were born in foreign countries, while 13.58 per cent have a mother-tongue other than Turkish. Of those who speak foreign languages the largest number, some 8.69 per cent of the population, are Kurds, the only minority group of any size

[8] *Annuaire statistique*, II (1929), 42.
[9] *Ibid.*, p. 49.

left within the Turkish frontiers, and the only one, despite its ostensible Turkish nationality, to express open dissatisfaction with the conduct of the government.[10]

With Turkey's population so thoroughly Moslem as a result of the wartime developments, one might be led to expect that she would try to make observance of her traditional law code compulsory for all within her borders. But the young leaders of the Ankara government had no interest in retaining a code based on religious sanctions, and it was found impracticable to alter the old code, or *Mejelleh*, to make it usable in a twentieth-century secular state. The new determination to eliminate religion from its place of control in the government and the desire to have one modern law code which should be uniformly applicable to everyone in Turkey caused the decision on the part of the Ankara leaders to adopt a totally new set of statutes based on Western models. With a civil code modeled almost exactly on that of Switzerland, any reservations felt by the Christian and Jewish populations who remained in Turkey about relinquishing their long-standing exemption privileges faded away. Most of them upon being promised equal treatment in the country accepted Turkish citizenship on the same basis as the Moslems, whose feelings in regard to their new laws will be discussed later. Thus the year 1926 saw all legal distinctions between Turkish subjects on grounds of religion officially removed. Though a clause in the Organic Law stated that the religion of Turkey was Islam, following the Gazi's interpretation that this was not incompatible with freedom of thought, it was decided in the spring of 1928 to remove this clause from the law along with one which required members of the Grand National Assembly to take their oath upon the Koran.

---

[10] A rebellion in 1925 was suppressed with considerable bloodshed.

Freedom of religious thought was insured by the insertion of article 75 into the Organic Law. This provided that "no one can be disturbed on account of the religion, rite, or sect to which he belongs, nor for the philosophic opinions which he professes. All ritualistic ceremonies which are not contrary to the public order or morale, or inconsistent with the law, are authorized." This constitutional provision was backed by articles 175–78 of the Penal Code,[11] which prescribed stringent punishments for those who transgressed this statute. Thus did Turkey seek to place all religions on a basis of equality in the eyes of the law, while the government maintained a neutral position, independent of and superior to the demands of any one sect.

In the law of citizenship, promulgated June 4, 1928, religion is not mentioned in any way as a qualification or handicap in the attainment of Turkish citizenship. This is all the more remarkable when one remembers the traditional Islamic practice that citizenship went automatically with religious allegiance. Until the year 1869, when a law was promulgated providing that citizenship should be determined by considerations of descent and residence, the only recognized method of becoming an Ottoman subject was by becoming a Moslem.[12] But even after the Nationality Law of 1869 was instituted, the protests of various European Powers which were unwilling to grant to an infidel government the right to determine its own citizenship laws won the continued exemption from Ottoman citizenship of Christian residents in Turkey. The Ankara government, however, by abandoning its official connection with Islam and patterning its laws after those of European countries, has been able to lay down

[11] Adopted in 1926 and based on the Penal Code of Italy.

[12] The question of citizenship in Moslem lands is excellently treated by Dr. Jean S. Saba in *L'Islam et la nationalité*. Note particularly Part I, chap. iv.

citizenship regulations comparable to those of Western nations.

Turkey has followed the lead of certain European countries which adhere to the *jus sanguinis* and a modified *jus soli*. The *jus sanguinis* is stated clearly in article 1, which says, "A child born from Turkish father and mother in Turkey or in a foreign country is a Turk." This applies even in illegitimate births if the father or mother or both are Turks.[13] The *jus soli comes* into the third and fourth articles. Article 3 provides that a child born in Turkey of foreign parents living in Turkey (diplomats, of course, excepted) may claim Turkish citizenship within three years after reaching the age of maturity, and, according to article 4, if the foreign parents were themselves born in Turkey after January 1, 1929, the children are considered Turkish unless within six months after attaining the age of maturity they apply for the nationality of their parents. Turkish citizenship may be obtained through naturalization if the foreigner has lived in Turkey continuously for five years, and is recognized by the laws of his own country as having reached the age of maturity.[14] In this case, as with other cases where doubt or change enters in, the Executive Committee of the Council of Ministers is vested with considerable discriminatory power in granting or withholding privileges.

Turkey's intentions, as manifested in her laws and published declarations, are unquestionably for the best. She is evidently anxious to abolish all religious discriminations among her subjects and to move as far away as possible from the old system which split her country up into rival and unsympathetic divisions toward a whole-hearted unification along national lines. But it takes more than the mere passage of laws to change attitudes and hatreds which have been long

[13] Art. 2c.
[14] Art. 5.

in growing. It is apparent to anyone who spends any time in Turkey that equality among Turkish subjects has not yet been actualized, and cannot be expected to be for another generation at least. The discerning French journalist, Paul Gentizon, who served as the correspondent of *Le temps* during the Turkish struggle for independence, points out in his book, *Mustapha Kemal:*

There still exist in the country two categories of citizens with unequal rights, the Moslems and the non-Moslems.

This discrimination made between citizens of the same state is not, however, dictated by the difference of religion. Its causes are, on the one hand, of a moral nature; on the other hand, of an economic nature. Let us examine first the former set of causes. The Moslem Turks, who alone fought for the independence of the country, remain still very much under the influence of the tragic struggle which took place in Anatolia. No more have they forgotten the attitude taken at that time by various sections of the non-Moslem communities. Certain betrayals rendered them suspicious. And in this state of mind they no longer consider the oral manifestations of civic loyalty on the part of the minorities as being of indisputable sincerity. They wish proofs more tangible showing that the Greeks, Armenians, and Jews have become heart and soul true citizens of Turkey.

The economic causes of discrimination, Gentizon goes on to say, are those which have arisen by virtue of the old Ottoman system which placed commercial affairs in the hands of the non-Turks, giving the Greeks, Armenians, and Jews a tremendous head-start in the attainment of business acumen, now so earnestly sought by the Turks.[15]

The issue in regard to the loyalty of the remaining non-Moslem peoples is indeed a very real one to the enthusiastically patriotic Turks. Newspaper men, government officials, and other Turks with whom I talked constantly stressed to

[15] *Op. cit.,* pp. 261 ff.

me their belief that Armenian and Greek propagandists were spreading false and derogatory reports about the Turkish Republic at every opportunity. Despite, too, the outward manifestations of friendship between Turkey and Greece, flurries of suspicion are aroused by the publication of such news as appeared in *Le milliett* of December 11, 1929, that in four years a total of fifteen thousand Greeks, supposedly citizens of Turkey, had fled the country to serve terms in the Greek army. Among Greeks and Armenians in the country there may be found a smoldering resentment over being forced to become Turkish citizens, indicating that they felt it somehow improper to be classified as Turks. The situation is one full of hard feeling and constant provocation on both sides, for the non-Moslems, who represent a defeated cause, seek to retain whatever they can of their old traditions and individuality, and resent the restrictions placed on them by the government, which sees in the continuance of those features a future danger to the internal welfare and peace of the state. The government, seeing the resentment on the part of the minorities, has reason still further to doubt their loyalty and restricts their traveling and citizenship rights.

In the economic sphere Turkey is especially anxious to have her subjects thrive commercially. She has set up laws requiring foreign business concerns to employ a certain percentage of Turkish citizens as employees, while certain occupations are entirely closed to non-Turks. But in the reckoning it appears that only Moslem Turks are regarded as citizens in this connection. It has sometimes been difficult for Christian Turks to secure or hold positions on this account. Naturally, because of the required employment of Turks, individuals who have frequently had little or no experience, efficiency sometimes suffers until the "green" employees become accustomed to their new work. In certain parts of the interior of Anatolia, where Turks are attempting to carry on the various agricultural and industrial enterprises left by the refugee Greeks or Armenians, or to learn the skill in craftsmanship possessed by their departed neighbors, the let-down is very noticeable. It is no doubt true that necessity will spur the Turks on to learn the new techniques more rapidly than might otherwise be the case, but it cannot be expected under the circumstances that efficiency and skill will reach a high level until more time has been allowed for the development of experts.

Until Turkey has had enough time, then, to develop her nation to the point where the Moslem citizens are able to hold their own without fear or favor in the ways of the West, a certain amount of favoritism cannot but be expected in their treatment. The sooner this condition is reached, the sooner will Turkey become a full-fledged, strong nation, ready to forget past blows and insults, and able to take her place as a progressive nation in which citizenship might be considered a privilege by anyone. It is difficult to find fault with any of Turkey's intentions. When she does not act exactly as equitably as might be hoped for, observers must be patient, take into account the difficulties which she has had to face, and be ready to give credit for the advances which have actually been achieved.

VIII

THE NEW SPIRIT IN TURKEY'S SOCIAL INSTITUTIONS

Profound changes were introduced into Turkey, as we have noticed, by the compelling force of Nationalism. But it must not be thought that the Western infiltration was limited to the realms of international policy and internal political structure. It is difficult to find any aspect of Turkey's life which has not been affected by the flood of new ideals which so suddenly broke through the Islamic dikes. In fact, the Turkish Revolution gives every indication of being one of the most, if not the most, far-reaching revolutions ever accomplished by so large a society in a corresponding length of time. As P. Gentizon has said:

The French Revolution was limited to the domain of political institutions; the Russian Revolution has brought about disorder in social relations; but only the Turkish Revolution has concerned itself all at one time with political institutions, social relations, religion, the family, economic life, the customs and even the moral bases of society. One transformation invites another. One reform conditions the following one. For all lay hold on the life of the people.[1]

The Swedish observer, Rutger Essen, one of the most notable political writers of Scandinavia, has declared in the *Svenska Dagbladet:*

In this remarkable development there is only one country comparable, and that is Japan during the last three decades of

[1] *Mustapha Kemal,* p. 198.

the 19th century. The differences also are very important. At
first sight Japan did not go so far in her occidental reform as
Turkey has now done. Japan adopted only occidental technique.
Mentality and reforms in the social life have preserved an
indifference. This indifference, after 1900 or 1910, tends rather
to grow than to diminish. But Turkey's point of departure was
quite different, and besides she found herself much nearer the
common civilization in the Occident. In that which concerns
mentality, the Turks are not so far from the common European
type as one might imagine, much nearer than the Russians, for
example.[2]

In the pages which follow, we shall see what these far-
reaching changes have been, spending some time on the more
important ones and noticing the way in which the government
has introduced them, often with the co-operation of private
or semiofficial organizations.

An alteration which may at first glance appear superficial
but which in reality is of almost fundamental significance in
the country's changing mentality was the adoption of the
European hat in place of the brimless fez, which, though it
had been adopted in Turkey a hundred years ago as a reform itself supplanting the turban, had grown to symbolize
the mentality of conservatism and opposition to change. One
day in January, 1930, when I was walking through a street
of the old bazaar of Istanbul near the Bayezid Library with
an American friend who had been for some years in Turkey
publishing Bibles, he remarked that ten or fifteen years ago
it would have been impossible for a person in a European hat
to walk down that street without being spit on. The hat indi-
cated the European *ghiaour* so earnestly hated by the religious
conservatives. The same person in a fez would not be mo-
lested. Nowadays Turks and Western *ghiaours* all wear the
same headdress; the visible mark of distinction has been removed; and by the psychological influence of wearing identi-

[2] Translated in *Le milliett,* June 21, 1930.

cal clothes the cause of friendly co-operation is greatly enhanced. To enforce such a prescription by law may seem to have been a somewhat extreme measure, but it was a tangible Westernizing measure and one which would affect every man in Turkey. To put a Western hat on the head of every Turk would serve as an ever present reminder to the country that new customs were the vogue. It betokened, too, the power of the new government, and at the same time was a blow against religious fanaticism, for the hat with its brim meant awkwardness in touching one's forehead to the ground as required in the Moslem prostration for prayer.

When Kemal Ataturk and his fellow-legislators had decided in 1925 that the fez must go, the Gazi, with characteristic directness, propounded his reform in one of conservatism's strongholds, Kastamuni, a somewhat isolated section between Ankara and the Black Sea. His feeling on the matter is well expressed in his own words in his Six-Day Speech of 1927:

> Gentlemen, it was important to remove the fez, which sat on our heads like a symbol of ignorance, of fanaticism, of hatred against progress and civilization, and in its place to put the customary hat, headdress of the entire civilized world, and to show thereby, among other things, that no difference in manner of thought existed between the Turkish nation and the great family civilization.[3]

In an earlier chapter we saw that one of the traditional restrictions which brought out great discontent and resentment was the application of religious principles to the laws of the country. It did not take the Ankara reformers long to see that their progress could not be achieved as they wished, if their country was kept under the handicap of an antiquated system based on the *sharia* law of Islam. True it is that attempts had been made in previous administrations to modify the force and the scope of religious applications in Turkey's

[3] *Die neue Turkei,* II, 386.

laws, for example, the introduction of rational Western principles in the Hatti Humayun of 1856 and in Midhat Pasha's Constitution twenty years later, and under the "Young Turk" wartime administration in 1917 the transfer of the *sharia* or religious courts under the jurisdiction of the Ministry of Justice. In 1920 the newly organized Grand National Assembly made an attempt to shape the old religious institutions to conform to the exigencies of the new state. On May 2 a law was passed substituting in place of the old offices of *Sheikh-ul-Islam* and minister of *Evkaf* ("Pious Foundations") a single commissary. At the same time in its law of organization the Assembly expressly asserted its powers to make laws which had previously been determined by Islamic treatises. In the Law of Fundamental Organization, No. 85, according to article 1:

The Government belongs unconditionally and without restriction to the nation. The system of administration is based on the fact that the people govern strictly and effectively, in fact and in person, their destinies.

And article 7 stated:

The promulgation and application of all laws, even religious prescriptions, the modifications to be made to them, and their abolition, the conclusion of treaties, the signature of peace, the declarations of defense of the country, etc., as well as all analogous prerogatives belong to the Grand National Assembly. In the elaboration of the laws the needs of the times, the interests of the people, legislative and juridical data, and manners and customs will be taken into account.[4]

On March 3, 1924, a new law abolished the Commissary for the *Evkaf* and *Sheikh-ul-Islamate*, and religious affairs were placed under a departmental head in the office of the prime minister.[5]

[4] Schlicklin, *Angora*, pp. 40 f.
[5] Cf. Toynbee, *Survey of International Affairs* (1925), Part I: "The Islamic World since the Peace Settlement," pp. 71, 572 f.

The new leaders were giving more and more evidence of impatience with inadequate and compromising measures, and showed that they would be glad to get rid of all Islamic incumbrances as soon as possible. The next question naturally to be faced was what to put in place of the antiquated *Mejelleh* (Turkey's adaptation of Islamic law). On this question the minister of justice, Mahmud Essad, is quoted as declaring:

We are badly in want of a good scientific Code. Why waste our time trying to produce something new when quite good codes are to be found ready made? Moreover, what is the use of a Code without good commentaries to guide in the application of it? Are we in a position to write such commentaries for a new Code? We dispose neither of the necessary time nor of the necessary precedents in practice. The only thing to do is to take a good ready-made Code to which good commentaries exist, and translate them wholesale. The Swiss Code is a good Code; I am going to have it adopted, and I shall ask the Assembly to proceed to a vote *en bloc,* as Napoleon had his Code voted. If it had to be discussed article by article, we should never get through.[6]

In accordance with this attitude, the Assembly in 1926 adopted from Switzerland a Civil Code and a Code of Obligations, from Italy a new Penal Code, and from Germany a new Commercial Code. These were put into force after Turkey's legists and common people had had six months to study them. The responsibility on the judges and lawyers who had to lay aside most of their funds of learning and experience in the intricacies of the oriental *Mejelleh* Code and switch in less than a year to practicing according to an occidental law which laid on the magistrate's judgment much more responsibility than the hoary and petrified religious system ever thought of was tremendous. Yet the change in law was but one of the radical reforms to which the citizens of Turkey

[6] Quoted in Ostrorog, *The Angora Reform,* pp. 87 f.

had to accustom themselves during the first decade of the Republic.

In the brief treatment which we are able to give to these reforms, any one of which could be made the subject of a long and deep study, it must not be thought that because small space is devoted to them that they are of minor significance. The fact is, in the case of the law codes, as Gentizon has pointed out:

The adoption of a European civil code by a Moslem nation, accustomed for centuries to obey only a religious law considered as revealed, is one of the most important dates and events in the history of the world. For the first time a people of Mohammedan religion applies with respect to personal and family law a legislation completely free from theocratic dispositions and able to rule indiscriminately all the inhabitants of the country, whatever their race or their religion. . . . [Turkey] no longer admits any difference between men according to their faith or their belief. And in doing this, in accepting that legally in her midst there are no more any but citizens equal in rights and in duties, Turkey, first among the Moslem countries, admits a rationalistic conception of the universe and of humanity.[7]

The benefits which Turkey believes will be safeguarded by her new legal system are numerous. While it is true that repressive measures have been taken and high-handed methods used in the introduction of reforms, the end in view has usually been to insure the success of Westernization and to root out reactionary and dissenting forces which might have set up fatal obstacles to the attainment of the new goals. The worst thing to be said of this type of superimposed advance is the criticism made of all beneficent dictatorships, that the progress is not the result of popular mass initiative and that too much depends on the continuance in power of the strong dictator. In the case of Turkey, however, the handicaps of illiteracy, fanaticism, fatalism, and lack of means of commu-

[7] *Op. cit.*, pp. 219 f.

nication might so seriously have retarded progress that Turkey without strong leadership might have been unable to hold off Western imperialists and the country might have been forced to undergo the tribulations of India, Egypt, or even China. If the present government, it may be added, were solely interested in maintaining itself in power, it would not be sponsoring so thoroughgoing a system of education and so determined a war on illiteracy along with its introduction of liberal laws. For with schools and the ability to read, the seeds of democracy are being sown which must sooner or later produce a nation which will not countenance any rule which does not make for the ultimate welfare of the nation.

I have not been able to find, and so far as I know there has not yet been published in any language, a complete history of education in Turkey. For the historical data on educational developments during the past century I am indebted to Hilmi Malik Adnan, who holds the degree of Master of Arts from Columbia University, and who prepared a study chiefly dealing with preschool education for presentation to a conference of former Columbia students in Geneva. Of education under the régime of the sultans the report has the following to say:

In the old régime, the religious side of education was the most important thing, and everything was based on it. The world to come was more important for the living creatures of God than the present world. The religious influence was supreme with the old régime in the educational system, so much so that physical and natural courses were religiously interpreted. The subject of evolution was discarded and ignored. The aim in education was to train the pupils to become faithful subjects and officials of the Sultans and their government. The school discipline was a model of the life of that period. Mechanical obedience was the soul of discipline.

For centuries whatever schooling a Turk could receive was in or near the mosque, where one of the chief functionaries was named the *hodja,* or teacher. Whatever training these ecclesiastics had had was obtained in a *medresseh* or theological school, and the bulk of what they taught was the memorization of the Koran in Arabic—a language which was not understood by most Turks. Elementary education was limited to this sort of teaching unless the student sought to become a member of the Ulema and make himself an authority on Islamic law.

Better things might be said of Turkey's scholastic system in the early heyday of the Empire during the fifteenth and sixteenth centuries. When the religious ideal was flourishing with the enthusiastic energy of the newly converted Turks, the great sultans, notably Mohammed the Conqueror and Suleiman the Magnificent, were lavish in their endowments for schools, and the best minds were attracted into religious, legal, and administrative service, and the curriculums of Turkish institutions measured up with the best in Europe. But with decadence in the house of Osman followed decadence in the religious and educational realms, and little disposition toward revitalization was met with until the reign of Mahmud II, who laid his reforming hand on these as well as other spheres. From his time dates the first compulsory education law in Turkey, which, however, was probably little more than a statute on paper. In the late sixties elementary education for the second time was pronounced compulsory, and parents were obligated to send their children to school at the age of six. In 1870 a set of rules and regulations for elementary education was issued by the Department of Education, from which the following program is quoted by Hilmi Malik Adnan: "There will be an Elementary School in every quarter of a city and in every village; its scholastic years will be four, and the teaching of Alphabet, Koran,

Courses on Morals, Writing, Arithmetic, Turkish History, Geography, and others, will be done according to modern methods." Apparently as part of the same movement which in literature was producing a Europeanized school of writers and politically was bringing to birth the Young Turk party and the Constitution of 1876, educational enterprise opened an experimental elementary school at Noury Osmanieh Mosque, studied the elementary-school system of Europe, appointed a commission to organize and improve methods of teaching, opened more elementary schools in Istanbul, and started to spread enlightenment into the provinces. About 1885 the first elementary normal school in the interior was established at Sivas. Further progress was then checked for some years by the growing reactionary conservatism led by Abdul-Hamid II.

After 1908 when the forces of progress came to power, education came back into favor. The government schools were expanded, students were encouraged to go abroad for study, and Turkish Moslems even began attending in large numbers the European and American schools long maintained in the country as missionary agencies. Most remarkable of all, perhaps, was the advance made in the religious schools maintained by the *Evkaf* or "Pious Foundations." Through the influence of Hairi Effendi, *Sheikh-ul-Islam* and a very broad man, serious reforms were undertaken. Halidé Edib, who played a part in the modernization scheme, has given an intimate and interesting picture of the movement in her *Memoirs*. She says:

The *medresses* for the first time were to have modern science taught by modern teachers instead of the old scholastic curriculum and the old teachers. The mosque schools, which so far taught only the Koran and which were housed in little holes, were to be modernized, and a dozen schools were amalgamated in one big and up-to-date building in an important center. Each was to have a modern staff with a modern curriculum. The boys' schools were organized by Ali Bey, a very capable and progressive section chief in *evkaff*. The girls' schools as well as the small mixed ones were to be organized by Nakié Hanum as the general director. [8]

Halidé Edib herself became inspector-general and adviser of the girls' schools and remarks that "the curriculum of the *evkaff* schools at the time was more secular than obtained in the schools of the public instruction." [9]

However creditable might be the innovations which were introduced into the various schools of Turkey, one thing which became clear to the Ankara leaders as they came into control of Turkey's destinies was that too much of Turkey's education was unsystematized and left to chance whims of individuals who happened to be in control. Little continuity existed between administrations, and Turkey's schools never really quite knew what their true end was or should be. The programs, too, had little connection with the practical facts of life. These weaknesses were sensed and criticized by the Gazi in his important pronouncements to the population at Ismidt following the Greek defeat. Turkey's future program of public instruction, he declared,

will be of such a sort that those who will have followed it will become good agriculturists, good manufacturers, good merchants, good shoe-makers—they will become practical and profitable men. Public instruction constitutes the ensemble of institutions and programs which will teach all that.

Gentlemen, a director of public instruction with whom I conversed in the course of this trip has lived during his career of between twenty and thirty years in different parts of the country. According to the information which he gave me, he has received many contradictory programs which he applied or caused to be applied. For each minister who came to power elaborated a pro-

[8] *Memoirs of Halidé Edib*, p. 351.
[9] *Ibid.*, p. 352.

gram according to his own views, distributed it, and worked for
its application. Another minister would come some time after,
who was not pleased with this program and would apply another.
What did all these programs produce? Men who had learned a
great many things. But what did they know? A certain number
of theories. And what had they not learned? To understand themselves, life, and their needs. They had learned nothing that it is
necessary to know to live, and they were hungry.[10]

. . . I do not wish, Gentlemen, to trace a program of public
instruction. But I emphasize that it is absolutely necessary that
primary and secondary instruction give science and the knowledge
which civilization and reality demand of men. But they must be
given in a practical fashion in order that the child leaving the
school may be certain that he will find work.[11]

As a keynote not only of educational matters but of the
whole governmental attitude on public enlightenment the
Gazi's plea for disillusionment and eagerness to face facts is
one of the most significant pronouncements of that new spirit
which seeks to arouse the Orient from its dreamy existence.
He insisted:

No, Gentlemen! It is necessary to be very honest! The greatest
of the errors committed up till now, the greatest sin of our men
of action, of our enlightened men, above all of our men of science, has been in not being straightforward. It is essential to be
honest, it is necessary to carry on honestly in the sight of the
nation.[12]

In education as in the other phases of Turkish life which
have been considered the Western point of view brought
sweeping changes. The goal now was to have an educational
system which would be scientific, realistic, and practical. It
was to produce Turks who should be equipped mentally and
bodily to serve the nation. It was to compete successfully
with the foreign institutions which Turks feared were edu-

[10] "Le Ghazi et la révolution," instalment No. 44.
[11] *Ibid.*, instalment No. 45.
[12] *Ibid.*, instalment No. 48.

cating their children away from their national environment.[13] It was to be a unified system, scientifically planned, and this meant that religious influences, feared as enemies of progress, were to be eliminated or at least brought under control. In order, then, that such a system might be realized, there was passed on March 3, 1924, at the same time as the law previously mentioned which made religious affairs a subdepartment under the prime minister, the Law for the Unification of Educational Systems.[14] By this piece of legislation all the religious schools connected with the *Evkaf* or other pious institutions, as well as educational enterprises connected with other ministries, such as military high schools which had been run by the Ministry of National Defense, were transferred directly under the control of the Ministry of Public Instruction. To the same Ministry was also diverted the income provided by the *Evkaf* ("Pious Endowments") for Islamic schools. Religious instruction, which had been the original *raison d'être* of education in Turkey, now played a distinctly minor rôle and was retained for a time by the secular ministry only in so far as it could be made to contribute in some way toward the building-up of the nation and the national spirit. Headed by a permanent commission of educational experts who retain their offices whatever political wind might blow, public instruction in Turkey entered upon a period of unprecedented activity in the war on ignorance and fanaticism and the building-up of a modern system of universal education.

The Ministry of Public Instruction is one of the most important departments of the Ankara government, leading and controlling as it does the agencies by which Turkey hopes to achieve that which is infinitely more difficult than any change in dress or legal system, a change in the nation's entire mentality. The Department of Public Instruction is intrusted

[13] The place of foreign schools in Turkey is discussed in chap. ix.
[14] Text in Toynbee, *op. cit.*, Part I, Appen. II, p. 574.

with the responsibility of producing a new generation which is literate, practical, versed in the ways of the West, and, above all, enthusiastically useful to Turkey's national society. For 1933 its budget was £T6,528,327 (about $3,000,000). [15] The post of minister of public instruction has often been held by men who are among the country's ablest.

Of central significance in the Department, however, is the permanent commission known as the National Bureau of Education and Instruction. According to Professor Ismail Hakki of Istanbul University, in his article on Turkish education for the *Educational Year Book of 1928,* the duties of this Bureau include the following:

To make decisions as to what educational aims, systems, and methods are to be accepted and applied; to examine books written for Primary and Secondary schools and to accept and authorize those which conform to the curriculum and which suit the educational conditions of the country; further to arrange and have printed school books for the various subjects of the curriculum; and to follow educational magazines and books written in foreign languages and to publish in whole or in summary those which will be useful for the teachers of Turkey.[16]

Compulsory education, which is still far from being universally enforced due to the lack of trained teachers and adequate equipment, begins at the age of seven and extends through the primary years, supposedly five in number. According to statistics given out by the Ministry of Public Instruction, there were in the year 1932-33 a total of 6,733

---

[15] According to the *Annuaire statistique,* Vol. VI, for 1932-33, certain other departments received the following appropriations for 1933 National Defense: £T33,326,640; Public Works. £T14,296,993; Finance: £T12,387,287; Gendarmerie: £T8,679,379; Justice: £T8,013,478; Hygiene and Social Assistance: £T4,196,884; Agriculture: £T4,487,- 611; Religious Affairs: £T619,586. Payment of public debts took £T146,210,355 in that same year.

[16] "Present-Day Education in Turkey," *op. cit.*

primary schools with 15,064 teachers, and attended by 567,-963 pupils throughout the country. The progress already made is evident when compared with the years 1923–24 and 1913–14. In 1923–24 the figures are 4,470 primary schools, 9,760 teachers, and 330,740 pupils, while in 1913–14, in the same area as modern Turkey, there were but 3,623 primary schools, 5,963 teachers, and 215,130 pupils. Encouraging though the progress be, however, it is estimated that the number of children who have reached school age but who do not attend school is more than 1,000,000.

Government education provides, besides the five-year primary course, a three-year middle school and a three-year lycée course, as well as special courses in professional schools and the University at Istanbul. More will be said about these higher schools in subsequent pages. Supervision of the educational system is maintained by the division of the country into thirteen sections, each administered by a regional superintendent who is directly responsible to the Ankara Ministry. The thirteen sections are in turn divided into smaller districts, each with a superintendent, and some districts are even subdivided. Close watch is kept on the schools through three types of inspectors: (1) primary inspectors who are responsible to the district superintendents; (2) regional inspectors, responsible to one of the thirteen regional superintendents and authorized to inspect all educational institutions within the specified region; (3) central inspectors, operating under the Ankara Ministry and having broad responsibilities in the examination of conditions, administrative and educational, throughout the whole system of public instruction. Financial support for the system comes as much as possible from the cities and vilâyets of Turkey, while the government budget takes care of whatever else is necessary. The training of teachers will be discussed later in connection with the higher education, and the recently opened adult schools will be described in connection with the promulgation of the new alphabet.

Since it is upon primary education that Turkey is laying great emphasis in the development of the type of citizens which she hopes will strengthen the nation, it will be of interest to examine the curriculum which has been laid out for primary schools and to note some of the objectives of the system as they appear in the instructions issued to primary-school teachers and in other publications.

The following curriculum for primary schools, which was adopted in 1926, exemplifies the extent to which Western educational ideas have penetrated the country. It is a far cry from the educational methods of the *hodjas* in the mosque schools which centered about the Koran and Islamic lore. It is a constant source of amazement to the outsider traveling in Turkey to see such things as school children dressed in neat European uniforms walking hand in hand with mothers who still wear the veil and *charshaf;* or to hear from a school-room window the strains of children's voices joyously singing a song to the tune of the "Barcarolle" from *The Tales of Hoffmann* while from a nearby minaret may be issuing the plaintive and distinctly oriental call to prayer; or to talk with a highly cultured Ankara official who follows American educational journals, including those of the University of Chicago, and who knows the history of American education more thoroughly than 999 out of 1,000 Americans. In the following curriculum it will be noted that the five years are divided into two stages, the first of three years and the second of two. The figures in Table I represent lesson periods per week. The table is taken from the previously quoted article by Ismail Hakki written for the *Educational Year Book for 1928.*

TABLE I

Lessons	First Stage			Second Stage	
	1st Year	2d Year	3d Year	4th Year	5th Year
A.B.C.	12	..	..	..	..
Reading	..	4	4	2	2
Writing	..	2	2	1	1
Composition ..	..	2	2	2	2
Grammar	..	..	..	1	1
Penmanship ...	..	2	2	1	1
Religious training *	..	2	2	1	1
Orientation	4	4	4	..	..
Arithmetic-geometry ...	2	2	2	3	3
History	..	..	..	2	2
Geography	..	..	..	2	2
Nature study ..	..	..	..	2 }	3
Object lesson ..	..	..	..	.. }	
Civics	..	..	..	2	2
Drawing-handicraft	4	4	4	3	3
Music	2	2	2	2	2
Physical training	2	2	2	2	1
Domestic science (extra)	..	..	..	..	(2)
Total	26	26	26	26	26

* Religion has subsequently been eliminated from the school curriculums.

After reading this program, which of course has gone through modifications from year to year, one can appreciate the message issued by the minister of public instruction to his teachers throughout Turkey at the opening of the school year in September, 1929:

Teachers, in your instruction, turning your eyes away from everything that has any vestige of the past, you will have as a sacred ideal the future of the new Turkey, prosperous and civilized. The ideas which you will inculcate will be the reflections of the ideals of the great Gazi, the creator of the new Turkish world, and the one who has turned a new page of our history.[17]

[17] Djemal Husni in Le milliett, September 18, 1929.

One of the vestiges of the past on which Turkey had most resolutely turned her back was the continuance of Islamic instruction in its old supernaturalistic and ritualistic form. Education no longer worked to produce good and faithful Moslems, but good and faithful Turks. Islam in so far as it could contribute to the new end was retained, but the religious instruction was not given by turbaned *hodjas* but by the regular secular teachers and was so presented, as will be seen in a later chapter, as to produce devoted Turks. As a matter of fact, recent developments have produced a new type of course called *Yurt Bilgisi* ("Knowledge of the Home"), which seems to play a part of more and more importance in the production of intelligent and patriotic citizens. A study of the educational objectives as they are presented in a popular *Yurt Bilgisi* series of textbooks and in the published instructions to the primary teachers will give an idea of what the Turks wish their educational system to accomplish and some of the means by which the students are imbued with the new ideals.

The four aims which seem to stand out most prominently in the writings mentioned are: (1) the attainment of knowledge for practical uses; (2) the development of a spirit of social co-operation; (3) the kindling of a devoted flame of patriotism; and (4) the promotion of good health. A fifth desideratum, which at present is frankly given but little emphasis due to the all-important need of gaining equipment for the struggle to keep alive, is aesthetic appreciation of nature and the arts. As years go by the finer and gentler sensibilities will no doubt bulk larger among the aims which Turkey wishes to attain in her education, but at the present time when every effort is being bent to bring Turkey back on her feet economically, and resentment is still rife against the leaders of the past whose dalliances and dreamy lack of practicality are blamed for Turkey's present plight, it is not to be wondered at that things dainty or delicate are considered of secondary consequence. And while it is recognized that music and the other arts are important parts of the civilization to which Turkey aspires, one must not be surprised to see painting take its greatest advances in the lines of commercial art, and music and sculpture find their expression in martial and patriotic subjects.

Turkey's desire that knowledge shall have a *practical application in life* is manifested frequently in the instructions issued by the Ministry of Public Instruction to the primary teachers in the little handbook entitled *Ilkmektepler Talimatnamesi.* Section 51 of this booklet has the following to say:

It is necessary that training should be practical, and it should be based upon the principles of observation of the objects with which the lesson is connected. If the object can not be brought to the classroom, then students must be taken to the place where they can see these objects; if this is not possible, then some equipment of the school such as maps or pictures must be used to make the lesson more interesting for the child.

Carrying this idea still farther, the minister of public instruction added in a special leaflet of instructions to the teachers which he inclosed with the booklet:

Children should be acquainted with the economic activities of their vicinity and the agricultural production and work of the place in which they live. Where vegetables and fruit grow, the lessons should have a close relation with the activity of the locality. If the village or city is near the shore of the sea, it is amusing and interesting for the children to have a knowledge of fishing and canning and the important part played by these in the economic life of the nation.

The same principle, says this educator, can be applied to mathematics, geometry, civics, geography, handwork, etc.:

The instructor should develop the tendency of the student, and the instructor who understands his work perfectly creates this type of interest in the child. Primary education does not help to realize a future career, but it creates and must create an interest. It should never be forgotten that primary education increases the productive energies, and this can only be obtained by having a close relation between the lessons and the economic activities of the environment.

Strong objection to any sort of teaching which is so abstract as to have no influence on the child's ability to face life more adequately is contained in sections 40 and 41 of the "Instructions":

It is necessary that teaching should have an educative nature. The lesson which does not have any influence upon the character and the spirit of the child is not an educative lesson. Students must be able to put into practice what they have learned. They must be able to apply their knowledge to overcome the difficulties of life.

Teaching must have a relation with the intellectual training of the child. It must also have a close contact with the feelings and will power of the child. So it is necessary to study the relations of the lesson to the points which are mentioned above [feelings and will power].

The lesson which is taught under the title of "Knowledge of Life" concentrates on the relations of the child with his environment. Therefore this lesson is the centre and the axle of the activities of the students.

Patriotic feelings are increased in teaching Turkish history, geography and civics. Arithmetic must be taught so as to increase the reasoning ability of the child. Drawing and handwork should serve to give a taste and appreciation of the fine arts; they also give a sense of pleasure derived from being able to accomplish something. Physical instructions should develop the body of the student and also strengthen the quality of daring. Games and excursions are to increase the power of observation.

One of the worst faults with the instruction in the old mosque schools was its emphasis on memorizing and repetition—features which made the students tend to be purely imitative and lacking in mental initiative. This meant that their education did nothing to help them think for themselves and apply their learning to constructive living. This error is specially warned against in the Ministry's "Instructions," again in section 41:

Students often fall into carelessness. They interpret the things which they see in accordance with their own feelings and imagination in a way often vague, sometimes wrong, and sometimes exaggerated. So teachers should correct them in games and in experimental activities. If a student is asked to repeat aloud what he has read in class, it will be found that he has read only with his eyes but not with his mind. The habit of playing on words must be avoided. One of the greatest duties of a teacher is to prevent his students from getting such bad habits and to strengthen the relations between the intellect and the talents of the child.

The second objective of education which we shall consider is that which aims to develop a *spirit of social co-operation* among the students. Sections of the "Instructions" which deal with this phase of the program are the following:

20. From the first day the younger generation starts school it should develop social powers and abilities so as to adapt itself physically and spiritually in the most useful way to the national community and to the Turkish Republic.

21. The first and the last aim of training in Primary Schools is the full adaptation of children to the national life. So there must be close harmony and relations between the schools and the national communities.

22. The social principles of the national communities must form the basis of school life and of the administration and discipline of the school and of the relations of teachers with the students.

23. In the schools of the Republic, discipline cannot be based on methods of compelling and restraining. Love and respect must be the axle of the relations between the pupils and between pupil and teacher.

24. The discipline of the school must be the result of work

done in the proper way. It must grow out of healthy and educative games, close social relations, mutual help and understanding. It must be a democratic, free, habitual discipline, inspired from the above-mentioned virtues.

25. Serious attention should be given that students in their characters and their words should be truthful and should behave properly in their relations with one another and should play games fairly.

26. Teachers should work hard to cultivate the sense of punctuality and regularity and to realize the value of time.

27. It is necessary that special attention should be paid to the fact that students should be persistent and faithful to the work which they have undertaken. They should not neglect the details of a duty and should be invested with civilized virtues so as to sacrifice their personal interests for the benefit of the community.

28. Care must be taken that competition either in lessons or in games, in the same school or between different schools, should be reasonable and moderate and that it should not create hatred in individual or in group games.

29. Students should know thoroughly and believe firmly that the school building, equipment, and furniture are to be kept in good condition and that they have no right to use public property more than any one else.

30. Students should be careful in their dress, behavior, and talk. It is important that they should avoid dressing and behaving carelessly. Especially should students avoid using bad language which shows a social defect.

31. Students from an early age should learn to discuss politely, to defend their own point of view without hurting others, to listen to the opinions of others, and to correct themselves without being hurt.

32. It should always be remembered that all social virtues may be obtained by experience in life and that habits can only be formed in this way. In order to lead the students to form good habits they should be given opportunity for activities so as to form these desired habits. This method is preferable to giving lectures and making speeches. Students must find themselves in an environment where the affairs of daily life are treated with honesty and purity and are closely related with physical and intellectual activities, and where there is no possibility of dishon-

esty and impurity, nor of a lazy life. Therefore teachers should concern themselves more with the environment than with the behavior of the individual student. The spiritual atmosphere of the school must be as pure as the material atmosphere.

33. Students must be saturated with the spirit of social service. For example, students ought to feel uneasy when they see window panes dirty. And where there are no servants, students should remedy the situation themselves. Students should not be indifferent to having the school garden ruined. Teachers should never forget that they will always be examples to their students.

A word of further advice to the teachers on this subject of building up habits which are desirable in modern Turkish society is added by the minister in his previously mentioned leaflet of suggestions to the teachers. He advises the teacher to study student activity, urging that he should study the influence of the work upon the child and the results of the work, and discover what sort of habits are formed; and the instructor should ask himself whether Turkish citizens have need of these habits. He goes on:

If you study the activities from this point of view, you will find what is to be avoided and what is to be allowed. Children should be trained to express their opinions freely. Insincerity and any tendency toward charlatanism and deceitfulness should be cut out at once. The student should understand that he is a human being and he should be treated as such.

Section 125 of the "Instructions" goes still farther into the subject of developing the right sort of members of society by establishing the right sort of life in the school.

It is necessary that the school should have the nature of a small society. It is not necessary that the student should only learn lessons and play games which are approved, but he must also use his own will and create some activities himself.

These activities may be put down as follows:

1) The students should feel responsible for the cleanness of the classroom, and for this they should have a committee for

cleanness and orderliness. Students elect the members of this committee.

2) A sense of responsibility may be given the students for keeping the school equipment in order.

3) The members of the fourth and fifth classes may be advised to form an honor committee. The committee is composed of four members, two from each class. Each member is to act in turn as chairman. . . . The members of the committee may give their opinions about cases connected with school discipline, if approved by the head teacher. Another important duty of the Honor Committee is this: that they should lead the students to obey the rules of the school and rules of friendship and health. Another duty is to pay special attention that vulgar language shall not prevail among the students.

4) With the help of the teachers the committee should try to form hobby clubs and savings societies, to help the Red Crescent and the Children's Protective Society [Himayei Etfal], to protect useful animals, and to take care of trees and gardens. (Besides these activities which are mentioned above, no other imitative activities are permitted in the schools.)

5) With schools in the same or in different cities the students may exchange postcards and give information about their own city. For this purpose the members of the higher classes may form a club.

6) Members of the fourth and fifth classes may be encouraged to put up a wall newspaper to give a record of activities in the school and of outside news which may interest the students. These wall newspapers may also have colored pictures. In order to obtain the best results, one of the teachers should take an interest in this activity.

7) The following points are important in the games and play program of the primary school: students should be encouraged to play, but football (soccer) is strictly forbidden. Basketball and volleyball [18] and other easy games may be allowed. In order to prevent competition and jealousy in collective games members of the teams should be exchanged. Sport activities, especially

[18] It is interesting to note that these two words have been taken over directly into the new Turkish and are spelt phonetically, as is all Turkish; thus *baskitbol* and *volibol*.

group excursions, camping and mountain-climbing, should be encouraged.

8) Regarding the relations of boys and girls,[19] special attention should be paid to politeness, but the boys should not be allowed to pay too many compliments to the girls. While having games of any sort or any other activities, it is not necessary that boys and girls should mix with each other. When it is noticed that boys wish to be alone on one side and girls on the other, it is not right to prevent such a division.

9) When it is possible, the children may form a club to help poor students, but in helping the poorer students extreme care should be taken lest the poor students' feelings be hurt. To help one group, the other group should not try to collect money openly. Public charitable organizations must be formed outside the schools, and students may receive help from them. These organizations may be the regular charity organizations of the city, or the teachers may form special organizations for this purpose.

10) Celebration of the National Holidays mentioned in the program is a source of love for the school, and later it develops into love for the community.

11) Schools should have a close relation with the environment and especially with the parents and guardians of the students. This relation may be established by communication with the parents and the holding of social exercises. It is useful to have these social exercises twice a year if the building is suitable. No obligation should be levied on the parents, and the program should be fixed by the students. If it is a play, it should have not more than two acts; national dances, monologues, and the recitation of poems may compose the program. Either the head teacher or another of the teachers must explain the nature of these exercises.

12) Besides these annual social exercises, class social activities may take place, provided that too much time is not taken

[19] Coeducation was introduced into the entire Turkish school system, the lycées temporarily excepted, in 1928. This radical change was regarded apprehensively by many parents. But as Père Ludovic of the French legation remarked, it has long been a custom in Turkish families to bring up small children in close proximity to each other and to their parents so that a child of six frequently has a rather complete sex knowledge.

for preparation. One or two of the activities which are mentioned in the above articles may be performed by the class, and the teacher may give a short lecture. Special care should be taken that the lecture be interesting and brief. Some educational authorities or government officials may be invited to these exercises. These social exercises should not last more than two hours and must be over at nine o'clock in the evening.

One last section of the "Instructions" may be quoted in connection with this objective of producing children who will be useful and co-operative citizens. This deals with the subject of thrifty economy. Section 35 states:

Another important phase of primary education is thrift. At every opportunity students should be informed and trained for national thrift. They must learn to economize their pencils, papers, etc. This idea of saving and thrift may be communicated to students in arithmetic classes by giving them special problems to solve.

One of the chief agencies used by the schools in developing the sense of social co-operation is the course mentioned earlier, known as *Yurt Bilgisi* ("Knowledge of the Home"). In the series of three books written by Mitat Sadullah for use in the third, fourth, and fifth grades of the primary schools, the child is given an introduction to all the institutions and activities with which the Republic wishes him to become acquainted, while backward customs are in various ways made to look either repulsive or ridiculous. Frequent use is made of letters or conversations between village worthies to explain new laws and to stress the importance of civilized living. Health activities are explained, the use of tax money is outlined, and the importance of willing military service is set forth. Particular emphasis is placed on the value of cooperative enterprises in purchase of agricultural machinery, etc. Turkey is shown to be made up of individuals and groups who must co-operate in order to make the most of their country.

In the book for the third grade is printed a letter purporting to have been written by a village lad to his uncle in Istanbul. The writer tells his uncle about the changes which have occurred in his village since the uncle's last visit. Among the improvements are mentioned the following: an extra teacher has come for the village school; the village guesthouse has been refurnished; the old coffee-house is now clean and well lighted with a *Lux* lamp where men come to read the Istanbul newspapers and listen to the gramophone; new homes have been built, with the chicken coops and stables located at a distance from the family dwelling; roads have been repaired and swamps drained—in fact, the village has raised itself to the standard of European civilization.[20]

In the volume for the fourth grade appears a set of "Civilized Rules Which Everybody Should Respect in Town and City Life." In regard to appearance in the street the writer has the following to say:

The problem of appearance in the street is very important. Civilized people can go out in the street only with a civilized appearance.

The Republican Government which has changed everything bad in the country has also taken appearance under some regulation and has adopted the hat for the headdress. There is no possibility hereafter of walking in the streets with a gown and *ketchekula* [bowl-shaped cap].[21]

Further advice is offered in regard to "behavior in public places like the cinema and theater":

One must be cleanly dressed when he goes to public places like the theater and cinema. You cannot go to a public place with dirty and dusty looking clothes. In such places one must not be

[20] *Op. cit.*, pp. 104 f.
[21] *Op. cit.*, p. 178.

in a condition which will disgust others. It is not allowed to smoke or speak loudly in the theaters and cinema halls, and especially while the film is being shown or while the play is being acted, talking is not a thing befitting a gentleman; and while listening to music, even if the piece is not to our taste, things like grimacing and laughing we must avoid.

In covered places one must take off his hat. . . .

It is not a thing befitting children who have gone to school and who have been taught politeness to attempt to get into the cinema or theater without a ticket, or to sit in the front rows with a ticket for the rear.[22]

In the third-grade book is printed the government's "Law of the Village," which contains twelve articles:

1) To pave the roads of the village with stone from one end to the other.

2) To build a laundry, a bath, and a marketplace in the village.

3) To grow forests at proper places in the borders of the village and on the hills.

4) To buy co-operatively agricultural machinery such as tractors, reapers, and threshers.

5) To bring in artificial fertilizer in order to get greater production.

6) To bring in books that will increase the knowledge of the peasant.

7) To kill insects which harm vineyards, fruitful or fruitless trees, and crops.

8) To keep the sown and planted crops and trees of the village people safe from every kind of damage and loss.

9) To irrigate co-operatively all the village land in order to water the village fields and orchards.

10) To make, to build, or to bring co-operatively a mill for the village.

11) To bring a sanitation officer in order to take care of the health of the village people. Otherwise to employ a man who will be sent by the village to the kaza [county] capital in order to attend and get instruction from the health courses opened in the city.

[22] *Ibid.*, pp. 178 ff.

12) To keep the medicines given by the Government in order to use them at the time required.[23]

Third in the list of objectives which we have mentioned as being striven for in Turkey's primary education is that of *inculcating patriotic devotion to the Turkish Republic* in the hearts of the children. Illustrations as to the methods used may again be found in the "Instructions" for the teachers and in the *Yurt Bilgisi* books. Patriotism may, of course, be regarded as one phase of the second objective, that of producing children who will be useful, devoted, and co-operative members of the Turkish society. Yet its importance in the eyes of the government and its contrast to the former religious loyalty stressed by the mosque schools warrant its being given separate treatment.

According to section 36 of the "Instructions":

The Turkish cause and Turkey will be the fundamental axle of training. The national feelings of the students should be strengthened at every chance. The significance and bountiful gifts of this Revolution must be explained thoroughly. Ceremonies and other exercises carried out on the anniversary of the Proclamation of the Republic [October 29] and the Bayram of April 23 [24] give a chance to increase the national feelings of the children.

Section 37 states:

Students should love and respect their flag, which represents the country and the nation. Thereafter in every primary school it is necessary that a flag ceremony should take place on the first and the last days of the week. The school building must have a flagpole, and this must be nearly as high as the school building. During official holidays and the days of Bayram there must be a flag on the mast. This flag must be prepared according to the flag instructions. The flag is raised one hour before sunrise and is

23 *Op. cit.*, pp. 39 ff.

24 National holiday in honor of children, anniversary of the first meeting of the National Assembly at Ankara, April 23, 1920.

lowered at sunset. It is not permissible for the flag to stay up during the night. Children must learn to salute the flag. . . .

Pictures as an aid toward the awakening of patriotic ideals are recommended in article 144:

It is desirable that the following items should decorate the walls of the assembly halls and public rooms:

1) A large picture of His Excellency the President, Gazi Mustafa Kemal.

2) Pictures of the Turkish leaders (a special list is prepared).

3) Pictures of great events in Turkish history and important places in Turkey, pictures of Turkish monuments and valuable paintings (a special list will be prepared).[25]

In addition to these symbolic and ceremonial methods of arousing a patriotic spirit, two other methods appear in the instruction given in the *Yurt Bilgisi* courses. These are: (1) the historical presentation of Turkish history as something proud and noble and worthy of admiration and (2) the appeal to youthful idealism to devote its energies to carrying on the progressive work commenced by the Republican leaders.

An example of the *historical-greatness presentation* is found in the third-grade volume of Mitat Sadullah's *Yurt Bilgisi:*

The Turks [26] are the oldest independent nation of history. Our nation is called the Turkish nation. The Turkish nation is one of the oldest and greatest nations. The masses of people who talk with the same language and who have been born of the same stock and whose feelings are the same are called a *nation*. There are many nations in the world, Turkish, French, Japanese, etc.

The Turks are of a very old nation. While the other nations

[25] The liberal use of pictures in Turkey, notably the ever present likenesses of the Gazi, indicates the strong trend against Islam's longstanding objection to any sort of artificial reproduction of the human face or figure.

[26] The term "Turk," because of its association with the rougher but more virile civilization of the Central Asiatic Plateau, has now supplanted the term "Ottoman" or "Osmanli," which connotes the refined but effeminate era of the sultans.

were in a state near barbarism, the Turks had a strong government and good laws. The Turks who lived in Central Asia some
thousand years ago have left many traces of their civilization.

The Turks are the bravest and best-hearted nation in the
world. To be brave, to be hospitable, and to pity those who have
fallen are some of the most beautiful qualities of the Turk.

Turks have formed great and independent states since very
old times and from time to time have taken many nations under
their domination.

There are millions of Turks in Europe and in Asia, but the
greatest Turkish state in the world is the Turkish Republic.[27]

This tendency to dwell on the historic achievements of the
Turks and to claim as ancestors many of the great conquering
peoples of Asia characterizes all history teaching in Turkey
today. A four-volume work entitled *Universal History* was
published in August, 1931, for use in the schools of the country. Much emphasis is laid upon the relationship of the Turks
and the ancient Hittites. Non-Turkish historians may dis-
agree with certain assumptions and interpretations which
play fast and loose with the previously accepted concepts of
Asiatic history, but when one considers the nationalistic bias
which pervades the history texts of every other nation in the
world, he would hardly be justified in singling out Turkey
for criticism.

Similarly motivated by a desire to build up national pride
is the current tendency to make the language more purely
Turkish and to purge it of foreign words, especially those of
Arabic and Persian derivation. So many names and titles are
being changed and the national vocabulary undergoing such
constant modification that those who write about Turkey are
under a severe handicap in their effort to find the proper
designation for the subject under discussion. Such alterations
in the national speech must be accepted, however, as inevitable in a nationalistic program such as that sponsored by

[27] *Op. cit.*, pp. 93 f.

Ankara. Kemal Ataturk himself, in an Introduction written in 1930 for an important linguistic work, *For the Turkish Language,* by Sadri Maksudi, points out:

The tie between national sentiment and language is very strong. A rich national language has great influence on the development of national feeling. The Turkish tongue is one of the richest of all; it only needs to be wisely used. The Turkish nation, which has known how to establish its government and its high independence, must free its tongue from the yoke of foreign words.[28]

An example of the *appeal to youthful idealism* in the inculcation of Turkish patriotism is contained in the *Yurt Bilgisi* for the fifth grade. In the concluding pages, the chapter called "Duties of the Young People," appears the following:

When the word *youth* is pronounced, you remember strength, valiance, agility, and newness. Our young Republic is waiting for every kind of progress and uplift from the youth. Our Grand Gazi was not satisfied with saving our country from the enemies; he brought about in our country a great national, mental, and social revolution also; he removed oldness and rotten organizations.

Are not all these things the removal of oldness from the country and its rejuvenation?

It is the greatest service to our country to save our beloved Republic, which we established as a result of great sacrifices, from every kind of danger, and, if necessary, to die for it. Because the country of the Turks will be lifted up only through the help of the Republic. The Turkish nation will attain the benefits and the advancements which she lacked for centuries by working in the way the Republican Government has shown. If we think of the many benefits that the very young Republic has procured for us, we understand what additional benefits we shall get from this fine Government.

We will not avoid any kind of sacrifice for the uplift of our

[28] Quoted by Sir Telford Waugh in "A Far Reaching Turkish Plan," *Journal of the Royal Central Asian Society,* XX, Part IV (October, 1933), 581.

beloved country. We will break every hand stretching out to damage the Turkish Republic even though that may result in our death. We will always work for the maintenance of the rule of our new and modern ideas in every corner of our beautiful country.

Young people, everything is yours hereafter; country, flag, and Republic are yours hereafter! Lift higher than all else our beloved Republic and our independence which we won for the price of the blood of hundreds of thousands of martyrs. Work always; work harder than any body and any nation. There are people ahead of us who have started much earlier than we. You must run in order that our victorious flag which has been waving in the skies may wave eternally.

Never expect anything from the past; take only advice from the past. Expect everything from the future. Let your eye and soul always face forward. Let your life be filled with joys and happiness.[29]

One of the most famous patriotic pleas is that addressed by the Gazi to his young fellow-countrymen and appearing in his Six-Day Speech:

Turkish youth! Your first duty is to guard and defend forever the national independence, the Turkish Republic. That is the sole basis of your existence and your future. This basis contains your most costly treasure. In the future too there will be both at home and abroad ill-will which will want to snatch away this treasure from you. If you are forced to defend your independence and the Republic, then, in order to perform your duty, you will have to watch out for the possibilities and conditions of the situation in which you may find yourself. It might be that these conditions and possibilities were absolutely unfavorable. It is possible that the enemies who sought to destroy your independence and your Republic represented the most victorious power that the earth had ever seen; that through intrigue or force of arms every fort and every arsenal in the fatherland was seized; that all your armies were dispersed and the land actually and completely occupied.

Assume in order to put before your eyes a still gloomier possi-

[29] *Op. cit.*, pp. 204 ff.

bility, that those who possess the governmental authority in the land have fallen into error, that they are fools or traitors, yea, that these ruling people have let their personal interests fall in with the political aims of the enemies. It might come about that the nation had fallen into complete want and extreme privation; that she found herself in a state of collapse and complete exhaustion.

Even under such circumstances and conditions like these, O Turkish child of the future centuries, is it your duty to save your independence, the Turkish Republic. The strength you need for this end surges in the noble blood which flows in your veins.[30]

The fourth thing which Turkey seems most eager to accomplish in her primary-education program is the *spreading of health knowledge and sanitation*. The articles in the "Instructions" for the primary teachers in this regard are indicative of a determination to stamp out the lazy fatalism which frequently prompted peasants to accept disease and squalor as a divine prescription, and to equip the new generation with knowledge which would permit them to fight infection and build up strong and healthy physiques. Following are the sections which deal with "Health Activities and Services in the School":

151. Special attention should be paid to the formation of health habits among the students. These should be encouraged on every occasion. Teachers must be watchful of the positions of the students in classroom and workshop, and specially while reading, writing, or drawing, the position of the book and paper is very important. In this case the normal standard is 30 centimeters. Some pupils may have eye trouble and be unable to see at that distance. Such students must be examined by specialists.

152. The air in the classrooms and in other rooms must be changed frequently. It is useful to have the upper part of the window open. During the winter it must be arranged to have the upper part of the window open.

153. Students should be assigned by turns to open the windows between classes.

[30] *Op. cit.*, II, 388.

154. It is necessary that the classrooms should be at a temperature between 16° and 18° Centigrade. It is harmful to have it less or more. In games, teachers should be watchful of the positions of the students.

155. If the heat in the morning is 25° Centigrade in the shade, classes are dismissed in the afternoon. It depends on local conditions of the environment whether the students should remain at the school or go to their homes.

156. Special attention should be given to care of the teeth. Frequent advice should be given for care of the teeth and students should be especially advised to use toothbrushes.[31] If possible, toothbrush exercises should be given in the class. At least four times a year, examinations of the teeth should take place, and if any student is found negligent, he should be advised, and if necessary, his parents should be informed.

157. Care of the hair should not be neglected. Once every week hair examination should take place, and students should be advised to wash their hair at least once a week, and also to have their hair cut every week.

Every morning examinations for cleanliness should take place. If any wounds or scratches are seen on the body or head, the student should be sent to a doctor.

158. If a student is ill with a contagious disease, he cannot be accepted in the school until he brings a certificate from a doctor that his illness is over. If there are no doctors in the town, twenty days must pass after the time of the child's recovery.

159. A small pharmacy must be established in the school, and the following medicines are required:

1) Iodine in a colored, corked bottle. . . .
2) Ammonia (liquid). . . .
3) Ether. . . .
4) A small quantity of pure alcohol.
5) Absorbent cotton.
6) A few packages of gauze.

Besides these above medicines there must be a good fever thermometer and pincers, and for examination of the throat, spatulas

---

[31] Here again an irrational religious prejudice is attacked. Because of the use of hog bristles in toothbrushes, Moslems have always regarded them with abhorrence and have preferred to use the primitive *misvak,* a bristly root grown in Yemen.

and medical scissors. All these articles must be kept in clean boxes in the head-teacher's room.

160. If a child falls and is hurt while playing, iodine must be applied at once.

161. The head-teachers who do not have the articles mentioned in No. 159 will be held responsible. In addition to the medicines above mentioned no other medical treatment may be applied to the students. Quinine may only be used for fever with the advice of a specialist.

162. It is desirable that a health club be formed among the students. The members of the club should be weighed every month and their height measured, and the results put down in the weight and height records. Members of the club should undertake and continue faithfully to take care of their health and teeth.

163. It is required that each student should have a general medical examination every year, and the result should be recorded in his health certificate.

164. Lectures should be given to cause the students to avoid and despise the use of alcohol and tobacco. In this connection teachers should be extremely careful not to arouse a sense of curiosity in the students. Pictures must be shown to depict the evil effects of drunkenness, and teachers should have conversations with their students on this subject.

It must not be assumed that the program and objectives which have just been set forth are being completely realized. Mentality does not change like a hat, nor is it possible in a few years' time to produce trained teachers capable of bringing into being a program conceived along lines so totally different from that of Turkey's traditional educational system. Furthermore, Turkey is faced with the problem of attracting her ablest young men and women to the all-important profession of teaching, for in the commercial world which the nation is just beginning to enter with such enthusiasm there is a need and an attraction of financial return. The teacher not only must go through a long period of training to receive a minimum salary of perhaps twenty-five dollars a month, but must also be willing to take a teaching assignment for a period of years at whatever place the government sees fit to indicate. There is still considerable reluctance on the part of young men and women born in the cities to run the risk of assignment to villages and communities in the far interior where conditions and intellects are still quite primitive. Objections of this kind are of course growing less year by year as the government develops its system of railroads and communication which makes life in Anatolia much less unattractive to the type of teachers, doctors, and administrators who are needed for the campaign against ignorance. Yet even at the time of my visit to Anatolia in October, 1929, I could not help being impressed with the high average of devotion and skill apparent among the young teachers and officials in the schools visited. Crowded conditions were everywhere encountered, and inefficiency and poor judgment were by no means absent, but from the way in which educators seemed to be buckling to their tasks and teachers were constantly receiving instruction from inspectors, publications, and vacation study courses, one is led to expect a rather successful realization of modern educational methods before the lapse of many more years. Whatever else may be said, it is an unquestioned fact that in Turkey's public instruction system a desire to propagate progressive ideas has completely supplanted any wish to preserve the institutions and practices of a religious system which lacked vitality.

It must not, of course, be presumed that the devout Moslems among the Turks—and there are still many of them— view with equanimity the changed point of view in education. As one learned *hodja* told me in Istanbul, "There is little probability of the new education succeeding in teaching morality. It is all experimental and has cast loose from the sure foundations on which education used to be grounded." Certain it is that in attempting to make responsibility to one's fellow-members of society the prime basis for moral and religious behavior Turkey is not only cutting loose from an inherited system in which everything depended ultimately on Allah, but is making a humanist experiment whose success or failure the world must watch with close attention and interest. The task placed upon Turkey's new young teachers of inspiring children to be moral and loving because of social responsibility instead of reasons based on fear of eternal punishment and hell fire is a tremendous one and requires the devotion of Turkey's finest young men and women. It

TABLE II

TYPE OF SCHOOL	NO. OF SCHOOLS	TEACHERS		PUPILS	
		Men	Women	Boys	Girls
University of Istanbul:					
Faculty of Theology ...	1	18	...	20	....
Faculty of Sciences	1	40	...	580	146
Faculty of Medicine ...	1	96	...	654	18
Faculty of Law	1	28	...	1,241	200
Faculty of Letters	1	25	...	133	186
Higher School of Pharmacy	1	45	...	65	22
Higher Dental School ..	1	*	...	208	75
School for Midwives ...	1	†	...	....	50
Schools under the Ministry of Public Instruction:					
Ordinary schools:					
Achievement schools .	2	8	...	229	29
Middle schools	83	750	241	22,590	5,929
Lycées	30	634	118	4,199	1,156
Special higher schools:					
School for Civil Service	1	24	...	130	4
Academy of the Fine Arts	1	33	...	136	20
School for High-School Teachers	1	4	...	41	49
School for Secondary-School Teachers ...	1	25	...	155	26
Professional schools:					
Boys' normal schools .	9	135	2	976	....
Girls' normal schools .	8	73	80	.....	974

TABLE II—(*Continued*)

Type of School	No. of Schools	Teachers		Pupils	
		Men	Women	Boys	Girls
Normal School for Village Teachers	1	10	...	76	10
Normal School for Music Teachers	1	22	7	21	19
Trade schools	17	206	78	1,780	801
Commercial schools ..	9	193	19	1,244	253
Schools under other ministries:					
Special higher schools:					
School of Commerce .	1	28	...	223	36
Forestry School	1	8	...	55	....
Veterinary School ...	1	28	...	84	....
Engineering School ..	1	30	...	328	5
Ankara Law School ..	1	17	...	435	33
Ankara Agriculture School	1	37	...	65	6
School for Marine Engineers and Captains	1	20	...	68	....
Professional schools:					
Agriculture and mechanical schools ...	5	34	...	231	....
Schools for silk workers	5	7	...	73	9
Schools for sanitary agents	2	5	...	104	12
School for Finance Ministry Employees	1	12	...	65	....
Istanbul Cadaster School	1	13	...	54	1
Istanbul School of Public Works	1	17	...	142	2
Istanbul School for Veterinary Health Agents	1	13	...	31	3
Izmir School for the Deaf, Dumb, and Blind	1	2	...	56	23

* The faculty of the Dental School is included with that of the School of Pharmacy.

† Instruction in the School for Midwives is carried on by the Faculty of Medicine.

might be expected that at this point missionary enterprises
would be able to furnish some real advice and help, and it is
true that some missionaries are anxious to do that very thing.
The difficulties attendant upon missionary contributions are
very real too, however; this problem is discussed in a succeeding chapter.

The advanced schools sponsored by the state are playing a
more and more significant rôle at the present time. An idea
of their extent and importance may be gained from Table II.
The figures are for the year 1932–33, and are taken from the
official *Annuaire statistique* (1932–33).

Although the question of non-Turkish schools is taken up
in detail later, it may be well for purposes of comparison to
note here the numbers of schools which, though their programs are subject to rigorous inspection by the Department
of Public Instruction, are supported from sources other than
that of the government. For the years 1932–33 the statistics
are as shown in Table III.[32]

TABLE III

Type of School	No. of Schools	Teachers		Pupils	
		Men	Women	Boys	Girls
Foreign primary schools ..	44	113	178	3,050	3,978
Foreign middle schools ...	15	92	165	1,512	924
Foreign lycées	13	268	143	457	251
Minority primary schools .	104	343	563	9,567	7,975
Minority middle schools ..	2	22	14	649	398
Minority lycées	10	238	112	334	218
Turkish private primary schools	17	38	40	1,515	919
Turkish private middle schools	6	60	28	990	329
Turkish private lycées	9	264	50	999	229

From what has already been written it is apparent that
Turkey is on the way toward the establishment of an educa-

[32] *Annuaire statistique* (1932–33), 183–85.

tional system capable of giving her citizens a thorough training in almost any branch of arts or science. More and more is she decreasing the numbers of schools supported by non-Turkish sources and increasing her own educational resources by inviting foreign experts to help in her own schools and by giving promising Turkish students an opportunity to study abroad and bring back technical knowledge to Turkey. A special law, No. 1416, provides specifically for the selection of students for foreign study, and so arranges matters that selection, inspection of studies, and payment of stipend are all supervised by the Ministry of Public Instruction, no matter what the field or what department is sponsoring the education. In the year 1932–33, according to the *Annuaire statistique,* there were 267 Turkish students, 44 of whom were girls, pursuing courses of study in European countries under government guidance. This compares with 31 in the year 1923–24. The countries of study in 1932–33 were as follows, with the number of students in each: France, 99; Germany, 97; Belgium, 29; Switzerland, 16; England, 9; Italy, 5; Czecho-Slovakia, 5; America, 4; Sweden, 2; and Austria, 1.

The subjects which these students are pursuing are especially interesting to examine since their character graphically reveals the absorbing desire of the Turks to master the technical craftsmanship of the West. The 267 government-supported students in 1932–33 were specializing as shown in Table IV.

Let it be again pointed out that these figures refer only to students officially sponsored by the government and does not include many others studying abroad on private means.

It might seem to the casual observer that the new Turkey would have her hands full carrying out the educational program which has been described thus far. Not so, however. Displaying a veritable mania for education and a determination to stamp out illiteracy, the new government in 1928 de-

TABLE IV

Subject	Boys	Girls	Subject	Boys	Girls
History and geography	24	..	Civil engineering .	5	..
Foreign language .	17	7	Agriculture	5	..
Physics and chemistry	20	3	Electricity	4	..
Mathematics	19	3	Manual training .	4	..
Commerce	16	..	Political economy	4	..
Law	12	..	Hydrodynamics .	4	..
Natural history .	7	4	Technical science	4	..
Tailoring	1	9	Pottery-making .	3	..
Mechanics	9	..	Lycée work	2	1
Philosophy.	7	1	Industrial and mining engineering	3	..
Geology	7	..	Blacksmith trade .	3	..
Carpentry and cabinetwork ..	7	..	Pedagogy	3	..
Motors and fitting	6	..	Medicine	3	..
Veterinary surgeon	5	..	Home economics .	..	2
Embroidery and needlework ...	..	5	Canning	2	..
Flower-making ..	..	5	Automobile repairing	2	..

One boy in each of the following: archaeology, wine-growing, pisciculture, cartography, shipbuilding, foundry-work, construction and engineering, creamery work, architecture, music and fine arts, dye and textile trade, forestry, drawing and decorative arts, psychology, factory head.

One girl in each of the following: gymnastics, dress-designing, drawing, child care.

cided to scrap the Arabic alphabet in which Turkish has been awkwardly written for centuries, and replace it with a Latinized alphabet which not only would suit the language better but which would also be much easier for the ordinary person to learn. It was contemplated in the amazingly short period of two years completely to eliminate the Arabic script from use in the country. But for government departments, periodicals, advertisements, and moving-picture captions, the time was much shorter. For these, the new letters had to be adopted December 1, 1928. The final deadline for changing all printed documents and discontinuing the use of Arabic script as shorthand for stenographers was June 1, 1930. Naturally the government had to spend hundreds of thousands of liras to subsidize newspapers and other periodicals, for with the suddenness of the change, most publications were deprived of virtually their entire reading public.[33] Moreover, in order that the change might be engineered with all possible dispatch, the Department of Public Instruction undertook the most comprehensive system of compulsory adult education that the world has yet witnessed. Every adult between the ages of sixteen and forty was to procure a certificate that he could read and write the new letters. If he was unable to do so, he had to attend school until he could pass the requisite examination. Classes were established in regular primary-school buildings, twice a week in the afternoons for women and twice a week in the evenings for men. At Samsun, where I discussed the matter with various Turks and the superintendent of public instruction, I was impressed with the thoroughness of the new law's application in a typical Turkish city somewhat removed from the capital. My friends told me with considerable glee of enforcement measures taken by police who visited cafés and backgammon dens, removing to school any culprits who could not produce certificates of their reading and writing ability. In the office of the educational superintendent I was shown the files of certificates and photographs which recorded the names and faces of all those who had successfully completed their tests. Penalties are prescribed both for those who neglect to attend the schools and for those who attend but are lazy. According to statistics in *Le milliett* for June 1, 1930, 12,902 schools were opened in 1928 and were attended by 589,858 persons. I was

[33] Critics of the government point out that this measure gave the government a tremendous leverage over the press, since newspapers which disagreed with the government could be deprived of the vital subsidy.

interested to learn in Ankara that these adult schools do not necessarily consider their work completed with the imparting of ability to read and write. Voluntary courses are provided for the second year providing instruction in geography, mathematics, and various other subjects of a somewhat elementary nature. It must be pointed out that distinctions have to be made in instruction for those who already know how to use the Arabic alphabet and those who have been completely illiterate. Some idea of the problem involved may be obtained from literacy figures obtained in the census of 1927. These show that out of Turkey's total population of over 13,600,000 only 8.16 per cent were able to read. The percentage of literate men was 12.99; of women, 3.67.[34]

Besides these popular schools literacy is being forwarded by the construction of reading-rooms in various cities, the publication of magazines on pedagogy by official and private sources, and the assistance of an important private organization known as the Association for Public Instruction. Alphabet classes have also been sponsored by private industrial enterprises for their employees. The task of providing a new dictionary has been undertaken by an official commission working in Ankara. After two years of labor it was announced in June, 1930, that this commission had completed the letter *A*. The whole country has embarked on a drive to bring about the day when, according to the Ankara *Hakimieti-Millie,* "an illiterate Turk will attract everybody's attention like a monstrous phenomenon of nature." [35]

It is obvious that Turkey's reform program will be vastly speeded up and strengthened by the attainment of a high degree of literacy, yet one's breath is almost taken away by the speed and comprehensiveness of the reform which Kemal undertook to this end. He fired the popular imagination by

[34] *Annuaire statistique* (1929), II, 18–37.
[35] Quoted in *La république* (Istanbul), October 26, 1929.

appearing himself in various towns and holding public examinations in the open squares to see whether citizens have acquired the desired reading ability. To the Western traveler like myself who had an opportunity to travel in Turkey both before and after the introduction of the new letters, the difference is especially noticeable in the new ease with which it is possible to read signs, etc. Today an English-speaking traveler feels no less at home linguistically than he may in Hungary or Czecho-Slovakia and probably more at home than in Bulgaria or Greece, where different alphabets persist. This very improvement illustrates one of the Gazi's great aims, to place Turkey on a level with other civilized countries of the West.

Before closing this treatment of Turkey's educational and anti-illiteracy program, those sections of Ismet Inönü's masterly speech to his constituents at Malatya in 1928 in which he deals with the importance of literacy in the Republican program must be quoted:

The Republic is not the name of a time which is quiet and stagnant. On the contrary it is a symbol of life which constructs and creates every day. To-day nations are obliged to be mobilized with high qualities in order to be able to fight and compete in their economic and social lives and in international relations. This age and the future require Turkish society to be invested with various qualities such as activity, hard work, knowledge and creativity. Or we may express these qualities in one single word, civilization.

We cannot close our ears to the things which this age and the future will require of the Turkish nation. And this is natural because we believe that we are the generation which has witnessed the complete and total decadence of the past periods.

I want to explain the reason why we are in favor of a radical reform to create a strong Turkish society to correspond with the requirements of civilization and science.

But, Gentlemen, we must know clearly that the first characteristic of the first living man was language. So the characteristic of human society is reading and writing. I want to point out particularly that reading and writing are not considered to be characteristics of education and civilization. They are the first signs of a community which is capable of assimilating education and civilization.

The ignorance of communities which lack reading and writing is a hindrance and obstacle to life and development.

To-day the Turkish nation has attacked this great trouble by the help of its great Gazi. The great Turkish nation with the leadership of its great and triumphant son, the Gazi, has decided to adopt Latin characters and to lift itself from among the nations which do not know how to read and write.

We have undertaken a great enterprise which will give glory to the coming generation. This enterprise is to teach reading and writing to every member of the Turkish nation.

It will not be easy to reply to the criticism of the future generation as to why such a promising reform has been so long delayed, but I shall tell them it was necessary for the Turkish nation to have a leader like the Gazi, who goes from one village to another and teaches the new Turkish alphabet like a village teacher and leads them away from their old habits.

Do you not see the rush of the people in Istanbul, Ankara, and other places to be lifted up from the state of ignorance? Our old women and mothers are glad to see that the black lines on white paper which meant nothing before start to talk to them like illumined figures.

To fight against ignorance is the leading point of our program. This program is the program of the Government and of the People's Party, and it is the program of the Turkish idealists.

To-day the whole country looks like a classroom, and the head teacher and the main treasure of this nation is its great son, the Gazi.

The Turkish nation will work hard to have full satisfaction from this classroom.[36]

In discussing the objectives of primary education it was noted that one of the chief ends striven for was health education. It is noteworthy, as we pursue our study of the mani-

[36] Quoted in *Seçme Yazilar* ("Selected Writings"), pp. 24 f.

festations of the new Western ideals in Turkish society, that health and sanitation activity stands out most significantly as a symbol of Turkey's drive toward modernization. One finds the government again taking the lead through its Ministry of Hygiene and Social Assistance, aided by a number of private but subsidized associations, in teaching Turks how to take care of their bodies and in supplanting the old fatalistic or superstitious mentality with an alert attitude which seeks to destroy disease.

The medical profession has furnished Turkey with many of its outstanding liberal leaders for many years. The faculty of medicine of the University of Istanbul has a distinguished reputation, and the various Turkish hospitals which I took special pains to visit in Istanbul, Ankara, and Sivas seemed well ordered and manned by a personnel of exceptionally high caliber. Although equipment was not always plentiful and modern, owing to lack of funds, in every case what equipment there was seemed to my lay eyes to be clean and well taken care of. Except for a shortage in well-trained nurses, owing to the fact that trained nurses are something new in Turkey and the social patterns have not shaped themselves as yet either to train a sufficient number or to employ in homes those who are trained, the medical profession in Turkey seems the best equipped of any professional group in the country, excepting only the military class. Thus the Ministry of Hygiene and Social Assistance in its attempts to carry out health and sanitation programs has had a reasonable number of trained men to call on.

Some notion of the accomplishments of this Ministry may be gathered from data in the *Annuaire statistique* (1932–33), VI, 137–49.

In 1932 there were 3,827 persons employed in public health work in Turkey, of whom 2,146 were paid by the state. Of the total number of workers we find 1,188 doctors, 116 pharmacists, 1,246 sanitary agents, 421 midwives, 216 nurses, and 640 listed in various other categories.

Hospitals in Turkey under the general direction of the Ministry of Hygiene show a remarkable development in usefulness over the years from 1926 to 1932 for which statistics are available (see Table V).

TABLE V

Year	Bed Patients	Dispensary Patients	Laboratory Analyses
1926	7,620	38,838	13,440
1932	16,971	109,032	40,603

The task of transforming Turkey into a healthy nation is making headway despite the inertia of the population, which for centuries has been taught that sickness and health are divinely dispensed and not to be questioned or interfered with by meddlesome mortals. Epidemic diseases such as smallpox, when they break out, are promptly and effectively dealt with by quarantine and vaccination. But particularly noteworthy is the aggressive program planned to check the ravages of four perennial scourges: malaria, trachoma, syphilis, and tuberculosis.

The figures shown in Table VI indicate the extent of the antimalarial activity.

TABLE VI

Year	Dispensary Centers	Expenditures (in Turkish Liras)	Persons Examined	Blood Tests	Treated for Malaria
1925 ...	3	£T576,000	67,000	30,000	36,000
1932 ...	11	£T623,000	1,677,000	557,000	432,000

In connection with the antimalarial work it is important to note that twenty-eight marshes were drained between 1925 and 1932, and thirty-two drainage-canal projects were completed between 1929 and 1932.

The progress of the campaign to control the spread of syphilis may be visualized from the statistics shown in Table VII.

TABLE VII

YEAR	DISPENSARY CENTERS	EXPENDITURES (IN TURKISH LIRAS)	PATIENTS REGISTERED Men	Women	CURED
1926 .	4	£T127,000	40,380	44,282	629
1932 .	9	£T168,000	Total both sexes 157,412		4,621

While complete figures for the early years of the campaign against trachoma are not given in the *Annuaire statistique* for 1932–33, the extent of activities for 1932 may be judged as shown in Table VIII.

TABLE VIII

Dispensary Centers	Expenditures (in Turkish Liras)	Bed Patients	Dispensary Patients	Operations
6	£T123,000	1,535	1,042,917	15,189

Smaller amounts have been expended in the fight against tuberculosis, the total for the three years 1930–32 being only £T78,000. This figure, however, apparently does not include the upkeep of the tuberculosis sanitarium on the island of Halki, which alone in the year 1932 required £T32,000.

Further study of the expenditures of the Hygiene Ministry reveals more regarding the comprehensiveness and diversity of its activity. In 1932 the items shown in Table IX are listed.

TABLE IX

Bacteriological work ...	£T8,000	Schools for sanitary agents	£T13,000
Vaccination work	7,000		
Health Museum	1,000	Aid to *vilâyets* in combating contagious diseases	66,000
Hydrophobia treatment	16,000		

The Ministry has also been active in sponsoring research, in drawing up laws for the protection of women and children, and in bringing about the sane distribution of pharmacies among the population. Health education along modern lines has been undertaken by posters and health exhibits, and especially through the medium of moving pictures. Among the health films imported from America for free exhibition in cinema theaters throughout Turkey [37] are such titles as the following: "Your mouth," "Tommy Tucker's Tooth," "Fly Danger," "The Error of Omission," "How To Live Long and Well," "Drinking of Health," "Confessions of a Cold," "Many Happy Returns," "Malaria," and "Child Welfare"; also a French film, "Il était une fois trois amis" (about syphilis).

Besides the official activities for maintenance of health which have been mentioned, a number of private organizations, some of them partly subsidized by the state, have been established to deal with specific physical and social problems. There is, for example, the Red Crescent Society which performs relief work in time of famine and distress in a manner exactly analogous to that of the Red Cross among Western nations. The problems of alcoholism, which have assumed a new form with the weakening of the Koranic injunction against liquor and the establishment of a government monopoly for the manufacture and sale of spirits, are dealt with by an organization known as the Green Crescent Society. There

[37] At the end of the year 1931 there were 144 moving-picture theaters in Turkey (*Annuaire statistique* [1932–33], VI, 482).

exist also two societies known as the Association for the War against Tuberculosis and the Association for Mental Hygiene. There is even a small Society of the Enemies of Tobacco.[38]

Noteworthy work is being done for children through the Turkish Himayei Etfal (Children's Protective Society) which was founded by Dr. Fuad in 1910 in his home city of Kasaba, and has grown to a place of nation-wide importance with a Central Committee of twenty members of the Turkish Parliament, and a headquarters in Ankara which is one of the most modern and best equipped in the city. An idea of the work being done by this organization for the benefit of children and mothers may be gained from the following excerpt from the report of its annual congress, May 8, 1927:

Our society desires to fight against infant mortality and occupies itself chiefly with children who need wet-nursing. Valuable results have been obtained from the wet-nurseries which we have established in Istanbul, Izmir [Smyrna], Ankara, and Tokat. We will try to establish other wet-nurseries in other suitable places.

3697 kilograms of milk have been distributed since the first of January [1927] at the milk dispensary in the Children's Palace [Ankara]. There is a great demand for the milk which is sterilized and pasteurized at our milk distributing plants. Doctors receive visits of patients in the afternoons for internal, external, ear, nose, throat, skin, eye, nerve and gynecological diseases, and in the mornings our specialized doctors take care of children. Since the first of January [1927] 7677 children and mothers have been examined and 3257 children and mothers have taken baths in our bath houses. Our bath houses are also used by mothers just before the time of childbirth, and by mothers who have nervous diseases.

Children who have been examined in our dispensaries and who are treated at their homes are visited by nurses, and the condition of their health is closely followed. Doubtless the ignorance of child treatment plays a great part in infant mortality. The nurses who visit the families give information about child treatment.

The love and interest which have been shown to our institution

[38] *Le milliett,* December 12, 1929.

increase every day. Last year we had 318 main branches. This year the number has been increased to 405, which are located in the districts where our organization is strongest, and 38 in other places.

It is worthy of note that Turkey celebrates a national holiday on April 23 in honor of her children. At the same time an entire week is devoted to special festivities for children, with important civic and other offices held by children.

Of special interest to Americans is the health and welfare work inspired by the late Asa K. Jennings and carried on since his death in January, 1933, under the leadership of his son, Asa W. Jennings, as executive vice-president of the American Friends of Turkey. Associated after the World War with the Young Men's Christian Association in the Near East, the elder Mr. Jennings was one of the first foreigners to recognize the new nationalistic self-reliance of the Turks. He saw that foreign philanthropy, if it was to be effectively administered in Turkey, could not be dictatorially manipulated by outsiders but must conform to the wishes and sensibilities of the Turks themselves. Between 1924 and 1928 in the city of Izmir (Smyrna) with the active co-operation of the great Turkish humanitarian, Aziz, who was governor and then mayor of Izmir, Mr. Jennings was instrumental in establishing a home for orphan babies, a playground with modern equipment (the first of its kind in Turkey), and a community sport field. Interest was also aroused in prison reform and a clinic for babies and mothers.

A wider field was opened to Mr. Jennings when in 1928 he was invited to carry on his projects in the capital city of Ankara. Aziz, who had become a deputy in the Grand National Assembly, continued to be an invaluable ally in winning the co-operation of Turks. At first the new enterprise functioned as an adjunct of the Children's Protective Society (Himayei Etfal), co-operating in the development of clinics, but, above all, playgrounds under the guidance of two American experts, W. T. Gannoway and Barent Burhans. Subsequently, in order to give wider scope to the American group, permitting them to aid other social service organizations besides the Children's Protective Society, a new arrangement was worked out. In 1930 the Turkish group organized a new Society for the Promotion and Support of Good Works (Hayir Islerine Yardim Cemiyeti), while the interested Americans became incorporated as the American Friends of Turkey; a mixed commission made up of representatives of each organization took over supervision of all projects. With money furnished by both American and Turkish participants, the arrangement has become a model in international co-operation and is exerting its influences in many other fields than those in which the experiment was first begun, notably in education. That, however, is another story.

An admirable summary of the sense of responsibility which the Turkish leaders feel for the health and physical welfare of their nation is fluently expressed in Ismet Inönü's speech to his constituents at Malatya:

Whatever others may say, the health struggle comes first for the economic plans as well as for duties of citizenship and humanity. The sick man is not only the emblem of a destroyed home; he is at the same time in the same position as the man who consumes his savings which some day may form the capital of some other man. When I say struggle against disease, I mean the fever which influences the general life and the social activities of the nation. This struggle has been started by the Republic. A scientific struggle has taken place in vast areas with limited means, but has ended with great success. The citizens who were once suffering from fever have become as a result of this struggle lively and active earning machines.[39]

In few spheres of Turkish life have the changed viewpoints had greater effect than on the position and status of

[39] *Op. cit.*, pp. 22 f.

women in family and public life. Contemporaneously with the weakening of traditional prescriptions in every walk of life, the seclusion and inequality of women, so long considered as characteristic of Islam, have lost their popularity, and one finds women forging to the front most rapidly in the last twenty years. In cities particularly came an abandonment of the veil. Schools for girls became more numerous. During the World War women received their opportunity to enter positions in industry and commerce which had been left vacant by men at the front. The story of woman's emancipation in Turkey would alone furnish material for many books.

The first great advance in the improvement of woman's legal status came in 1917, when the law of October 25 introduced certain innovations in the marriage provisions. This law is clearly analyzed and explained by Mahmud Essad in his Introduction to the new Civil Code of 1926. His explanations are worth noting in detail:

From the Islamic point of view, the Moslem marriage was analogous to that which one calls in Europe to-day civil marriage. The consent of the two to be united given before two witnesses was sufficient for the contraction of the marriage. Such was the custom, it is true, at first, but the union was then pronounced by the "imams." The new law had extended this principle; it had sought to give to the act a character more official. It declared the presence of two witnesses insufficient and rendered obligatory the presence of the magistrate or his deputy.

If the fact of contracting the marriage in the presence of the judge already had regularization and consolidation in view, there was added yet another thing: the registry of the union. Henceforth every act of marriage and divorce had to be entered on the registers of the tribunal.

The third measure envisaged for the regularization of this question was the preliminary publication of the banns.

As for divorce, there was admitted a system in conformance with the words of the Imam Maliki: if a difference arises between the husband and wife which prompts the latter to demand divorce, the tribunals will designate two members of each family to attempt to reconcile the couple; in case it is impossible for these arbiters to attain a reconciliation of the parties, recourse will be had to the judge, who will pronounce the divorce. If a disagreement arises among the arbiters, a new superior arbitral council will be appointed outside the members of the couple's families, and action will be taken according to its decision. It can be seen that while safeguarding the rights of the wife, freedom is not allowed her lightly to break one of the most powerful social ties.

In order to put an end to forced marriage, the commission referred to the words of the Imam Shafi, and it wrote in the law that forced marriage was not valid.

As for polygamy, here is what the commission adopted: at the time of contracting the union, the wife may set the condition that in case the husband should wish to conclude a new marriage, the first or the second would be *ipso facto* annulled, a procedure which would prevent the husband from having several wives contrary to the wish of the first.

Another question still had been settled: that is the sum which the husband must pay the wife in case of divorce. The commission, to settle the case, referred to the Imam Yusuf: at the time of marriage, the husband must propose to his wife an adequate dowry.

The law also took into consideration matrimonial capacity. Young girls could not marry before the age of nine years, and men, before twelve; the former were free to contract marriage according to their desire and with whoever they might wish after the age of seventeen years, and the latter, after eighteen. Between these two age limits it was necessary to have the assent of the judge for men, and that of the parents or guardian for girls.[40]

Mahmud Essad goes on to point out the special arrangements made for marriage among non-Moslems. But when the new code of 1926 came into force,

the new project established no difference between Moslems and non-Moslems. From the very moment when there was found the

[40] *Op. cit.*, pp. ix f.

word "Moslem" in no article, it was necessary to conclude that after its promulgation the law must be applicable to all subjects of the Republic. The chief principle adopted was monogamy. Nevertheless, as it did not seem possible altogether to prevent polygamy, because in Anatolia, said the President, men were less numerous than women, it was believed necessary to retain polygamy, but imposing on it such severe conditions that it was only possible in cases of absolute necessity.

In the case of divorce there was set the principle of reciprocity.[41]

In the spring of 1930 the Grand National Assembly passed a law granting women the right to vote in municipal elections, and at nearly the same time a woman, Beyhan Hanum, was appointed to be a judge.[42] But the climax in the struggle for equal rights was not reached until the end of 1934 when women were granted full rights to vote and to hold office in the National Assembly itself. Turkey had come a long way since the days twenty years ago or less when a Turkish woman who appeared on the streets without a veil was an object of police attention.

In almost no phase of activity in Turkey today is it possible to find anything but new energy and new methods. Small villages are being linked to the rest of the world by gendarmerie telephones; dirty and tumbled-down cities are being cleaned up and improved with paved streets and parks. Particularly is this true of Ankara, which is being reconstructed according to the plans of a famous German specialist. Trees are being planted, and reforestation is one of the country's watchwords. Elaborate irrigation schemes are under way, and an unprecedented activity in railroad-building is taking place. These lines, built by foreign engineers for the most part but financed almost wholly by government revenue, are expected to play one of the most important parts in de-

[41] *Ibid.*, p. xi.
[42] *Le milliett*, April 30, 1930.

veloping both the commerce and the mentality of the remote regions which were formerly notable chiefly as places of exile. Model villages are being set up to lead the peasants toward a cleaner and more comfortable life. On model farms, particularly that of the Gazi near Ankara, experiments are constantly being carried on to develop the most satisfactory agricultural methods and products. Automobiles are becoming less and less a novelty, and with the influx of light American cars, especially the Ford, which is assembled in a plant at Istanbul, the day cannot be far distant when good roads will insure passage all the year round. Great interest is being manifested in Western music and in Western art. With the change in alphabet, the old school of calligraphy which used to develop such fascinating designs and mottoes from the Arabic characters has turned its attention to developing beautiful monograms and designs from the new Latinized alphabet. Safety razors now form a stock in trade alongside the traditional blue beads which are supposed to ward off the evil eye and which in many places are twined around the radiator caps of modern automobiles. A new desire for efficiency and exactness is manifested by the establishment of a national Bureau of Statistics in Ankara and by the spread of civil service methods in the selection of government personnel. To attend the opening of Parliament in Ankara on November 1, to note the dress and manners of the guests at the presidential ball on October 29, the anniversary of the Proclamation of the Republic, and to witness the cosmopolitan appearance of the city and citizens of the new Ankara would cause anyone to ask himself most dubiously whether this were an Oriental land he was visiting.

True it is that the Turks are far from used to their new habits and surroundings and frequently produce strange interpretations of Western clothes and customs which might be amusing if they were not so dead in earnest. It is even difficult to reckon historical dates now, for on January 1, 1926, the old Hegira calendar was definitely abandoned after several years of a clumsy combination of lunar and solar calendars. Aeronautics is constantly kept in the public eye by means of a national Airplane Society which raises money for Turkey's air force through the medium of frequent nation-wide lotteries. The metric system has been adopted for all official measurements, and the set price is even beginning to displace the hallowed custom of bargaining in the larger centers. A law taking effect January 1, 1935, compels every Turk to take a family name in accordance with the practice in Western countries. At the same time all titles such as Pasha, Bey, Effendi, and Hanum, customarily added after a name and indicating something of the social status of the individual, were outlawed, their place being taken by simple Turkish titles, Bay and Bayin, placed before the name. The need for this revolutionary departure from traditional Moslem avoidance of family names is apparent to anyone who has glanced through a long list of Turkish names, such as a telephone directory, and been puzzled by the appalling duplication therein. Efficiency is clearly enhanced by this innovation, and one more custom which made Turks different from westerners is eliminated. For the sake of conforming to European commercial standards and to place its banks on a plane of equality with those of its Western neighbors, the Turkish government might consider the abandonment of Friday as its distinctive day of worship and rest in favor of Sunday so that valuable business time might not be lost.[43]

Turkey's aim, now that she has gained her political independence, is to adopt the ways of the West so that Western ways and methods may strengthen her own national and eco-

[43] Since this statement was written, the Turkish Parliament has actually enacted this change by a law passed May 28, 1935.

nomic life in order that she will be able to take her place on a par with any other nation and be compelled to ask favors from no one. In the words of a writer in *Le milliett:*

Our movement can not be compared to the Hindu movement which aims to return to the spinning wheel. Our movement is no more negative than reactionary. It is a movement forward, a positive movement. We do not say to the people "Return to the industry of the fireside; boycott foreign merchandise; become positive again." On the contrary we say to them, "Let us industrialize; let us perfect technique; accord importance to those branches of industry whose development is possible among us, and assure their success." Our doors are open to the merchandise which is not or cannot be produced in our country. To be able to buy more of them we wish to augment our national revenues.[44]

[44] February 1, 1930.

IX

MISSIONARY EDUCATION IN THE LIGHT OF NATIONALISM

It was only natural that Turkey's determined attempt to rule her own destiny and to master the technique of Western civilization should have an effect on the foreign philanthropic work which had been established within her borders. These enterprises, evangelical, educational, and medical, had been carried on for decades by mission groups representing the important nations of Europe and by Americans. Under the governments of the Ottoman Empire the missions had enjoyed much freedom to carry on their work, for the Sublime Porte was everywhere being forced to accede to requests from nations of the West. Furthermore, since a large proportion of the mission work was directed toward the various Christian minority groups within the Empire, and since the Moslem Turks were nearly immune from the Christian virus due to their fancied superiority and the solidity of Islamic society, there was for a long time little reason for agitation on the part of the Moslems. When, however, the Empire dwindled away and the Turkish population concentrated and solidified into a nation, eliminating by violent means the disloyal Christian groups from its midst, the situation went through a radical change. Turkish territories were now populated almost solely by Moslem Turks; the Christian missions were left in the country with these Moslem Turks as the only object of their activity; and those Turks, due to the sudden disorganization and readjustment of their society, were no longer immune to disturbing influences. It became essential, then, in the eyes of the strongly nationalist government, to make profound alterations in the status of these foreign enterprises and to subject them to more rigid governmental control than ever before lest they offer an obstruction to the attainment of strong, united nationhood.

It is true that the number of foreign schools in Turkey is smaller than before the war, though accurate comparison cannot be made because of the tremendous alteration which took place in Turkey's territory between 1914 and 1923. As we have already pointed out,[1] there still functioned 72 foreign schools in Turkey in 1932–33, attended by 10,172 pupils, not counting the minority schools operated by the Greek, Armenian, and Jewish populations. While the *Annuaire statistique* for 1932–33 does not separate the foreign schools by nationality, it will give an idea of the comparative extent of the enterprises of various nations to cite figures released by the Ministry of Public Instruction for 1927–28, when there were 36 French schools, 17 Italian, 8 American, 5 Bulgarian, 3 English, 2 Austrian, 1 German, and 1 Jugo-Slav.

It is a noteworthy fact that the foreign schools are thought of primarily in connection with their nationality rather than with their religious denomination, although the large majority of them are supported by religious groups. This is explainable largely because secular governments frequently interfered on behalf of the schools from their own country and because the language used for instruction in a foreign school was always that of the country from which the teachers came. Certain of the European schools have even received subsidies from the governments of the countries of their origin. The Turks are no doubt justified from past experience in suspecting that other motives than religious and philan-

1 Cf. chap. viii, Table III.

thropic ones have entered into the establishment of foreign schools on their territory.

The Turks' connection of religious belief with nationality is explicable not only by their observance of the behavior of European governments but by their own history in Anatolia. In the days of conquest, he who became a Moslem became an Ottoman citizen and participated in the privileges of the dominant group. The Christian remained apart as a member of a semiautonomous inferior body known as a *millet* and was not an Ottoman citizen in full standing.[2] In the grim days between 1914 and 1923 the budding Turkish nation was seriously threatened by those Greek and Armenian *millets,* people who dwelt in the same land but whose religious differences, among others, led them to revolt and seek to set up new states at the expense of the Moslem Turks. It is not to be wondered at that a Turk instinctively thinks of a change from Islam to Christianity as an indication of treason to the nation. It will take Turkey many years to forget her enmity to Christianity, and, meanwhile, no matter how many declarations she may make about separating church and state, sacred and secular, one must regard it as only natural that Turkish citizens whose religion is other than Islam or agnosticism should be accepted into Turkish society with distinct reservations.

Turkey's present attitude toward the foreign schools in her midst may be brought out more clearly by a careful study of the position of one group of such institutions, the American schools. While their influence may be smaller—as are their numbers—than the French schools, they are by virtue of the quality of their instruction highly regarded in the country and hold a place of prominence in its educational life. Furthermore, data concerning them are more readily available, and it may be presumed that what is true for the schools of

[2] Cf. p. 80 above.

one nation will be true in general for the schools of all foreign states represented in Turkey.

The American educational work in Turkey comes under two main categories: one consisting of schools administered by the American Board of Commissioners for Foreign Missions, the other consisting of two colleges, Robert College and Constantinople Woman's College, which co-operate for purposes of finance and appointment of American teachers with the Near East College Association.

The American Board of Commissioners for Foreign Missions, an agency of the Congregational church, which in 1933 operated five schools with a total attendance of 582 students, has been carrying on work in Turkey for more than a century. In fact, Turkey as the Asiatic country most accessible to the United States has served as the center of American mission work to Moslem countries since the time when Levi Parsons and Pliny Fisk were sent out in 1819 as the first two missionaries.[3] Oddly enough, these men were expected to minister not specially to Moslems but to the Jews of Palestine, and this same policy of working with non-Moslem peoples in the Turkish Empire prevailed until recent years. It was not the Jews, however, but the Christian Armenians who received the bulk of attention from the American missionaries. It was not a deliberate plan on the Americans' part to specialize on the Armenians to the exclusion of Moslem Turks and others. It was largely due to the coincidence that the Armenian Gregorian church was going through a disruptive experience brought about by a conflict between the reactionary, unintelligent clergy in control and a progressive, reforming element which was seeking to end the obscurantist tendency of their church—a struggle which was becoming bitter at the period when American missionaries began to appear on the scene. Here the newcomers

[3] Barton, *Daybreak in Turkey,* p. 87.

found a definite opportunity for service open to them, and they immediately embarked on the venture of aiding the reforming Armenians in their attempt to liberalize their church.[4] The Armenians were responsive to American work, and when schools were later opened in connection with the missions, they made up by far the largest racial group in attendance. Figures for 1913–14 for the twenty secondary schools operated by the Americans show that the registration included 4,385 Armenians, 339 Greeks, and 122 Turks.[5]

Robert College and the Constantinople Woman's College, founded in 1863 and 1871 respectively, pursued a similar policy, and though not carrying on Christian propaganda as intensively as the mission schools, catered to a clientèle predominantly non-Turkish. Prior to the Young Turk revolution of 1908 the number of Turks in their student bodies was negligible, and even in 1913–14 there were registered in Robert College but 90 Turks in a total of 644, and in the Woman's College only 55 Turks in a total of 277.[6]

The outbreak of the World War and its consequent upheavals brought tremendous readjustments both in Turkey's internal affairs and in the status of the missions. Most notable was the elimination from the territory of Turkey of virtually the entire Armenian and Greek population. This meant that the people with whom the missions had spent the greater part of their effort were no longer in the country and that the missionaries must now shape their work to deal with Moslems. But some of the institutions which were regarded by the nationalists as having been so active in their assistance of Christian populations as to be anti-Turkish were asked to withdraw from the country, thus leaving for the new work only those Turkish-speaking missionaries and other edu-

---

[4] Cf. *ibid.*, pp. 108, 144 f.
[5] C. A. Reed, *Problems of American Education in the Near East.*
[6] *Ibid.*

cators who were sympathetic toward the new national ideals. The Ankara government showed that it intended to run things as it saw fit, and the missionaries of every nationality came to realize that they were no longer to enjoy the free hand they had had under the sultans. Facing the new situation courageously, however, the Americans determined to continue their educational enterprises to the best of their ability, even though they were to be seriously restricted in any religious work they chose to undertake.

The years immediately following the Graeco-Turkish War and the Allied occupation of Constantinople were fraught with uncertainty and painful readjustments. The new nationalistic government, suspicious of all things foreign, kept a most careful eye on every move made by the foreign schools, while the directors and teachers of those schools, determined to spread the message of unselfish devotion to which they had dedicated their lives, shaped their plans to conform to the demands of the new régime. Courses were laid out with their chief purpose to meet the needs of Moslem Turks. Turkish teachers were added to the faculties of the schools; courses in Turkish language, literature, and history were added; in fact, all possible steps were taken to shape their curriculums so as to attract the younger generation of Turks, who were for the first time as a result of political circumstances exposed in large numbers to such Western influences.

To patronize the American schools was for the Turks something new. More than the French Jesuit schools, which had succeeded in the past in maintaining work definitely for Turkish Moslems,[7] the American institutions had held a repu-

[7] French has long been the accepted second language in Turkey, and today among the younger officialdom one meets many loyal Turks who have attended schools under French influence or control. A young army medical officer who had attended such a school told me he would never have thought of attending an American school, though there was one as conveniently located for him as the French.

tation for being interested chiefly in the minority Christian populations, and the impression clung tenaciously in the Turkish mind that a treasonable taint attached to American schools. Nevertheless the proportional number of Turks began to increase in the registration so that in 1923 seven American Mission schools had 257 Turkish students out of a total of 836, and in 1927 the proportion had become 919 Turks out of a total of 1,257, two additional schools having been reopened to make nine altogether.

The reasons for this growth in popularity of the American schools among the Turks after the World War are not hard to find. First of all, one should recall the background of Turkey's condition in the years which followed the cessation of hostilities. The country had passed through years of war, suffering, and deprivation. She had bled herself of men and money nearly to death, had passed through a period when all seemed utterly lost, and then by a titanic effort had re-established her right to exist as a nation. Disillusioned with the oriental way of life, to which she attributed her decadence, she turned eagerly toward the West to learn from it the skill and technique which she believed necessary for the maintenance and improvement of her existence. Two conflicting attitudes were discernible in the young nation: one a debasing sense of the inadequacy of her tools and material equipment inherited from the past; the other an exalting sense of confident determination to master the new civilization, born of the victory over Western foes. It is not surprising, then, that the Turks individually should turn eagerly to the American schools, for their equipment seemed in general vastly superior to the Turkish schools, which had suffered as a result of war-depleted treasuries, and they offered to teach the Turks that very knowledge of the West which the new nation was so eager to learn.

In an analysis of the causes which prompted individuals

to send their children to the American schools, there appear manifestations of the fundamental life urges [8] which one would normally expect to find. With the entire nation busy in learning the new civilization, the *explorative* and *investigative urge* naturally played an important rôle. There was much that Turkey did not know about Western ways, and so the foreign institutions attracted a certain patronage from those who were curious to find out more about this novelty. Of importance, too, was the *acquisitive urge,* for Turkey had made up her mind to take care of her own finance and commerce. Believing that acquisition of wealth was of importance for comfort and stability, having reduced the Greek and Armenian populations which formerly carried on the bulk of her commerce, and having cast aside her old prejudice against participating in trade, Turkey sought how best to make money. Since America is looked upon as the nation most adept at amassing fortunes, it followed that her schools should be able somehow to impart this ability to Turkish students. A young official of Robert College reported to me that it was almost impossible nowadays to interest Turkish seniors in staying on at the college to teach, since all were inclined to enter commercial positions as soon as possible after graduation. A young graduate of an American College, in speaking of the attractions of American education, admitted that he felt he should be enabled to make a better living as a result of knowing the English language, and that this language attraction had first drawn him to consider attending the American college.

The *urge to mastery* gives indications of being one of the most important factors in the popularity of American schools among the Turks. Mention has been made of the impoverished and inadequate condition of Turkey's schools as a re-

[8] Cf. M. Price, *Christian Missions and Oriental Civilizations,* pp. 537 ff.

sult of years of warfare. In contrast to them stood the American schools, which were in at least good if not flourishing condition and manned by staffs of teachers who carried themselves with assurance. In Turkey's anxiety to grasp and control the new techniques which she deemed essential for her well-being, is it to be wondered at that her citizens saw in the American and other foreign schools the surest means of achieving their ends? Better equipped than most Turkish schools, with able teachers, and providing a curriculum in the very fields which Turkey felt she must master, schools of the West must have seemed to many Turkish parents, eager that their children should be provided with an up-to-date education, a veritable answer to prayer.

In close alliance to the urge for mastery as it expressed itself in the selection of a foreign school to learn the new technique must be recognized the *urge toward recognition* or self-regard. Would not the parent who sent his child to one of the supposedly "superior" foreign schools feel that he had elevated his own status by educating his child in the best possible manner, enjoying the reflected glory which would come to him as the parent of a child who felt at home in the new Western ways, and who could converse in a European language with foreigners?

Both the mastery and the recognition urges as we have described them are revealed in an article by an anonymous parent which appeared in a magazine of Istanbul. The article is titled "How I Gave My Daughter to the American Girls' College." The writer begins:

Five years ago, while seeking a school for my daughter, I had recommended to me the American Girls' College, and to convince me they made me visit the school one day.

As soon as I saw the modern and elegant building situated on a beautiful and commanding site on the Bosphorus and the students inside who like flowers were flitting here and there, did

I not give my decision? It would not be possible to find in Turkey a better or more perfect school than this. After inspecting under the guidance of a student the classrooms, the laboratories, the library, the dining room and the dormitory this conviction took on new strength. This without any doubt was a place the like of which could not be found in the country. This most important matter was settled, and I decided in a satisfactory way the question of education for my daughter, which had bothered me so long. When that evening I took the good news to my daughter, her joy was unbounded. . . .

We went to a good deal of expense. We had new clothes made as if we were preparing a trousseau for our daughter, and finally we sent her to school.[9]

In an article which appeared in *Hayat*, an Ankara magazine, the writer in discussing the attractiveness of foreign schools makes mention of the element of recognition and self-regard. He remarks:

The idea of education which the heads of families have, especially and quite generally in the high classes, is narrow and mistaken. The educational ideals of some of those who belong to the high class can be turned exactly to these three points: a foreign language, piano, social manners. . . .

Snobbery also is another important element which insures full attendance at foreign schools. It is the desire to appear refined and aristocratic.[10]

This same writer suggests that a further motive, that of *self-protection*, enters into consideration in that parents, eager to escape from the nuisance and responsibilities of educating their children, choose to send them to boarding schools, especially foreign ones. He writes:

A large number of heads of families on giving their children to a school are happy, counting themselves henceforth free from all educational responsibility. For such as these, boarding schools

[9] *Resimli Ay*, May, 1929, p. 18.
[10] "The Christianizing Incident," editorial in *Hayat* (Ankara), February 2, 1928.

are attractive; as for foreign boarding schools, they are ideal, for in a great degree they save the families from educational responsibilities and inconveniences.[11]

Turkish parents who sent their children to foreign schools under the impulsion of the various urges described above no doubt felt that their position was fully justified by the circumstances. It was not to be expected, however, that the path of the foreign schools was to continue smooth despite the respect with which they were regarded in certain quarters. Republican Turkey was jealously insistent on maintaining and developing her national genius, in which, as we have seen, there was a liberal sprinkling of religious feeling inherited from the past. She was furthermore extremely anxious to attain a position of complete independence and self-reliance in every realm, including the educational. Schools under foreign Christian auspices, no matter how wholeheartedly they sought to play the game as the Turks wanted them to, could not hope to escape friction with the authorities since they stood for cultures and religious ideas which were alien to those of Turkey, and since their very presence was a constant unpleasant reminder to ardent Turks that their own educational system was regarded as inadequate.

Early in the year 1928 the Americans and others who maintained foreign-supported schools were brought to realize that their position was extremely precarious. This came about through a chain of unfortunate circumstances which resulted in the closing of a school at Bursa which had been supported by the American Board of Commissioners for Foreign Missions, and the imprisonment in the school buildings of the teachers judged guilty of breaking the laws of the Ministry of Public Instruction. Personal spite on the part of one of the Turkish teachers in the school who had been discharged as the result of discontinuance of her course

[11] *Ibid.*

at orders of the government was no doubt responsible for the securing of evidence on which to prosecute, but, be that as it may, the prosecution occurred, and whatever the sense of injustice felt by the missionaries, the case must be regarded as an important one, symbolic of the trend of the times.

The charge brought against the Bursa school-teachers was that they had converted four young Turkish girls in their school to Christianity, and they were prosecuted in accordance with article 526 of the Turkish Penal Code, which provides punishment for those who disobey the regulations of a competent authority. The regulation deemed broken was that of the Ministry of Public Instruction, No. 37, originally adopted on August 20, 1915, and passed again by the Ankara government July 30, 1922. This paragraph reads as follows:

It is not allowed to encourage or force students to take part in the instruction or the services of a religion or denomination other than the religion or denomination to which they belong or to prevent students from attending the school because of non-participation or to permit the participation of students who attend by their own consent.

To understand the issues and sentiments involved in the case it will help to study the twelve charges and the defense arguments as presented by the lawyer for the mission, Ali Haydar, at the fifth session of the trial held April 25, 1928:

The charges against us can be analyzed under twelve heads, and we will treat each in turn:

1. "Kameron and her sister Nemika and two other girls have become Christians." It is easy to become a Moslem; one simply repeats the "word of witnessing." But Christianity is different; it is necessary to be baptized and partake of the communion before one is considered a Christian. We can say categorically that these girls did not become Christians. It is more true to say that they felt a love for Protestantism and for Jesus. Are we to suppose that Kameron came to love Protestantism because she had made a careful study and found it better? She is not

able to make such a study. The reason for her love for Protestantism is rather to be found in the early influences of her mother, who was an Armenian, and her grandmother, who to this day remains a Christian. Without the least desire to cast any disrespect upon the family, or to blame them in any way for such influences, we must see that it is not the school but home influences which are largely responsible for her love for Jesus. She herself has said that she is a Mohammedan and a Turk, and in the secular republic of to-day none of us has any right to question or criticize her.

2. "The diaries of Madelet Hanum are before us." In these diaries are found a number of references, including the fact that Miss Day told her the resurrection story. This story, as you know, is to the effect that Jesus was buried and later when some women went to his tomb, they were met by angels who told them Jesus had ascended into Heaven. In our own religion the story is only slightly different, relating that before being put on the cross he ascended into Heaven. In any case, the diary of an emotional young girl, filled with her imagination, is not sufficient to convict any one of a penal offense without further proof.

3. "Miss Day was guilty of religious propaganda during walks with the children." We shall explain later whether she did this or not and the degree of responsibility involved.

4. "Religious records were played as a means of religious propaganda." The "Ave Maria" record is particularly referred to. On my way down here on the S.S. "Marmora" I heard this "Ave Maria" played on the gramophone. Are we to accuse the stewards of the boat with trying to make us Christians? Religion is not propagated by piano and violin pieces which have no words. Many of the pupils testified that they did not even imagine this record was religious until they were recently told so. How can it be regarded as religious propaganda?

5. "Religious songs were taught to the children as a means of religious propaganda." "I would be true" has been cited as an example of this, but the translation submitted to the court shows it to be not religious. It advocates virtues which belong to our religion also. Is it only Jesus that teaches truthfulness, purity, courage, etc.? The government is encouraging the teaching of morals without religious teaching in the schools. This song is just such as should be approved.

6. "Miss Day gave a New Testament to Kameron Hanum."

7. "Miss Sanderson gave Madelet Hanum the *Girls' Year Book*." Is the giving of a book a penal offense? In Pera there is a shop devoted exclusively to selling Bibles. This is not stopped by the police because the government grants freedom in this respect. By what law is it a penal offense to give some one such a book? Just in these last weeks Ismet Pasha and his associates have made a proposal for revision of the constitution which has been adopted. This leaves every one free to do as he likes in matters of religion. The government does not interfere in such matters.

8. "Distinctions were made between Friday and Sunday." No distinctions were made by the school. The forbidding of tennis on Sundays is a perfectly natural thing, as the teachers have a right to have that day quiet for rest. They did not scorn or slight our Friday in any way. It is our humane and religious duty to respect their Sunday also. Four points are clear: 1. The school gave the same permissions to pupils on Fridays and Sundays. 2. The teachers have a right to have quiet on Sundays. 3. The Department of Education has accepted the principle of Sunday observance in foreign schools. 4. Clothing worn on Sundays can have no relation to religious propaganda.

9. "Greater privileges were accorded to the four girls who are said to have been converted." Although it had been charged that they received better food when sick, Shàhide Hanum herself, who worked in the hospital, testified that all received the same food. If some were introduced to American guests, it was because they spoke English better or made a better impression. The fruit garden was forbidden to all the pupils. Is it supposed that there was a church in this fruit garden?

10. "There were religious pictures in the school." All witnesses, including those against us, have testified that there were no religious pictures in the school. If there were some in the private rooms of the teachers, which the pupils were not supposed to enter, no complaint can be made. In one's own room one can hang any pictures one likes and perform any kind of worship one chooses.

11. "Before meals, the pupils were made to stand a moment and participate in a prayer said secretly by the teachers." It is very natural that the pupils be made to stand a moment and all sit down together for purposes of discipline, as is done in the Naval Academy and other Turkish schools also. Even if the

American teachers did say a prayer to themselves, it is not a crime to thank God for one's food, but it is taught by all religions. It is a Turkish custom to say "Bismillah" at this time. All the witnesses agree that no prayer was said aloud and that the pupils were not forced to pray.

12. "Prohibited books such as Longman's *Grammar* and *Silas Marner* were taught in the school." This point was not raised at first but only brought out later. What sort of religious propaganda can be made by scattered references or religious phrases in a grammar? Moreover, this book has been shown to be included in the lists submitted every year to the Department of Education and approved by them. *Silas Marner* has been declared by a translator appointed under order of the court to be a novel, not religious in nature, and not referring to Christ. We can thus declare that these two books are not forbidden by law.

From the foregoing presentation it is plainly apparent what sort of atmosphere was being maintained in a typical American school. The missionaries no doubt were sincere in their protestations that they were doing nothing not strictly permissible in the eyes of the law, and although each point of accusation when taken by itself seems to be only of trifling consequence, when presented *en masse* the effect is one over which the Turks can hardly be blamed for becoming worried. The missionaries may have felt impelled to present their message of Christian love by whatever means were open to them, but the Turks would have been blind, indeed, if they had failed to see that under the surface forces were stirring which would be bound to have a profound influence on their religious, social, and national life.

Before proceeding to a further study of protests which have been raised by Turks against the alleged proselyting and denationalizing activities of the foreign schools, a brief glance may be taken at representative pronouncements by American missionary educators concerning their religious position.

In 1908 at the period of the constitutional revolution in

Turkey, an American institution, the Central Turkey College, stated its aims and purposes, three of which are worthy of note in our present problem. The religious aim is stated as follows:

The college is a Christian college. It makes Christian character the basis of educated manhood, and believes education without character building to be worse than folly and more harmful than ignorance. Consequently, it guards itself against all influences which are antagonistic to religion in general and to the Christian religion in particular. It can tolerate nothing, however popular or plausible it may be, at the risk or expense of the religious welfare of its students. It seeks to develop the spiritual life of every student, under the conviction that Jesus Christ alone can supply the needs of the human soul.

Another paragraph deals with the college's denominational aims:

The college is not a denominational college. It is based upon evangelical Christianity, but its object is not to propagate any particular form of Christianity among its students. It is first and foremost an educational institution, which promotes religious education so far as it believes religious life to be as natural as physical and intellectual life. Consequently, the college is open to young men of all religions on exactly the same terms. Formal distinctions with reference to religious sects and ideas cannot be made by the Faculty, and will not be tolerated among the students.[12]

The statement of a prominent American educator in Turkey written after the war again stresses the vital importance of religion in the missionary educational work:

So long as American colleges are loyal to the religious convictions that have made them possible, and broadly tolerant while absolutely loyal to their best convictions, they may expect the respect even of those who differ from them. If through fear or favor, they seek to withhold their witness to the essential

[12] Quoted from Reed, *op. cit.*, p. 381.

truth of their religion, they will not only lose the respect of those who differ from them, but also the possibility of broadening and liberalizing the young people who do not know in their own countries any forms of religion which are largely not corrupted by superstition and meaningless forms. If education means enlightenment, certainly the American colleges owe it to their students to exhibit religion in its highest and purest forms. We should condemn them if in art they exhibited only inferior forms, if in music they allowed no one to play Beethoven or Chopin because these were not Orientals. And they would be equally blameworthy if, with their high ideals of religion, they did not present to every student the truths which have made possible their own service to the world.[13]

A representative Turkish reaction to the type of religious living and character-building carried on at Bursa and defended by the viewpoints expressed above is set forth in an editorial which appeared in *Hayat* magazine, an Ankara journal, at the time of the excitement over the Bursa trial. However high the ideals which missionary educators profess to exemplify, it must not be forgotten that they may not wear a halo in the eyes of the people in whose land they are working. The editor writes:

It is reported that several of the Turkish girls in the Bursa American School have become Christian. If the event is taken by itself, it is a simple, ordinary event: a few individuals of the Mohammedan mass which numbers several hundred millions of people have come out from the mass and joined the Christian mass, which also numbers several hundred million persons. But if we think of the reactions to which the event has given birth, the publications of the newspapers, the emotion experienced by the parents whose children were studying in this school in Bursa, and the taking of their children from the school by these families at once after the event, then we realize that we are not face to face with an ordinary question. The affair has made a deep impression upon the Turkish mass, to such a degree that the educational administration of the secular Republican government felt

[13] *Ibid.*, pp. 510 ff.

the necessity of entering into the affair. In this respect the problem is not simple; it is worthy of discussion and analysis in a comprehensive manner and taking full account of the meaning of the word "social."

It is fitting to begin our analysis first of all by asking why an "American" school is situated in Bursa, which is our most Turkish city. Yes, why is there an American school in Bursa when there is not even one American family there? Why are there in Constantinople American, French, Italian, English, German, Austrian, etc. schools for boys and girls? It is well known that the duty of the school is to give education; the function of education is to inoculate the younger generation with the thoughts, feelings, desires, and ideals of the society *to which it belongs*. The thoughts, feelings, etc. common to a society, however, can only be firmly established in the spirits of conscious and cultivated mature members of that society. And only these can inoculate the younger generation with these things. If this idea of ours is correct, then American and other foreign schools in general in Turkey are meaningless, and therefore functionless, empty institutions. We are sure of the truth of our ideas about education because these are not merely a matter of personal opinion; in every civilized country they are current and respected ideas. From another point of view, the foreign schools in Turkey are not meaningless, functionless, and "empty."

The object of the foreign school is foreign culture; foreign language, foreign national ideals and foreign religion are the chief bases of this culture.

The purpose of the foreign school then is to inoculate native youth with this culture. . . .

The writer goes on to speak of the professed intentions of the directors of foreign schools to help Turkey and their care to obey the demands of educational laws. He goes on:

Now let us also pass on to the educational activities of the school. Here we are first of all face to face with moral training. They constantly mention character building to you. This character building duty is always taken in charge by the American teachers. And all the activities of the school are directed toward this center. Let us not forget that the most attractive of the activities of the school is sport. The one directing this is sure to be a teacher brought up with care and under strong religious suggestion in the special schools of the Y.M.C.A. This teacher is on intimate terms with the pupil. The directors of American schools have learned by experience that indirect religious suggestions are more influential upon young people; especially the influence of a good sports teacher upon the spiritual nature of the youth is deep and continuing. . . .

An important activity of the schools is also student discussions. These discussions are conducted with great skill and always drive the student toward a definite idea. This idea is a virtue such as faithfulness, cleanheartedness, etc. Only, the roads which, always secretly in the beginning and on the condition of remaining nameless, lead to this virtue, all lead through Christianity. . . .

He goes on to mention points which were brought out in the Bursa charges such as the importance placed on Christian holidays. He asserts:

The result is that there is Christianity and Protestantism in the school. But the influences upon the pupil are all indirect, all without name. . . .

Perhaps there are also those who will say, "Very well, what of this? In a secular Republic is a religious question to be discussed?" Indeed every Turk who has reached the age of majority can choose the religion he wishes. . . . But we must not forget that every religion is an ideal, and every ideal is an intense love that needs to be satisfied. The longings of soul of a young Turk who is a Protestant cannot be satisfied in Turkey within a Turkish society; he will turn his eyes to the great Protestant nations. However, it is necessary that the glance of a young Turk be directed to his own society, and education is charged with assuring this. . . .

In a word these schools are institutions which by their lessons, by their training, turn Turkish youth away from the society to which they belong to another society and carry them toward a foreign ideal. The conversions which occasionally take place openly are the high points of the indirect influences which are at work every day and every hour upon the Turkish students who fill the schools, and the most harmful influences of the foreign school are especially the indirect influences. . . .

Character is very much a matter of nationality. It takes shape only in a national environment, and only with the good and bad actions and reactions of that environment. I stress the phrase "both the good and the bad." Character cannot be brought in from outside, for it is not an external, a corporeal thing. The foreign school moulds a character only according to foreign ideals; as for this character, be it in a religious form or in a political form, it is harmful for the national Turkish ideals. . . .

The continuance in Turkey in an enterprise harmful for Turkish nationality under the name of educational activity of some countrymen of those Americans who do not look with pleasure upon institutions harmful to the Americanization movement and to American national activity in America, can be harmonized neither with the humanitarian purpose which they advocate on every occasion nor with the principle, "Do not to another that which thou dost not desire to be done to thee," which they attribute to Christianity. . . .[14]

Numerous examples could be cited of Turkish writers who have protested against the presence of foreign schools because of their indirect religious influences which are regarded as distinctly dangerous to the development of Turkish nationality. Mehmet Emin, one of the most influential educators in Turkey, writing in the same magazine, *Hayat,* two weeks later makes the declaration:

The worst schools are those institutions which do not create capacities useful for the social and national environment. The foreign school not only fails to create these capacities, it produces young people who gradually get out of harmony with the spiritual life of their environment, due to the religious and national influence which the institution makes its object.[15]

In a novel entitled *Pervaneler* ("Moths"), the woman novelist, Mufidie Ferid, has written a strong criticism of the effect of American college education on Turkish girls, from which certain passages are worthy of attention. Describ-

[14] "The Christianizing Incident," *op. cit.*
[15] "Is the Conversion to Christianity Incident a Result of a Culture Crisis?" *ibid.,* February 16, 1928.

ing the emotional conflict undergone by one of the characters
in her novel, she writes:

Nesimé's trouble was like that of all Turkish children who
study in this school [Byzantium College] . . . American life
and the desire to live in America!
This was their last year, and as it was the time to leave the
school, this desire was more acute. To return home at the end
of the year—God spare them from it! Every day putting her
head together with Leman [a fellow-student], the two of them
were seeking an escape from this fate. But they were not bad
girls. Perhaps they loved their families, but the training which
they had received from this college in their early years [16] had
caused them to dislike their environments.
Because they were changed and transformed.
The trip to America was a psychological need for Nesimé.
Nesimé was the daughter of a well-known Mevlevi sheikh, Amir
Tchelebi. Her mother died when she was born. She grew up in
a *tekké* [dervish monastery] without any love and kindness
among the armies of dervishes and *badjis* [negro nurses], and in
a continual flood of visitors. When she entered the cold stage
of the school, which resembles the world of struggle, she thought
there were two sorts of women on the face of the earth: one, the
women whom she had seen in the *tekké,* silent, aimless, and
filling their lives with menial tasks; the other, women whom
she met in the college, able to earn their livelihood, fight against
men, and rely on their own strength without the help of relatives.
Perhaps there might be a third sort of women who are loved
and married . . . heroines of love. But they were beautiful
women, and Nesimé knew that she was not beautiful.
Therefore there remained for her two alternatives of life:
either to thrust herself into the struggle as she did when she
was in school, or, as her father wished her to do, go back to
the *tekké* and marry and thrust herself into a monotonous desert
of life and do small and menial tasks.
But was this life possible for her now? Was it possible for
her to leave the college and go back to the *tekké* and mend
clothes before a *mongal* [charcoal stove] in low-roofed rooms,

[16] The college, like its real prototype, the Constantinople Woman's
College, included preparatory courses in its curriculum.

obey her husband without love, and live among the *badjis* a life in which one day is just like another? Was it possible after this?

Now it was too late. In her empty heart the worship of America was sown as a seed. The vision of being master of her own life was shining before her like a great happiness. To earn her livelihood! Perhaps to be famous! Of course these were mere wishes, but that sort of desire may lead to happiness. So who would go back home? [17]

Another notable passage describes the impression made on relatives of one of the students who have come to the school to protest against having the girl sent to America on a scholarship; they are being shown around the school by one of the teachers, an Armenian.

Andrée [a French girl married to a Turk, brother of the student] was looking at the pictures hanging in the classrooms and corridors. There were masterpieces of the world's art. They were chosen to be shown to the children. They had photographs and lithographs, starting from the Apollo Belvedere, up to Memnon the Giant, including the Statue of Liberty in New York, the Acropolis, the Capitol, stones from Karnak, the palaces of Westminster, and the Gothic castles of feudal times; small or large, they had all these pieces, but they did not have a single thing which concerned Turkey.

The only thing that was Turkish was the air and sunshine which came through the large windows. Andrée, as she looked out from the window, saw the crimson line of minarets and mosques which forms the unique Turkish picture, looking like a winged and imaginary painting.

Then they went to the Ethnographic Museum. There they had everything from Armenia, Greece, Russia, Bulgaria, Yugo-Slavia—but not a single thing from Turkey. Better to say they had a few Turkish kerchiefs and towels from Aintab, but they all came under the name of Armenian work. They did not find a single thing, neither a Turkish carpet, nor an antique faïence, nor a gilded book cover, nor a silken headdress that looks like a flower, not a thing made by Fatma [a name representing

[17] *Op. cit.,* pp. 47 f.

Turkish women in general]. They had forgotten the Seljuk bridges and castles, the Blue Mosque of Bursa, the Mosque of Selim in Adrianople, and the Suleimaniyeh of Stamboul. As they had forgotten Turkey among their art works, so they denied her in the Ethnographic Museum.

Andrée wondered at this treacherous frame of mind toward the country whose hospitality they had accepted. Now she, and all three, understood why the Turkish girls like her sister-in-law did not remember their nationality. . . .[18]

Sami said, "They live apart like a different state in our country, without recognizing us or our laws, under their own rules, organization, environment, civilization, even in their own streets and lighting. And by so living they think they can exert the influence and power of their country more effectively. You are right. It is a lantern which attracts moths." [19]

Enough evidence has been presented to show that the position of missionary and foreign education in Turkey is in a precarious position as a result of Turkey's evangel of nationalism. The work of all institutions which are not regularly administered by the Ministry of Public Instruction is bound constantly to be subjected to a rigid scrutiny by patriotic Turks, and any denationalizing influences, direct or indirect, especially any which have Christian religious significance, will be certain, if found, to meet with a punishment similar to that accorded to the teachers at Bursa. Turkey at the present time is not a place for a missionary who is not willing to forego all ideas of proselyting and to devote himself whole-heartedly to the task of helping Turkey develop according to her own genius, supplying only such Western or Christian viewpoints as the Turks themselves call upon him to suggest. Pragmatic as Turkey now is, and ready to accept from the West whatever she feels will contribute to the strengthening of her national society, philanthropists may assume that any essential features of their culture and re-

[18] *Ibid.*, pp. 112 f.
[19] *Ibid.*, p. 116.

ligion will be eventually requested by a nation so avowedly eclectic as Turkey now is. It would be a great tactical blunder on the part of those who wish to share Christianity with the Turks to make an effort to force their ideals down Turkish throats. The antagonism which would be aroused by such activity would delay indefinitely the achievement of those very ends so earnestly desired by Turkey's well-wishing foreign friends.

Now that the new Turkish government and American mission workers have had more than a decade to become acquainted with each other, there should be a constantly diminishing number of causes for friction. The missionaries remaining in Turkey understand the definite limitations placed upon religious teaching and are altruistically committed to the service of the Turkish people in whatever manner is possible. Turkey's responsible officials, for their part, are co-operative and ready to extend a cordial welcome to American enterprises which have shown themselves ready to conform to the policies of the republican government.[20] Turkey's enthusiastic appreciation of the work of the Messrs. Jennings and the American Friends of Turkey has already been cited.[21] And there seems no reason to suppose that other American activities will be treated with hostility so long as they continue to be genuinely helpful in Turkey's transition and development.

An example of the intelligent work of the American mission group was its initiation of a wholesome magazine, *Muhit*, with the co-operation of Turkish publicists, when the change in alphabet and reading habits of the nation made it ex-

[20] Curtailment of American educational activity since 1931 has not been due to Turkish unfriendliness. The closing of three American Board schools and the college at Izmir was necessitated by financial and administrative difficulties and was carried out voluntarily by the responsible American executives.

[21] See pp. 135 f. above.

tremely difficult for any except crude pictorial journals to secure enough circulation to survive. In many other practical ways these missionaries of the new day have sought to lend a hand where the need was greatest. In addition to the schools already referred to, five medical centers have been established, playground and social service work have been set up in Adana, and an experimental farm placed in service at Gaziantep.

A paragraph from the *Annual Report of the American Board of Commissioners for Foreign Missions for 1932* summarizes the practical work being attempted in Turkey:

A survey of the whole Near East Mission reveals how much there is of great promise in the work being done, both in city and in rural areas. The definite rural activities center around Merzifon, Talas, and Gaziantep where during the past year experimental work in village education by means of "movies" and village visitation has been carried on. Suspicion and mistrust have been replaced by confidence and friendship as a result of this quiet, intensive work. The Village Boys' Hostel in connection with the Talas School has been a worth-while experiment. Fifteen village boys who brought their own beds and food were provided quarters and a cook, so that with a minimum of expense they might have some educational opportunity which would otherwise be beyond their reach. The Gaziantep Farm is the outstanding rural project in the Mission. The village boys who serve as apprentices on the farm are being trained in better methods of agriculture and in turn will become demonstrators of these methods in their villages. There are results in character building which are quite as real though less tangible.[22]

From the Turkish viewpoint it is clear, despite hostile hysterical flurries, that Turkey will welcome American philanthropy when it is given without ulterior motives. A statement in this regard has been made by Mehmet Emin in his previously quoted article in *Hayat:*

[22] *Op. cit.*, pp. 15 f.

Those of philanthropic temper who wish to help us must do this exclusively with Turkish hands and for the needs of Turkey. The Americans have given vast assistance to the University of Brussels, but in return for this assistance they did not seek to open an American University in Brussels. Humanitarian assistance which can be given to Turkey can only be of this kind.[23]

From the missionary viewpoint the tendency is more and more to respect the wishes of the Turks with a growing realization that missionary educational work is a co-operative enterprise. It is clear that students must be educated as loyal Turkish citizens to be of maximum service to their community. Recognizing the prevailing Turkish attitude on religion, this precludes any attempt to make these students professing Christians. Patience and forbearance must be manifested until the wounds caused by Christian-Moslem rivalry have healed and until Turkey as a whole outgrows her suspicion of religion as a benighted superstition and an enemy of progress. When Turkey, along with the rest of the world, comes to understand real religion as a great dynamic, liberating force, designed to serve the needs of humanity, and when she realizes the close identification between the aims of her own leaders and the humanitarian purposes of vital religion, there will be an end to inhibitions and the mutual distrust existing between Moslem and Christian. Leaders of each faith may then work in harmony, releasing their full energies to seek together the ideal society wherein man may live at his best, thus fulfilling the fondest hopes of Jesus and Mohammed. But how long it will take to reach this ideal era, who can say?

[23] "Is the Conversion to Christianity Incident a Result of a Culture Crisis?" *op. cit.*

X

THE PLACE OF ISLAM IN THE NEW TURKEY

In nearly every phase of Turkish life it is possible to point definitely to changes and reforms which have occurred and which represent results of clearly defined policies. The great exception, however, is met with when it comes to religion and the attitude of the government toward the forms and institutions of Islam. True it is that definite changes have taken place, and great ones, such as the removal of Islamic influences from the government, laws, and education in the country. And when one considers that Islam has always prided itself on being an all-inclusive system which prescribed rules for every phase of human activity, any alteration which pretends to draw a line between realms subject to and independent of the religion's influence must be recognized as well-nigh revolutionary. It is not questioned that great changes have been wrought on the status of Islam in Turkey; the puzzling point to the outside observer is just how much vitality remains in the shrunken institution or organization which persists in Turkey and calls itself Islam.

The difficulty in reaching an accurate conclusion is increased by two things: one, that almost everybody has a different view on the matter; and the other, that almost everybody is extremely cautious and reluctant to talk about religion because the republican government is none too tolerant of religious ideas which may direct the thoughts of the people toward reaction or superstition.

It is an unfortunate fact that to the average Turk the

169

word *din* (religion) connotes all that is bigoted and backward, instead of unselfish devotion and nobility of character. The resentment against traditionalism, which we saw to be so important a factor in paving the way for Kemal Ataturk's Westernizing reforms, directed much of its furious anger against Islam, which for centuries had been the only thing the Turks knew as religion. Their contact with oriental Christianity was such as only to confirm their idea that religion meant fanaticism, ignorance, and opposition to progress.

When, with the emergence of nationalism as Turkey's great ideal, alterations were made in every section of Turkey's social structure, Islam as a religious system had also to be dealt with. The problem was one of the most delicate which a government was ever called upon to solve. All of Turkey's leaders and those who fought so valiantly for Turkey's independence were Moslems, if they professed any religion. In many hearts Islam had represented an ideal worth dying for, and such repetitive features as the required worship five times each day meant that religious practices were habitual in millions of lives and regarded as among the most vital performances in the technique of living. Yet it was painfully plain to the new leaders that a continuance of traditional Islam in the country would never do if Turkey meant to attain parity with the nations of Western civilization. On the one hand, it was impossible to keep Islam as it was; on the other hand, because of its deep roots in Turkish hearts, Islam could not be violently extirpated. Under the circumstances the new government did the only thing it could do: (1) remove from Islamic jurisdiction its laws, educational system, and other phases of life which Western nations were observed to have removed from religious to secular domination; (2) destroy or remove all leaders and breeders of bigotry and reaction; and (3) divert religious energy so far as possible into channels which would make for progress and co-operation with the governmental program.

Explanation of the government's rôle and interest in the reshaping of the Islamic forms lies in the historic association which always existed between religion and state in Turkey as in all Moslem countries. Islam had always been a part of the state, so that when it became *persona non grata* with the government, it had no separate organization which would permit it to stand on its own feet. Hence its guidance and leadership had to continue to come from governmental sources. According to one who is out of sympathy with autocratic features of the present régime, the great difference in Islam's status now from what it was formerly is this: in the old days the Turkish governmental authority was wielded by two rival forces, the military and the religious, each acting as a check on the other; now the military force is supreme, and the religious element is completely under its thumb.

Frequent examples have appeared in preceding chapters of the way in which secular matters have been taken away from the control of Islamic prescriptions—in other words, a separation of the state from the church. The most significant operation in the removal of bigotry breeders was the law of 1925 which closed all dervish *tekkés* and theological *medressehs* after the reactionary Kurdish revolt of that year. As for the third step, the warping of Islamic institutions so as to cause them to play into the hands of progress and the republican program of modernization, that is what we must study most attentively, seeking to understand the point of view of the government, the present organizational set-up, and the proposed or attempted changes in Islamic beliefs and teachings for the current needs of the country.

What, first, is the point of view toward Islam of those who control its destiny? Here one can find a variety of answers.

Some people declare that the government is frankly hostile and apprehensive of everything connected with religion, and that, being avowed freethinkers themselves for the most part, the leaders would like to obliterate as soon as possible all traces of Islam or any other religious system, and are only preserving enough of the old forms to preclude violent reactionary movements from those millions who still cherish Islam. Others, representing the other extreme opinion, seem to regard the Kemalists as cordial friends and well-wishers to Islam, eager to purify it and strengthen it. As Count Ostrorog has put it:

The object was not then to destroy religious beliefs: religion was simply caused to recede from the halls of human conflicts and ascend into the stronghold of conscience, to dwell there in much greater dignity and security than when its ministers pretended to rule earthly interests as well as moral aspirations.[1]

As a matter of fact, the truth seems to lie somewhere between the two extremes of hostility and cordiality, with the adjective "experimental" perhaps best describing the government attitude.

There are numerous reasons why the Kemalists should not be utterly hostile to Islam. In the first place, religious sensibilities played an important part in the success of the War of Independence. Accounts of the Greek invasion tell of frequent insults and defilements cast on the Moslems and their holy places by the arrogant infidel Greeks. The thought of Christian enemies invading the precincts of Islam was one of the most important factors in awakening the Turks to their famous desperate resistance. A notable event recorded by the Gazi in his Six-Day Speech was the ceremonial attending the opening of the first Parliament in Ankara on April 23, 1920. The deputies all gathered together for prayer in the

[1] *The Angora Reform*, p. 96.

mosque of Hadji Bairam in a manner reminiscent of crusading knights.[2] In his statements on religion made to inquiring fellow-countrymen as recounted by Mahmut, Ataturk expressed no compelling bitterness against the religion of Islam, though he criticized freely the errors into which its leaders had led it. In fact, one interview reports him as declaring that the religion of the Turkish state should continue to be Islam, but an Islam which should provide freedom of thought.[3] This point of view was later changed when it became evident that a state religion was not in line with twentieth-century specifications for a modern state.[4] Accordingly, those sections of the constitution which affirmed that the religion of the state was Islam and which required deputies to take their oath by swearing on the Koran were modified to eliminate the religious references.[5] A Turkish educator with whom I was discussing these matters described Turkey's treatment of Islam within her borders as similar to a father's discipline of his own child: a spanking does not imply hatred! Turkey's new government would indeed be foolish if it cast impatiently aside so important a factor in national unity as religious similarity or spent valuable effort in antireligious, repressive tactics which would only serve to deplete her resources and to arouse resentful protests.

Reasons why the Kemalists should not be whole-heartedly and actively sympathetic to Islam are also easy to find. Preeminently, of course, there is the feeling, frequently appearing in these pages, that Islam is responsible for Turkey's backwardness. This is not a basis for a cordial attitude. Furthermore, with progress and social uplift the leading ideals in the new program, too much favoritism could hardly be

[2] Cf. Gasi Mustafa Kemal, *Die neue Turkei,* I, 407 f.
[3] "Le Ghazi et la révolution," Instalment Nos. 21 and 22.
[4] Cf. Gasi Mustafa Kemal, *op. cit.,* II, 250.
[5] Cf. p. 179 below.

expected to be shown to an institution which had usually made for opposite ideals. Another item to be noticed is that among the new leaders there was included no young man vitally interested in reforming Islam or theologically trained and qualified to undertake it if he had so desired. Islam's antiquated educational system [6] had filled the ranks of *hodjas* and *imams* with men who were sterile in new ideas. Thus if a wholesome reform movement had been contemplated within the ranks of Islam, where was the trained leadership to be found? The prevailing notion among the nationalists seemed to be that expressed by Yusuf Kemal when he declared to me that the thing of chief importance for Turkey at present is to get herself on her feet economically. Religious idealism, he feels, can wait until Turkey has assured herself of bread to eat. Religion he classes as a sort of luxury which wealthy nations like the United States can indulge in. It was a puzzle to many students at Istanbul University, I was told, why anyone should bother to come to Turkey to study her religion when the country was solely occupied in scraping together enough food and money to live on. A further factor to be borne in mind in connection with the new government's lack of cordiality toward Islam is the traditional jealousy and suspicion which has in the past attended the relations of military and ecclesiastical elements in the state, leading to the presumption that when the military group assumed full power, they would repress their old religious rivals as much as possible. Evidence of the close watch which is being kept by the government over the acts of religious leaders was brought home to me in Istanbul when after an attempt to interview an important *hodja* I was informed that he dared give no interviews. Something he had said in a previous in-

---

[6] A picture of the life of hypocrisy and ignorance in a theological medresseh is contained in the novel by Rechad Nuri called *Yeşil Gece* ("Green Night").

terview had apparently been misinterpreted and had brought down on him a sharp warning from Ankara. This same spirit of apprehension toward the government was manifested by every man of the turban [7] with whom I talked, including the members of the Diyanet Ichleri (Presidency of Religious Affairs) whom I interviewed in Ankara.

From the foregoing evidence of friendliness and suspicion, it is plain that one cannot categorically assert either that the government is favorable or that it is hostile to Islam. The truth of the matter seems to be that it is distinctly opportunist in its attitude: that it is favorable to whatever in Islam is consistent with the republican ideals, relentlessly opposed to anything which might endanger Kemalist success, and, for the rest, more or less neutral. The apparent goal toward which the government would like religion to move is to cut loose from its roots in seventh-century Arabia, eliminate those features which cramp originality, keep away from political and governmental matters, and contribute what it can toward the social and moral welfare of the Turkish Republic.

A glance at some of the more important acts of legislation and regulation affecting the place of Islam in the country will perhaps illustrate the trend of the Ankara attitude.

In 1920, as was mentioned in a preceding chapter, shortly after the Ankara government had established itself, the old *Sheikh-ul-Islamate* and Ministry of *Evkaf* (Pious Foundations) were combined in Ankara under a single *Vekil* or Commissary. On November 18, 1922, a caliph with solely spiritual powers was elected by the Grand National Assembly to supplant the old office of sultan-caliph which combined spiritual and temporal powers. But on March 3, 1924,

[7] Until recently the only Moslems exempted from wearing European headdress were the religious dignitaries, who wore a fez of brick color with a turban wound around it. Distinction of religious garb is no longer permitted. See pp. 181 f. below.

[8] Toynbee, *Survey*, I (1925), 71. See p. 88 above.

came the most stringent changes yet legislated: the caliphate was definitely abolished, all educational institutions, including theological schools and others under religious control, were combined under the control of the secular Ministry of Public Instruction, and the *Vekil* for religious affairs established in 1920 was abolished, in its place being set up a subdepartment under the Prime Ministry which should handle Islamic affairs. At the same time new regulations concerning the rich *Evkaf* moneys were passed.[9] The law regarding the new religious organizational set-up is important:

ARTICLE 1. Whereas the laying down and execution of the Law in cases concerning civil transactions in the Republic of Turkey falls within the province of the Great National Assembly of Turkey and of the Government which it has constituted,[10] there is now (hereby) established, in the capital of the Republic, an office, designated "Presidency of Religious Affairs" [Diyanet Ichleri], for the dispatch of all cases and concerns of the Exalted Islamic Faith which relate to dogma and ritual, and for the administration of religious foundations.

ART. 2. The Commissariat for the *Sherieh* and *Evqaf* is abolished.

ART. 3. The President of Religious Affairs is appointed by the President of the Republic on the recommendation of the Prime Minister.

ART. 4. The Presidency of Religious Affairs is attached to the

[9] The collection and administration of income from these endowments in real estate and other properties are most complex. Some of Turkey's most valuable properties are held by the *Evkaf* as a result of past donations by wealthy Moslems. Today one finds some of Turkey's finest office buildings, hotels, and apartments constructed from *Evkaf* funds.

[10] Civil regulations had hitherto been considered to have their origin in the *sharia* law, based on the word of Mohammed, who in turn had received his revelations from God. It should also be pointed out here that the administrative arm of the government at the time this law was passed was chosen by and solely responsible to the elected Assembly as a whole. The arrangement has since been changed so that the cabinet is appointed by and responsible to the president, but is made up of deputies of the Assembly.

Premiership. The budget of the Presidency of Religious Affairs is appended to the budget of the Premiership. . . .

ART. 5. The President of Religious Affairs is charged with the administration of all mosques . . .[11] and of all dervish houses within the boundaries of the territories of the Republic of Turkey, as well as with the appointment and dismissal of all rectors of mosques [imams], orators [khatibs], preachers [va'yz], abbots of dervish houses [sheykhs], callers to prayer [muezzins], sacristans [qayyims] and all other employees (of a religious character).

ART. 6. The Presidency of Religious Affairs is the proper place of legal recourse for jurisconsults in the Islamic Law [muftis].

ART. 7. With a view to a settlement in conformity with the genuine interests of the nation, Evqaf affairs are provisionally placed in the keeping of the Premiership in the form of a general administratorship.[12]

In 1925 the government was brought to a sharp realization of the danger and strength of reaction and ignorant fanaticism in the country when a revolt broke out in the eastern provinces chiefly among the Kurdish tribes. At the same time there were revealed the power and popularity of the Ankara reformers in the swell of indignation which arose against the reactionaries. But the government, at least the Gazi and his clique, decided that there had been enough temporizing with ignorant fanaticism. As the Gazi said in his Six-Day Speech two years later:

Could one regard as a civilized nation a mass of men who allowed themselves to be taken in tow by a rabble of *Sheikhs*, *Dédés*, *Saïds*, *Tchelebis*, *Babas*, and *Emirs;* who entrusted their fate and their life to chiromancers, magicians, casters of lots, and amulet sellers? Ought it be allowed to retain in the new Turkish state, in the Turkish Republic, elements and institutions

[11] The census figures as shown in the *Annuaire statistique*, Vol. I (1928), list 28,705 mosques in Turkey for 1927. The number of schools was 14,425, by way of comparison.

[12] Text in Toynbee, *op. cit.*, I (1925), 572 ff.

like these which for centuries had given the nation a different appearance as if it were real? [13]

In order to put an end to these retrogressive influences there were passed on September 2, 1925, three decrees:

The first closed all religious houses [*tekkehs* and *zawiyehs*] and abolished all religious orders in Turkey; [14] prohibited individuals from living as members of orders and from wearing the costumes or bearing the titles associated therewith; closed all chapels [*mesjids*] attached to religious houses and all mausolea [*türbehs*]; and abolished the office of custodian of such establishments. The second decree defined the categories of persons who were to be reckoned as *ulema,* and their costumes, and prohibited the wearing of these costumes by unauthorized persons. The third decree laid down that all public servants who were not required to wear a special uniform were to dress in the ordinary clothes in use among the civilized nations of the world—including the hat [*shapqah*]—and were to uncover the head indoors, and also out-of-doors, as a sign of salutation.[15]

Superstition and everything that might be a breeder of it were to be eliminated from Turkey. I was even told by a young Turkish woman in Istanbul that when she had proposed to translate Grimm's fairy tales into Turkish for children's reading, she had been politely requested by the Ministry of Public Instruction to give up the idea, as the government wished to discourage anything which had to do with distortions of the imagination.

When in 1926 the Westernized law codes were put into effect, the long-standing prescriptions of the *sharia* law in regard to marriage, divorce, and family relations, along with

[13] *Op. cit.,* II, 386 f.

[14] The groups affected by this decree, most of them dervish orders, have long played picturesque rôles in Turkish life. Though some of the orders encouraged enlightenment, their history in general is bound up with chicanery and intrigue. Some of the orders were monastic and held mystical beliefs which orthodox Moslems regarded as heretical.

[15] Toynbee, *op. cit.,* I (1925), 72 f.

all other statutes of Koranic origin, were put into the discard. At the same time four articles (Nos. 175–78) in the Penal Code provided punishment for anyone who interfered with religious liberty in worship. Article 163, however, provided strong penalties for religionists who sought to meddle in politics in their ecclesiastical capacities:

Those who make use of religion, of religious sentiments, or of things considered as sacred by religion, to stir the people to acts of a nature to bring injury to the security of the state in any fashion or quality whatever, as well as those who organize associations for this purpose, will be punished by heavy prison sentence, even if these excitations and organizations have achieved no results. . . . It is forbidden to form political associations based on religious sentiments and opinions. Associations of this kind will be dissolved, and those who have formed them, as well as their members, will be punished according to the dispositions mentioned above.

Two interesting developments in the religious situation came about in 1928. On April 10 the Organic Law of the Republic was modified to remove all references which might seem to give the religion of Islam a favored place in the Republic's constitution. From article 2 was eliminated the clause that the religion of the state was Islam. Articles 16 and 38 provided that in taking oaths of office, deputies and the president should be sworn in on their word of honor instead of on the Koran. Two months later there was presented to the Assembly the report of the faculty of theology at Istanbul in regard to changes proposed in rites and practices of the Islamic religion. The theological faculty had been set up in 1924 at the time of the abolition of the caliphate and the unification of the educational system, and had been assigned the task of making such suggestions. Their proposals when made four years later were extreme. The report called for such innovations as the introduction of pews and instrumental music into the mosques; the retention of shoes on the feet during worship, which, of course, meant an end of the hallowed custom of washing the feet in the ablutions preceding worship; and the use of the Turkish instead of Arabic language in the services. The innovations were branded by a writer in the *Review of Religions* as "absolutely un-Islamic." [16] It is noteworthy, however, that although the report was not enacted at the time into legislation, the recommendation to use Turkish in place of Arabic wherever possible has been carried out. It is now prescribed that the Koran is to be used in Turkish translation, and that the call to prayer is to be given in Turkish. The Turkish word for God, *Tanri*, has been substituted for the Arabic *Allah*.

Before we proceed to a consideration of current writings on Islamic subjects which bear a mark of more or less official approval, something should be said in regard to the present-day personnel of the Islamic religion, its character and its training. It must be realized that the attractiveness of going into religion professionally is much less than it used to be. No longer do men of the turban preside in courts of law, no longer is their religious instruction eagerly sought after, and no longer does life in the *medresseh* offer the attractions of a comfortable, easy life with material wants amply taken care of. Rather, indeed, it seemed to me that in some places a certain stigma of backwardness went with leadership of a religious congregation. Much, of course, depends on the locality involved, for the farther one travels eastward away from the metropolitan centers of progress the less does the influence of the *hodjas* seem to have dwindled. The time is past, however, when the country can be flooded with irresponsible holy men who can prey on the generosity and superstitious fears of the populace, for *imams* and other functionaries are regarded as state employees and only those officially licensed may wear robes of office and gain the salaries and fees which rightly

[16] "Turkish Religion," *op. cit.*, July, 1928, pp. 1 f.

accrue to men of the cloth. Since the *Evkaf* moneys, from which financial support for mosques and their staffs comes, are under the close supervision of the state, *hodjas* who are out of step with the government's ideas are not retained on the pay-roll.

An interesting sidelight to the status of *hodjas* as employees of the state was given me in Merzifun, where it was reported that the local administration had utilized *hodjas* as tax surveyors. The ordinary salaries paid these men are far from adequate to live on, but additional fees may be picked up by performing funeral and marriage ceremonies. A *hodja* in Izmir, who is compelled to run a bookstore and sign-lettering business in addition to his religious duties to make enough to live on, reported that there was as much demand as ever for his services at a funeral, people apparently not yet having reached a point where they dared pass away without satisfying religious requirements. The case with marriages, I was told, was somewhat different. In his own district, the civil ceremony performed at the town hall in conformity with the state law was usually regarded as sufficient. In poorer and more ignorant districts, however, he understood that people frequently called on the *hodja* to give some sort of blessing after the civil ceremony performed by the governor or his deputy.[17]

The Government's regulation of November 27, 1934, forbidding the wearing of clerical garb except during religious services, seems to have been designed partly to eliminate the publicity attendant upon the public display of religious garb, likely to be reminiscent of "the old days," and partly as a phase of the larger program to eliminate social and class

---

[17] Islam does not, as a matter of fact, consider marriage as a sacrament in any fashion corresponding to Christianity. Though performed according to *sharia* law, marriage does not normally require more than an agreement and witnesses.

distinctions within the Turkish Republic. The law applies not only to Moslems but to Christian clerics as well.

Most of the individuals who carry on the rites of Islam at present are men who have been trained under the old régime and are well along in years. It was an odd coincidence that two young Turks still in their twenties, with whom I became well acquainted, had fathers and grandfathers who were holy men but had themselves decided against following the profession because they felt it to be out of date in the present century.

For the young man who wishes to enter professionally upon a religious career there is today in Turkey virtually no incentive and no public theological school or *medresseh* where the study may be undertaken. During the first ten years of the Republic there existed two types of religious training school: one, emphasizing the historical and philosophical aspects of Islam, the Faculty of Theology at the University of Istanbul; the other, designed to train practical leaders who should also serve as village teachers, special schools for Imams and Khatibs under the Ministry of Public Instruction.

With the reorganization of the University of Istanbul projected in 1933, the Faculty of Theology loses its identity, for the four faculties as newly constituted are in letters, law, medicine, and science. Among the special institutes to be set up in the new organization, one will deal with Islamic research, but it is plain that no facilities are planned to equip young Turks for active religious leadership.

The special schools for *imams* and *khatibs* established by the Ministry of Public Instruction seem, after an eight-year experiment, finally to have been abandoned. Though the *Annuaire statistique* for 1932–33 still mentions the schools under its list of professional institutions managed by the Ministry of Public Instruction, the report for 1932–33 reveals no schools, no teachers, and no students. In 1924–25 there were 26 of these schools with 302 teachers and 1,442 students. The number of schools was cut in 1926–27 to 2, with a combined faculty of 41 and an enrolment of 278. As attendance shrank from year to year, the schools were discontinued in 1930–31, though the registration of a small number of students for the next two years indicates that provision was made for those who had begun their studies in these institutions to continue them in other government schools.

It is easy to see why Turkey with her new policy of complete separation of religion and politics should have concluded that the secular government was illogical in sponsoring schools for religious leaders, yet the very fact that she did maintain such institutions for a number of years and conscientiously set up a wholesome curriculum for the training of an intelligent religious leadership is plain evidence that the Kemalists are not narrowly and fanatically antireligious as are the Communists of Russia.

It was my privilege to visit one of the schools for *imams* and *khatibs* in Istanbul while it was still actively functioning under the Ministry of Public Instruction. The director of the school wore no clerical garb and appeared to be a keen and thoughtful educator. His previous experience had been confined entirely to lay schools, and he appeared to have no theological qualifications other than an enthusiastic belief in the possibilities of reforming Islam to become a vital and inspiring force in the life of the new Turkey. His eyes shone eagerly as he told how people had frequently complained because *hodjas* were ignorant and unable to assist their congregations spiritually or morally, and he told of his plans to see his students go forth into the villages so equipped with new knowledge and devotion that they would transform the populace from lazy, ignorant, and superstitious folk to active, intelligent, and keen-minded citizens of his beloved Republic.

The course of study laid out for these new style *hodjas* would never have been accepted in an old-fashioned *medresseh*. Such subjects as the Koran and Hadith occupied but a few hours each week, while the bulk of the work was made up of modern disciplines like biology, chemistry, and French. Now that this type of school is closed and the government has ceased to take responsibility for religious instruction, it remains for some sort of private initiative to provide the facilities to train leaders for Turkey's Islam. It is possible, of course, that the theological education could be attained outside Turkey—at Al-Azhar in Cairo, for example. But since every such institution would employ Arabic or some other language than Turkish, it is not likely that foreign study would attract many Turks. The new facilities for religious training will have to be in Turkey and adapted to the Turkish mentality. To the degree that the problem of leadership training is solved, to the same degree will the survival of Islam as a vital force in Turkey be assured.

In the legislation and regulations which were noticed to have grown out of the opportunist attitude of the Turkish Republic toward Islam there was manifested no all-compelling bitterness against religion as is the case in Soviet Russia, nor was there any apparent eagerness to keep Islam as a state religion and use it to give the new government a sacrosanct position as defender of the faith. The policy seemed rather to meet situations as they arose, dealing harshly with any religious manifestations or attitudes which were at cross-purposes with the all-important national ideals, but lending cautious encouragement to moves which might produce a more progressive Islam, a religion which would be of value to the state in developing intelligent, co-operative, and moral citizens. It has been frequently asserted by individuals supposedly in touch with the situation that such moves on the part of leaders of the Islamic faith in Turkey were so few as to be nonexistent. It seems to be a fact that reform moves within the Islamic body are not great in volume, but there is unquestionably a move in the direction of harmonizing the teachings of the Prophet with modern conditions, of discovering vital points in the old teachings, and of contradicting those critics who have averred that Islam was a faith only for Arab nomads or that a modified Islam was Islam no longer. It will be worth while to examine carefully certain writings which have been published within the last decade, including sermons issued by the Presidency of Religious Affairs (Diyanet Ichleri) for use in the mosques of Turkey, sermons written by one of the members of that Presidency and preached from the pulpit of Hadji Bairam Mosque in Ankara, textbooks written for use in the government primary and middle schools while religion was still a curricular study, and miscellaneous magazine articles. In considering these progressive pronouncements it must not be forgotten that there is a large, non-vocal, conservative mass, which would not subscribe to such interpretations as are given the sacred writings. Furthermore, books on religion of any kind have very little sale at the present time, according to booksellers with whom I talked, so that these ideas must not be thought to have too wide a vogue.

The first selection deals in general with the religion of Islam and is taken from the first book on "The Religion of Islam" (*Islam Dini*) by Yusuf Ziya. This book, and its companion Volume II, are the only religious textbooks which were approved for use in the middle and normal schools of Turkey in the list of schoolbooks issued by the Ministry of Public Instruction for the year 1929–30.

It is said in the great Koran, "Islam is the religion in the sight of God." Islam is the religion of all the Prophets who came from different parts of the world. Their religions were based on the needs of human beings and their times. Finally, when men became perfected, Islam showed them the path which should lead to their happiness.

Religions have come out of different races and at different times. But all of them were more or less altered. Finally there came Islam, which has not been altered at all and suits the needs of all nations.

As Islam comprises all religions, so it orders us to believe in other prophets and books, and that is why it is a world-wide religion. Each race and every nation may progress in its own way, and Islam does not interfere with this progress, because Islam has universal principles in itself.

Islam requires men to have perfect morality, unity of faith, and beauty of worship, and then says, "The field is yours; you can go on as you please," and that is why Arabs, Turks, Egyptians, though they are all Moslems, yet they all have their own characteristics. But this does not prevent them from coming together on the general principles of Islam. . . .

At the time when Islam was spreading, the Turks were residing in Transoxania. Then they came in different groups to Moslem soil. They became Moslems, and established states that filled the world.

The Turks are a nation that likes independence, freedom, and sovereignty. Yet they never interfere with the doctrines and conceptions of others, or the freedom of others. At the same time they meant no one to interfere with their conceptions. They are not fanatics. Their hearts are full of courage, faith, and obedience. Kind deeds, honesty, and justice are their inborn qualities. A Turk is patient, devoted, and energetic. And as Islam required these qualities, Turks became Moslems and have adapted themselves to Islam more than any other nation.

Differences between the Moslem sects are deplored, and the writer goes on to say:

In such cases the best and most useful method is to separate religious and worldly affairs. To separate national affairs from religious affairs and to avoid having misunderstandings will be the duties of the nations.

The principles of religion: Morality, Faith, Worship, should be fixed. And so all the difficulties of different schools [sects]

should be removed. . . . Once Shah Ismail, in order to succeed
in his political intrigues, accepted a school and caused enmity
and wars between Shiis and Sunnis. In all these fightings of
different schools there are political intrigues and opinions. As
all these schools are bound up with Islam, so Islam appeared in
different forms in different places. In spite of these troubles,
the fundamental principles of Islam have remained the same
in every Moslem country. This shows the soundness and the
truthfulness of these principles. It is for this reason that Islam
has spread in different countries.[18]

In another passage the same author brings out other
strong points of Islam and complains against misconceptions
of its true meaning.

In Islam there is no priesthood. Moslems are all equal in the
sight of their religion. One does not have precedence over another. One cannot say to the other, "I can give you a place in
heaven." One cannot say to the other, "I am nearer to God
than you are."
The Great Koran says: "The person who is nearest to God is
the person who is kind and virtuous." In the sight of God one
person cannot have a better place than another. A person can
obtain a place near God by being virtuous.
Let us purge Islam of these vain and false ideas, and let us
guide the persons who have misunderstood the religion of Islam.
In Islam there are no false ideas at all. Islam is the highest
and most perfect religion. It is misunderstanding Islam to think
that it is composed of *namaz* and fasting. *Namaz* and fasting
are merely signs. Islam stands for a good character and a high
morality.
Worship must be the result of the love of God and humility
of heart. Then the delight of being a Moslem is enjoyed. In the
Great Koran it is said that being a Moslem is not to worship
God by facing the East or the West. It is doing kind deeds to
everyone, being faithful to one's undertakings, facing the hard-
ships of life with determination; for these are verses in the
Koran. Islam is a narrow path, but it is high. Islam should be
understood in this way. If we meditate, we shall find out that

---

[18] These selections are from Yusuf Ziya, *op. cit.*, pp. 28 ff.

Islam is the most progressive and most perfect religion, and urges humanity always toward reform.[19]

One further statement in regard to the meaning of Islam today in Turkey may be quoted from the same book:

Islam means to show submission, but not in the sense of hurting one's self-respect.

Islam means to forgive, but not so as to make itself an instrument of evil.

Islam means to be kind, but not in the form of forgetting one's rights and overstepping one's authority.

Islam combines in itself morality, faith, and worship. So it has a wider meaning than the word faith, alone. And that is why our religion is called the religion of Islam and the belief of Moslems.[20]

Moslem theology, like theology all over the world, is undergoing in Turkey a period of great stress. Belief in God is still insisted on by the writers under consideration, and one finds the familiar emphasis on the value of God's unity. But there is a new tendency to warn against the evil effects of resignation and fatalism and to stress rather the obligations of a true believer to be moral, hard-working, and patriotic. The following passages reveal something of the trend of thought.

Yusuf Ziya devotes his third chapter to "The Principles of Faith" (*Imanin Esaslari*):

The principles of Faith are to believe in God and his Prophet, and in the future life. We believe in God as follows: God exists; he is one; he is the Lord of all the universe, and is omnipotent. Allah has no partner and has nothing in his image. He has no beginning or end, and is free from all needs. He existed before time and space existed. He is the creator of the universe and its order, and gave life to living things, and gave senses, comprehension, and will to human beings.

Allah has created us in the highest form, and granted us a

[19] *Ibid.*, pp. 20 ff.
[20] *Ibid.*, pp. 11 f.

great many gifts, and helped us without limit. For this reason Moslems love God and fear him. The love of God is the beginning of all worship.

The man who has love of God in his heart will also be a man of good morals and kind to everybody. Those who fear God will never trespass on the rights of others, will keep themselves from sin, and never live dishonestly and apart from justice.

This is the way which leads humanity to perfectibility. To believe in the unity of God is an important principle of Islam, and it differentiates Islam from other religions. Jews believe that every country and each nation has its own God. Christians believe that God has a son and say God is one, but composed of three. But Islam has raised itself above these conceptions and has reached the principle of unity.

That is why a person who has attained Islam and raised himself to the degree of believing in this unity can never become a Christian or a Jew. And that is why missionaries who have been working for years could not convert a Moslem who believed in the unity of Allah. Though they were able to deceive a few persons who did not know Islam, yet Moslems, without having missionaries, have spread their religion through all the world. The reason for this is that Islam is a more practical religion, and it is based on the unity of Allah.[21]

A somewhat more novel note is struck by Professor Abdulbaki in his religious lessons for children in primary schools.

We must not pray to God on account of our being afraid of God or desiring to serve some self-interest; we must pray to him because we love him. He has brought us into the world; he has given us many good things. He leads us always toward the good, toward righteousness through our hearts and minds. Is it at all possible that such a great God would not be loved? If only we think of the good which is rendered to us by our government, our fatherland, our nation, the love of our father and mother, we understand his greatness. The greatest worship of God is to love him, to be a good man, to serve our government, our fatherland, our nation, and afterwards, all mankind.[22]

[21] *Ibid.*, pp. 13 ff.
[22] *Religious Lessons for the Children of the Republic* (Bible House trans.), I, 21.

An interesting chapter in the volume for fourth-grade children conveys Professor Abdulbaki's interpretation of the proper way to put trust in God:

Our grandfathers and grandmothers say often, "We must trust God." I wonder what this means. Is it not to rely on God and keep one's heart whole?

Now I will explain thoroughly to you what this means in the Moslem religion. Trust is: to think carefully, to consult wise saints, and to prepare, one by one, whatever might be necessary for a piece of work when we begin it; after these things, to have faith that our work surely will turn out well and that in the end good will come from it. This is to keep our hearts whole.

For instance, we are going to take a trip on a boat. In the first place in order not to give our money to foreigners, we look for a Turkish boat. We make sure that the boat we want to take is strong and durable. We buy things which will be necessary on the way. We notice whether the barometer indicates "good weather" or not. This done, we buy our tickets, settle ourselves in the cabin, believe that we shall surely reach our destination in safety, fortify our hearts, and fear not.

For instance, we want to get a good mark in our lesson. We work hard; we ask our teacher about the things we do not know. We study and discuss with each other; after this we do not succumb to vain thoughts such as, "I wonder whether I will be able to get a perfect mark." We trust and believe that we may get a good mark.

On the contrary, it is not true, but foolishness, to take an unseaworthy boat in stormy weather to sail out to rough seas, or to want a perfect mark without working for it, and instead of being careful and industrious say, "I trust in God, no danger will come to me." In the religion of Islam there is no such thing. What the mind does not accept, the Moslem religion also never accepts. You know, we have a proverb: "Fasten the camel to a strong post and then trust." This is a word both of our forefathers and our Prophet.

One day a foolish man came to our Prophet and leaving his camel untied, entered, stayed a while, talked, and afterwards went outside "to find winds blowing in the place where his camel had been before." Returning to the Prophet, he told him what had happened. The Prophet said, "To what did you fasten the camel?" The poor man answered: "I trusted in God." The Prophet replied, "You should have tied the camel and then trusted." . . .[23]

In the books for children little stress is laid on other-worldly matters, the greatest emphasis being placed on those phases of Islamic faith which make for betterment in this life. In the sermons for the older citizens, however, the familiar terms are used, but in such a fashion as to give them a value for modern times. The following selection from a sermon by Ali Vahit—called "For Whom Is Heaven?"—provides an admirable illustration:

These [joys of heaven] are the rewards for good deeds and honesty in the world. A person who while in the world believed in God and his Prophet and did not follow any other way but that which his religion showed him, and the person who has not cast his hand over the lives and properties of others and who has not cast his eye on any one unchastely and who has trodden down his bad ambitions by thinking of his God, has gotten rid of his bad desires [sic].

One day when he is called for military service and has fulfilled his duty without thinking of his children and property left behind, and has not turned his head away from danger and sacrificed his life willingly—will these persons be left without any reward? No! God has created these heavens and gifts for such persons.[24]

In the midst of the confusion which has attended Turkey's resentful abandonment of many of Islam's unworthy features, one finds a tendency to cling fast to the Koran, whose truths are regarded as eternal. Conservatism and features incompatible with progress are blamed on later misconceptions and misinterpretations which have incrusted a really vital truth with a host of petrified anachronisms. Ali Vahit speaks his mind strongly on the subject in one of his sermons:

[23] *Religious Lessons for the Children of the Republic* (Bible House trans.), II, 13 f.

[24] *Turkish Sermons* (2d ser.), pp. 340 f.

Let us come to the revolt against the Koran. The revolt against the Koran is due to not understanding it, failure to learn it from a competent authority; and this is a great lack, because it is the Koran which creates faith in the heart, refreshes it, and keeps it free from doubts and different storms. It is the word of God which removes vices, immorality, and rusted sins from the heart of man. It is a treasure in which we could find remedies for all spiritual diseases. But we must know which remedy is for which disease. . . . It is a great revolt against the Koran to commit wrong things in the name of Islam, because by so doing we do not carry out its orders. The person who carries out wrong orders does not get any benefits, and creates enemies against the Koran. He gives a chance to others to say that those who carry out the principles of the Koran become lazy and backward. That is why it is necessary to understand the Koran thoroughly and study it from a competent authority. A man sees a *hodja* with a white turban on his head and thinks he is a competent person, and he wishes him to teach the command of God, and the man teaches him something as the command of God. He may either explain it in a wrong way or give him an answer which may not be the right answer to his question. He may be misled. A half-trained doctor causes death, and a half-trained *hodja* causes atheism. For our health we seek a competent doctor; so for our religion we should look for a competent guide. It is not wise to learn everything from persons whom one meets along the way.

Is it right for a person who has a toothache to go to a pharmacy and swallow anything he finds there? It is the same with religion; a man may have a good will, but he may get wrong information. The wrong information is like wrong medicine. You may have faith and confidence in God, but this doesn't help to cure your disease, though the confidence and faith may be practised in some other way.[25]

Delivering a tirade against those who have forgotten the true meaning of the Koran in employing it for hidden and magical purposes, Ali Vahit says:

---

[25] *First Sermon—from the Pulpit of Hadji Bairam Mosque,* pp. 66 ff.

O you foolish persons, did God send us the Koran that it should be kissed and kept in bookshelves? Did he send it to be read for the salvation of the souls of the deceased? No! It is not for the dead. It did not come that it should be kissed and praised and used as a fetish. It is the remedy for persons who fight and struggle every day against the thousands of troubles of the world. It nourishes souls, it gives a joy to hearts, and points out the right way.[26]

With regard to specific duties and practices of Islam one finds little said in the schoolbooks for primary children. Routine or mechanical features are little spoken of. In the writings for older people, however, the duties of prayer, fasting, pilgrimage, etc., are described, but so interpreted as to minimize their mechanical features and to stress their value for the attainment of richer living and better citizenship in the nation. Yusuf Ziya devotes a number of pages to the presentation and discussion of the various grades of performances regarded as meritorious or discreditable, and presents a table indicating the times for prayer and the number of repetitions which are obligatory, strongly urged, and creditable. He also lists the seven requisites which must be fulfilled before the act of worship (*namaz*) can be performed. But in his remarks commenting on these things he reveals the extent to which rigid prescriptions may be modified by exigencies of the times. He points out:

Some of the scholars have admitted that one may combine the evening prayer with that of *yatsi* [two hours after sunset]. Because there is nothing burdensome in Islam. Those who work in factories or some other important business may perform all *farz* [obligatory acts of worship] at one time, and God doubtless will accept their prayers.[27]

[26] *Ibid.*, pp. 61 f.
[27] *Op. cit.*, p. 85.

As for the *ezan* (call to prayer), he says: "It is permissible that *ezan* be performed in any other language than Arabic, provided that it be understood as being the *ezan*." [28] This is in line with the Turkish tendency to carry on as much of the Islamic ceremonial in Turkish as is possible, in preference to the traditionally sacred Arabic, which is not popularly understood. *Namaz* (performance of the act of worship) is valuable not so much as a perfunctory fulfilment of a command, but rather, according to Yusuf Ziya, it "keeps one from remaining altogether in the world of material things; it gives a spiritual joy and pleasure." [29] One of the seven requisites for performance of *namaz* is to turn in the direction of the *Kaaba* at Mecca. But, says the writer, "When it becomes impossible for one to point out the direction of the *Kaaba* from the position of the mountains, rivers, and sun, then one may turn to the direction which he thinks to be the direction of *Kaaba*. This," Yusuf Ziya explains, "shows the importance of the decision of conscience and freedom of opinion in Islam." [30]

Under the Republic one finds a new importance attaching to the prayer on Friday.[30a] Turkey has adopted Friday as a day of rest comparable to the Christian Sunday, and the tendency among some seems to be to consider it as a day of special sanctity, a new feature for Islam. Special sermons on patriotic and educational topics have been prepared in the Turkish vernacular by the Diyanet Ichleri (Presidency of Religious Affairs) for delivery to congregations on Fridays or special Bairam days by the *khatibs* (preachers) of the mosques. Yusuf Ziya and Ali Vahit have a good deal to say concerning the new importance of collective worship on these days.

[28] *Ibid.*, p. 105.
[29] *Ibid.*, p. 60.
[30] *Ibid.*, p. 88.
[30a] On Sunday as day of rest see page 141.

Yusuf Ziya in good Moslem fashion goes back to the precedent of the Prophet's practice to justify his position:

> Our Prophet used to preach in all his *khutbes* [sermons] about topics of the day and summarize the events of the week and inform his hearers about their religious obligations. During the times of war he used to speak about *jihad* [holy war]; during the time of famine he spoke about thrift; and in times of disturbances he spoke about tranquillity. As after the death of our Prophet the number of Moslem countries was increased, so this duty was performed by deputies and preachers. At that time preachers were chosen among the enlightened and scholarly men. These preachers inspired the people with their literary lectures and bound people more sincerely to their government and nation. Later on, as a result of the preachers' ignorance and lack of knowledge, the sermons became mere routine or were given in a language which the people could not understand.
>
> Now think of the situation that we are in. We are in the hands of ignorant *imams* who cannot prepare speeches by themselves. We must thank God that we have not been ruined and swept from the world with our present condition. Most principles of Islam have been changed by ignorance. See the reason for the Friday prayer and study its present situation. The purpose of the Friday ceremonies and sermons is to enlighten people and strengthen their faith and increase their national and religious emotions. Those who could not perform these obligations of course found a shelter in Arabic, and insisted on giving lectures in Arabic. The *khutbe* [sermon] is a lecture. If it is not understood by the people, it loses its significance. As our nation has been awakened, it realizes these truths.[31]

Friday prayers, Yusuf Ziya points out further, "are performed in the cities and not in the villages. The reason for this is to collect the peasants of different villages in a city and to enlighten them under the leadership of a well-known person and to give them a chance to know each other and to love each other." [32] The gatherings are good to develop

[31] *Ibid.*, pp. 111 ff.
[32] *Ibid.*, p. 113.

such qualities, he maintains, as collectivity, democracy, obedience to a leader, exactness, and friendship. There is no obligation, however, to worship collectively in times of bad weather or terror. "Islam," he reminds, "does not impose difficult performances. Persons who look after sick people and persons who are engaged in reading sciences are excused from collective worship." [33]

Ali Vahit gives rather explicit instructions for Friday observance which in places are distinctly reminiscent of Sabbath observances in the Jewish and Christian religions:

You Moslems should consider Thursday as an eve of preparation. You should prepare yourselves for Friday on Thursday, and you should give instructions to the members of your family that they should prepare themselves for Friday on Thursday. In order to find ample time for your prayer on Friday and perform it with ease, you should complete your work on Thursday and get ready for Friday. Friday is a day of *Bairam*, and it is a holiday of Believers.

That is why one should finish his work on Thursday, and after having performed his afternoon prayer, he should read the Koran to enlighten his own soul and to give solace to the souls of the dead.

On that day members of the family should be fed and clad properly, and the orphans and poor people should not be forgotten. They should also be helped, at least they should be encouraged with sweet words. It should never be forgotten that a good deed done on Friday is twice blest. It is not the same as ordinary days. When Friday comes, you should express your thanks and be joyful just because you have lived another week, and you should get ready for prayer. You should cut the nails of your fingers and toes and clean your body and use the *misvak* [a toothbrush made from a dried root, thereby avoiding the abomination of hog bristles]. To have a bath on Friday is *mustehap* [i.e., optional, but creditable].[34] Some say it is *vajib*,

[33] *Ibid.*, p. 108.

[34] The eight gradations of credit or discredit in the Moslem's religious performances are as follows: (1) *farz*, something obligatory; (2) *vajib*, something strongly hinted to be obligatory; (3) *sunnet*, something ad-

and so you should do your best to have a bath on Friday. You should put on your best clothes and use nice perfumes, and you should go to the mosque early. If you find a place to put your shoes outside, leave them there, otherwise clean them, take them in your left hand, go in without stepping on any one and without passing in front of any one who is praying, and when you find a place empty, then perform two *rekat* for the will of God. If it is the time of *zeval* [i.e., exact noon—the time of Christian prayer], then do not perform your prayers, just sit down. If the Koran is read at that time, listen to it carefully and respect the Word of God and do nothing else. Do not even read the Koran by yourself. Do not use your beads. Do nothing but listen to the Word of God. If the Koran is not read, do not turn your face from the *kibleh* and use your beads, mentioning the names of God. Then listen to the sermon carefully and without speaking. You should not only keep silence, but not even read the Koran to yourself. And do not ask any one to keep quiet. If it becomes necessary, then you can make the sign of silence by putting your finger over your lips. If you open your mouth and say something, the virtue of Friday is spoiled. While the sermon is going on, you should listen to it carefully and keep your tongue close to your palate.[35]

Fasting (*oruj*) is another Islamic practice which finds approbation from these religious writers, though it is not stressed in the book for primary-school children. The traditional custom is to take no food between dawn and sunset during the sacred month of Ramazan. The commencement of Ramazan was formerly determined by the sighting of the new moon at Bursa (Brusa), whence word was sent throughout Turkey. Now, as with all official matters of reckoning

---

vised or performed by the Prophet, and very creditable; (4) *mustehap*, something not urged, but creditable if done; (5) *mubah*, neutral acts, bringing neither credit nor penalty; (6) *haram*, the opposite of *farz*—absolutely forbidden; (7) *mekruh*, something discreditable—of two degrees: (*a*) *kerabati tahrimiye*, the opposite of *vajib*, and (*b*) *kerabati tenzihiye*, opposite of *sunnet* and *mustehap*; (8) *mufsit*, something which destroys the efficacy of worship (Yusuf Ziya, *op. cit.*, pp. 66 ff.)

[35] *Turkish Sermons* (2d ser.), pp. 108 ff.

time, the beginning is determined by the scientific observatory located at Kandili on the Bosphorus. Although fasting is at present irregular, particularly in the cities, various observers have told me that in 1930 the number of Turks observed to be keeping the fast was considerably more than in the years immediately preceding. Yusuf Ziya declares that *oruj* (fasting) "leads one to obedience, patience, and endurance. Out of devotion to God one avoids eating, strengthens the character, and increases the will power. It also helps one to understand the condition of the poor and hungry." [36]

Zekat, or the giving of one-fortieth of one's property, is another disciplinary practice of Islam which is considered as important, for it stimulates one's sense of generosity. Yusuf Ziya points out, however, that people are not required to give *zekat* on property which is taxed. Indeed, "to pay a tax to the government is *farz.*" [37] *Zekat* is to be given on property which is not seen—for example, cash in the safe. Professor Abdulbaki in the lessons for primary grades praises almsgiving, but he advises the children instead of giving their small donations to individual poor people to give to the public charitable societies like the Red Crescent, the Children's Protective Society, and the Aviation Society, "which buys the aeroplanes that protect our country from enemies, this being the most useful society." [38] In this same connection I am told that special notices were posted by government authority at the time of the *Kurban Bairam* of 1929 urging Turks to give their slain lambs or the equivalent amount of money to the Aviation Society rather than waste the lambs in a short orgy of feasting.

There is finally the duty of making the pilgrimage to Mecca (the *haj*), which one might expect to be soft-pedaled by a

[36] *Op. cit.,* pp. 60 f.
[37] *Ibid.,* p. 139.
[38] *Op. cit.,* I, 6.

Turkey which is bitter toward things Arabic. This is to a certain extent true, and the number of Turks making the pilgrimage since the advent of the Ankara government is small indeed. Ali Vahit, however, in his sermons, describes the joys and benefits which come to the believer who visits the holy places, provided that he has fulfilled his obligations at home. Yusuf Ziya is less enthusiastic:

The *haj* is *farz* for those who can afford it once in their lives. For this it is necessary to have security on the way, to have sufficient means to sustain one's family, and sufficient money to cover one's expenses on the way. But to waste one's wealth and to spend the money of his country in those places may be harmful from the point of view of his family situation and the economic conditions of his country. So one has to be careful about it.[39]

Paul Gentizon has quoted the statement of a prominent Turkish journalist, Agaoglu Ahmed Bey, on the subject which is worth including here as representing the lay viewpoint of a modern Turk:

The Turk will continue to go to Mecca, but he does not wish to return from there more fanatical, more ignorant, and with his brain more filled with superstitions. He wishes to come back with his soul elevated, his heart purified, as a man who has known the world and whose experience has been formed by his intercourse with all humanity. In kissing the Black Stone he will experience the sensation not of kissing a piece of stone come from the sky but an emblem sacred for all the traditions of the entire history of his religion. In imbibing the water from the well of *Zemzem,* he will consider it not as a remedy for all his ills, but as representing a communion with all that is signified by the religion he venerates and with the sacred personalities who established it. In running between the mountains *Merwa* and *Safa* he will not yield to the superstition of pursuing the demon and absolving his sins; but he will be moved by the remembrance of all that was suffered between those two mountains by the

[39] *Op. cit.,* p. 136.

Prophet and the saints for a faith, a conviction, a law. Finally, in walking seven times round the *Kaaba* he will not do it with the superstition of going round an edifice inhabited by God, but he will recall that it was in this very monument that the divine unity replaced polytheism. That is what the Turk will teach to the Moslem nations and the true divine worship which he will cause to live again.[40]

From the foregoing statements it is apparent that the practices often known as the "Pillars of Islam" are not regarded as utterly incompatible with the requirements of a modern nation. Through scission of inharmonious features and re-interpretation of certain essentials, Moslems have found that their religion need not be discarded because its efficacy and vitality have been impaired by ignorance and reaction in the past. Needless to say, the ethical notions of the religion have also been given a thorough scrutiny, and the tempering fire of progressive patriotism has given the whole such a burning test that only the strong and creditable features have survived, while there has been both a loss of antiquated ideas and an addition of new ones required in the present day and age. In the following pages it will be our task to notice what are the retained and added features in the ethical teachings of Islam in Turkey. If a comparison is made with the objectives of primary education listed in an earlier chapter, the same points will in general be seen to be emphasized.[41] The religious writers, however, touch upon them in a manner slightly different, thereby requiring a somewhat different classification. Of the original Islamic ideals there seem to be five—or four and one more which may include the other four; these are: (1) good character or morality, under which the other four may be grouped; (2) honesty; (3) justice;

[40] *Mustapha Kemal,* pp. 275 f.
[41] Those four objectives were: (1) inculcation of practical knowledge, (2) development of a spirit of social co-operation, (3) foundation of health habits, and (4) development of patriotic loyalty.

(4) generous helpfulness; and (5) sobriety. Besides these five one might list eight others which are sometimes claimed to be inherent in Islam, but which have of late been honored more in the breach than in the observance and which appear as novel emphases in the light of Islam's recent history. These are: (6) self-reliance and hard work; (7) thrift in time and money (these seven points would harmonize with the second educational objective: the development of co-operative and useful members of society); (8) progressive adaptation to new conditions; (9) encouragement of intelligence and science; (10) stress on the practical as opposed to the theoretical (these three points are related to the first educational objective: the inculcation of practical knowledge); (11) tolerance; (12) good health; (13) patriotism.

The first ideal which we have mentioned is *good character* or *morality* in general. Although this ideal naturally includes the next four if not all the other ideals, it is sometimes regarded as a separate and special desideratum in the writings under consideration. In the book of sermons issued by the Presidency of Religious Affairs (Diyanet Ichleri) for use in the mosques in 1927, the seventh sermon deals with good character:

Do you know what good character is? Not to have an eye on others' property, life, and honor, not to be jealous, to keep oneself away from pride, to show humility, not to be cruel-hearted, to keep away from wrath and anger, not to lie, not to cheat, to hate rebellion and disobedience, to show kindness to God's creatures, etc. . . .

It is by having good character that a man feels comfortable in the world.[42] Through having good character a great many

42 In the attempt which is made to get away from supernatural and other-worldly sanctions for good behavior and character, there is a frequent substitution of the somewhat sordid sanction of self-gratification. Obedience and gratitude to God are sometimes guardedly employed as reasons for good conduct, while devotion to the best interests of the national society is the strongest sanction with an altruistic tinge.

enemies have become friends and prevented a great many disasters. . . . No one loves the man who has a bad character. No one pities him in his time of greatest need. A person who has good character is useful for himself and all humanity. Everybody loves the person who has a smiling face and a true heart and a sweet word. His request and application are never refused. Good character is not bought and sold. It does not do any harm, but on the contrary does thousands of good things.[43]

Yusuf Ziya writes that "the philosophy and aim of the Prophet's mission were the quest for morality."[44] A little later he makes a declaration which hits at a much-criticized weakness of Islam: a tendency to substitute pious phrases for pious acts. He says:

We have learned that the most important and the highest principle of the religion of Islam is good character, and we have read the requirements for good character in the verses from the Koran and the Sayings of the Prophet [Hadith]. But to read and to understand them are not enough. The most important thing is to apply them. Because to have a kind heart and to know what is good, are different from practising deeds of kindness. To do a good deed is better than to wish it.[45]

Honesty and straightforwardness, second among the virtues as we have listed them, are stressed in Turkey's Islam as in most religious systems. The official sermons of 1927 include the following admonition:

In order to succeed in this struggle, it is necessary to be honest and true. One should not cheat the other; one should behave honestly and not stain his honor and credit for the sake of passing interests.[46]

Yusuf Ziya takes occasion to criticize hypocrisy and dissimulation:

[43] *Turkish Sermons in the Age of the Republic,* pp. 16 f.
[44] *Op. cit.,* p. 40.
[45] *Ibid.,* p. 45.
[46] *Turkish Sermons in the Age of the Republic,* No. 8, p. 19.

Dissimulation is religious counterfeiting. If a man, in order to show himself good and kind, speaks of kind deeds and of religion and worships falsely, then he is a hypocrite. In the Great Koran dissimulation is described as one of the worst habits. "Pity those who are not cordial and faithful in their prayer, and those who are hypocrites." Persons whose hearts and actions are not in agreement hurt themselves and become hypocrites. Hypocrisy in the Great Koran is rebuked severely. To be two-faced, to cause trouble between two persons, to lie, to be slanderous, to twist the truth, are very bad habits.[47]

Justice, the third virtue listed, is praised and given practical applications in the tenth sermon of those issued by the government in 1927:

O Moslems, justice, which God commands and the Prophet praises, is necessary for all of us. The Prophet in his Hadith says . . . you are all shepherds and responsible for what you have under your care. That is, everybody in his house, institution, shop, or factory is a ruler who has a responsibility for treating the persons around him well. Therefore justice, which is the base and foundation of governing, becomes also the base and foundation of the home, institution, and factory, which are kinds of states. In these places, justice is necessary to obtain stability and discipline. Those who do not deal justly in their homes and do not treat their servants justly, spoil the happiness and discipline of their homes. It is the same with persons who own factories and institutions. If they do not treat the persons who work for them with justice, then they cannot keep order and do harm to themselves. Because justice is a reward for a good deed, and it is also a punishment for those who deserve it. Some small mistakes may be excused, and this excuse may sometimes be a part of justice. That is why God has commanded us to be just and forgiving. . . . O Moslems, act justly though it may be against your own interests. Do not trespass on the rights of others. Treat every one equitably. Do not show favoritism to any one. You may show mercy by forgiving the wrongs which are done to you, but you have no right to forgive the wrongs done to others.[48]

[47] *Op. cit.,* pp. 51 f.
[48] *Op. cit.,* pp. 23 f.

The writers under consideration speak highly of *loving and generous helpfulness*. It is not advocated, however, to the complete forgetting of self nor to a point where it might cause great inconvenience. The following passages will indicate the importance given to helpfulness. According to Professor Abdulbaki:

> Moslems always do good and derive pleasure from it. A man who is of service to no one is not a real Moslem. We must do good first to our family, to our nation, to our fatherland, and later to all mankind.[49]

Yusuf Ziya quotes liberally from the words of the Prophet and adds admonishments of his own on the subject of helpfulness:

> If one wishes to test his acts, then he must remember the three teachings of the Prophet: "Wish to others all that you wish for yourself." Do not do to others things which you do not wish to be done to yourself. Our Prophet says, "The beauty of one's belief in Islam is revealed by not committing acts which are useless." Also: "The best of people are those who are useful to others."
>
> It is seen that to be a good and useful person and to wish good to others are the commands of Islam. There is no limit to being good and useful. To be good to one's mother and father, brothers, friends, neighbors, country, and nation come one after the other. Islam requires every one to be good and kind to the extent of his ability. . . .
>
> To help one another, to hold the hands of the poor, to help those who are in need, to be kind toward children, to respect our elders, to take care of orphans—these are all required by good character and are the teachings of Islam. These commands show us the importance of helping those who are crippled in the world. Under the influence of these teachings, some good persons have established the Red Crescent, the Dar-ul-Ajesi [Home for the Poor], and the Himayei Etfal [Children's Protective Society], and we are obliged to help them by our religion.[50]

[49] *Op. cit.*, II, 7.
[50] *Op. cit.*, pp. 46 f.

According to Ali Vahit:

It is easy to repay a good deed with a good deed. But the main bravery is to return a good deed for a bad deed. If this cannot be done for everybody, it should be done for one's mother and father. Their nonsense must be borne. You should try to please them because it is the command of God. We have no other way to act than to try to please them.[51]

Strong drink has always been particularly prohibited by the teachings of Islam, and at the present time when Western vices are sweeping into Turkey along with the better things, one finds a special concern on the part of the religious leaders to emphasize *sobriety* and to carry on the war against liquor. When I talked with the members of the Diyanet Ichleri (Presidency of Religious Affairs) at Ankara in 1929, the subject of conversation very shortly after it became known that I was an American turned to the subject of prohibition in America. These venerable Moslems, who expressed great admiration for American efficiency,[52] felt that if America's battle against alcohol could be won, the world would soon follow its lead and Mohammed's precept would receive universal recognition. A passage from one of Ali Vahit's sermons expresses the feeling of the Islamic leaders toward liquor:

O Moslem community, it must be known to you that one of our great troubles which cook and fry us is the matter of drinking. We have suffered a great deal from wars and epidemic diseases, but we have suffered from drink a great deal more than from any other cause. A war is like a gale. It comes to an end, though it may last a long time. An epidemic disease is like a flood. It will recede and go away, though it may be very severe. But drinking is not so. If it comes once and seizes its

[51] *First Sermon—from the Pulpit of Hadji Bairam Mosque*, p. 55.

[52] One of the members, Ali Vahit, whose sermons have been frequently quoted, had commenced the study of English, declaring his belief that Turkey has more to learn now from America than from Arabia. Though well along in years, he cited the injunction of Mohammed that learning never stops from the cradle to the grave.

victim, it never leaves him again. . . . Now our religion became a remedy for this disease over thirteen hundred years ago and spared humanity from this trouble. In Islam a drop of strong drink is *haram* [absolutely forbidden]. There is nothing else than Islam which attacks drunkenness so severely. Other nations have gradually started to realize the bad effects of drinking. Now they try to save themselves from this trouble.[53]

One of the dangers to which Moslems have been most subject as a result of their belief in the omnipotence of Allah is a tendency to resign themselves lazily to fate. This fatalistic reliance on *kismet* is considered by many Turks to have undermined the Turkish character quite seriously, and consequently great emphasis is laid by those who are leading the way in promoting new religious ideals on the importance of self-reliance and hard work. The praises of the virtue of industry are sung in one of the Diyanet Ichleri's sermons:

God in His Koran says man will get nothing but the fruits of his work, and he acknowledges that we will get nothing in this world or the next if we do not work. If we think a little, we will see that the greatest miseries, needs and troubles are the results of laziness. Those who do not work and waste their time lazily obtain nothing in this world or the next. Let us take ourselves as an example. If we had not wasted our time as we did, we should have become the richest and most progressive nation of the world. God has created our country as one of the richest places of the world. He gave us mind and wisdom and power more than any other nation. If we had worked, then we would have benefited from the treasures of our country and we should not have any misery.

O Moslems, let us come to our senses, and obeying the commands of God, let us start to work. . . . O you creatures of God, I advise you to keep away from laziness and obey the commands of God and his Prophet to obtain happiness in this world and the next.[54]

---

[53] *Turkish Sermons,* pp. 170 ff.
[54] *Op. cit.,* No. 4, pp. 10 f.

Ali Vahit's remarks and exhortations on the subject are also important:

O Moslem community, let it be known to you that one of the things we misunderstand is Fate. That is the place where the feet of many persons slip. There is many a person who leaves work unfinished, saying that it is *kader* or *kismet,* and becomes lazy. He does not work and struggle, and he goes on saying that whatever is *kader* or *kismet,* that will happen. Some deny fate altogether. One may refuse to do a work thinking that something may go wrong. He becomes a coward. He passes his whole life in suspicion, and leaves the world without having been useful for any purpose.

We want to find the mean between these two extremes. We shall use our minds and judgment in the work we are going to do, and we shall not tie ourselves to Fate. We shall do whatever we can and then trust in God.

If we don't act as I have said, and if we don't keep our accounts properly, then God may ask us, "O my creatures, I have left these things in your hands, and I gave you mind and wisdom and sent you a Prophet and a Book. You were free. No one hindered you. Why did you not use your mind?" What would our reply be? We cannot save ourselves by saying, "O God, you knew everything." It is not necessary that our hands and arms be tied up because God knows what we are going to do. And our excuses do not hold good. Because when we want to do a good turn, we can do it with our own will. No one will tie our hands. And when we want to do a bad turn, we again do it with our own will. No one forces us to do so. We can rule our hand and foot. So "whoever saves his ship is the captain." If you wish, you can do a good deed and go to heaven, or you may do a bad deed and deserve hell.

So never misunderstand the teaching that whatever happens, good or bad, is the will of God. It must be known to you that though a good and a bad deed are created by God, yet it is we who do them. God creates a good deed in the hands of persons who want to do good deeds. And again God creates a bad deed in the hands of those persons who want to do a bad deed. One deserves heaven, and the other, hell. . . .

There would not be a single free man in the world if man could not behave as he wished. Then what would be the value of

hard work and struggling? Would there be any meaning to a
good or bad deed? What would be the use of the religion and
the Prophet? What would heaven, hell, and book mean? God
wished that man on earth should be free. He wished that man
should be the master of himself and use his mind. Each would
get the things which he deserved. He wished that a good deed
should be rewarded and a bad deed punished. So God created
man in accordance with his desires. He created man in such a
way as to be able to do good deeds and bad. And this is
Fate. . . .

The proper thing is to tackle the work whether easy or difficult, and our behavior should be mastered by our thoughts. If
anything happens that is beyond our power, then we may say it is
our Fate. But it is not right to depend on Fate and do nothing.[55]

Many observers who have traveled through Turkey and
seen the cafés filled with indolent individuals who seem to
have an unlimited amount of time to spend in idleness have
expressed the opinion that absence of ambition, wastefulness
of time, and inability to be thrifty are inbred characteristics
in the Turk which will prevent the strong development of
national character. Leading Turks are themselves aware of
this handicap; so along with the plea to work hard which
we have just read there comes a stirring call to awaken the
seventh virtue in our list: that of *thrift in time and money.*
Two striking passages from Ali Vahit's sermons will indicate
the depth of Turkey's feeling on this matter. In the first
passage to be quoted he strikes at the ideal of poverty so
frequently praised by Moslems:

One of the greatest gifts for those who appreciate it is wealth.
It is a great thing to live with open hands and not to bow
to any one. It is a great gift for a man to make his children
independent of others. . . .

Though the case is as I have explained, yet there are some
persons who dislike wealth. They put aside such a gift of God,
and wish poverty. I do not know what poverty has to be

[55] *Turkish Sermons,* pp. 294 ff.

admired, and I do not know why they become enemies of wealth. As if poverty and dependence were good things! They never think that poverty is a shirt of flame. It has no features to be liked. There are times of poverty which compel a person to commit all sorts of sins. That is why our Prophet used to pray, "O Lord, I need thy protection from poverty." If poverty was a good thing, do you think our Prophet would have prayed that way?

How can poverty be better than wealth? A poor man cannot become a *hadji* [one who has made the pilgrimage]. He cannot give *zekat*. He cannot fulfill two great obligations of Islam. He cannot sacrifice lamb, and he cannot do charitable works. He cannot help poor people. Are wealthy people the same? They make the pilgrimage; they give *zekat;* they build mosques and fountains; they educate orphans and arrange for the marriage of poor girls and do many other charitable things. Poor people can do none of these things, for all of these things depend on wealth.

So wealth should not be cast aside. Wealthy people should not be disliked. Our religion does not teach us that we should not become wealthy. It teaches us to be wealthy, but commands us not to worship wealth. It criticizes those who forget God as their wealth increases. There are no words against wealthy people who appreciate their gift. They are the cream of the country. They are necessary for the world. . . .[56]

In a colorful passage from the same sermon, Ali Vahit berates those who waste their time and money:

We spend like those who have inherited wealth, and we never keep a record of what we spend. We fail to realize the values not only of our leisure, but of all our time. We destroy our world and the world to come by wasting our lives and these long years. On the other hand, Europeans and Americans, whom we don't admire, find the teachings of our Prophet by using their heads. They do many things that Moslems are required to do. One is perplexed to see how they whom we call *ghiaours* utilize their leisure. Leaving aside the weeks and days and hours, they even calculate the value of minutes, and these minutes have a great importance for them. . . .

Here is the secret of the progress of other nations. They do

[56] *First Sermon,* pp. 111 ff.

their work exactly on time. They know the value of their lives and pay great attention to the minutes. The cause of our backwardness is in not realizing the value of our lives. If we had known the values of our health and our life as our Prophet teaches in his sayings [Hadith], we would not be behind the others. We would not be lacking knowledge and arts as we are now. But we did not appreciate these gifts. Not only hours and minutes have passed, but during the years and centuries we have slept and hibernated. We played the truant and became ignorant. We forgot the things we knew. We lost what we had in our hands, but then we were punished for all these things, and we suffered and are still suffering. . . .

We have a very queer habit. If we lose anything out of our pockets by chance, we search our pockets and pound our knees. But, on the other hand, we never regret the time we have wasted. But for the person who realizes the value of time, to lose a year is a great loss; and especially for us who are so backward, the loss becomes a disaster.

. . . We merely sit down and smoke our *chibouks,* and we preen our feathers at the corner. On the other side our cart is broken, and our stable is leaking. Our vineyards and our garments are overgrown with weeds. Our soil becomes sterile, and our children are in wretched condition. We are up to our necks in debt, and work is left as it is. They all await our care. Let them wait for our care! Let the Day of Judgment come! We won't move from our places! What can we do? [*Neapalum.*] We can't be forced. We don't feel it. We never think of putting our things in order. We want to work only enough to keep from starvation and nakedness! [57]

It has often been asserted that progress is incompatible with the teachings and spirit of Islam. This is vigorously denied by the present apologists, who stress *progressive adaptation* as one of Islam's strong points. Yusuf Ziya has the following to say against fanatical people who are enemies of progress:

Though fanaticism is rejected completely in Islam, nevertheless we see unfortunately that fanaticism has entered into our religion. It is fanaticism to call others misbelievers, to become

[57] *Ibid.,* pp. 90 ff.

enemies of reform and progress, to hate without cause, and to at-
tach oneself blindly to old habits. The religion of Islam is free
from these bad morals. . . . Moslems do not hesitate to accept
new movements.[58]

Professor Abdulbaki is also emphatic in his insistence that
Islam regards progress favorably. He takes the prohibition of
painting or carving likenesses of the human figure as an example of a temporary or changeable prescription:

The religious hypocrites used to be against civilization and
progress. In order to deceive the people, for instance, if you had
asked them, they would say painting was a sin. As if pictures
would ask for life from the men who made them! What nonsense,
is it not? How can a picture ask a man for a soul? Even if it
should, how could we give it a soul? The Prophet in his time tried
to set those uncivilized people who worshiped stone and bowed
down to earth, on the right path of civilization. They were accustomed to worship idols and pictures. If he had not forbidden
painting, after the Prophet's death they would have begun to
worship his body, because of this habit which was rooted in them.
However, to-day when we see the statue of some one who served
the country, for instance, our great Gazi, or hold a picture of
our mothers, fathers, or some of our friends in our hands, do we
bow down to it? We respect it, but respect is one thing and to
bow down is another. Thus to-day, no fear of pictures or
statues remains, and they are not considered as sins. The Moslem
religion does not mean to stick to customs blindly or to tie oneself to tradition. For real religious thinkers have said that "Opinions change according to the times." Religion never accepts nor
finds suitable that which the mind does not accept or civilization
does not find suitable. [59]

Professor Abdulbaki again argues from the history of
Islam to maintain his contention:

After the death of the Prophet, a new set of needs arose,
times advanced, and ideas changed. For that reason, wise men
searched in the Holy Koran, in the words of the Prophet and

[58] *Op. cit.*, pp. 50 f.
[59] *Op. cit.*, II, 23 f.

in the actions of the Apostles (that is, those who were Moslems at the time of the Prophet); they accepted the main ideas of Islam without tampering with those conceptions concerning the existence of God and his Unity, or the righteousness of the Prophet, and they derived their ideas about purification, *namaz*, and other orders of God from the Koran, the words of Mohammed, and the behavior of the Apostles; and having accepted these in a fashion acceptable to their intelligence and knowledge, they adopted a course of action of their own. From this you may understand that Islam is a religion suited to any century. According to the changing of ideas and according to the needs of the century it can be accepted in a manner suitable to the mind. Of course the freedom of thought which is in Islam does not exist in any other religion, and it is because of this that it has spread so widely.[60]

Professor Abdulbaki in like vein upholds the use of Turkish instead of Arabic for the services of Islam in his country:

Islam, because of being a religion which belongs to all mankind, cannot have a single language special to it. Every nation addresses God in its own tongue, makes known its desires in its own tongue, and gives thanks in its own tongue. A Turk addressing God in Arabic, the meaning of which he does not know or understand, quite resembles a parrot talking. Such a speech or such a prayer does not of course come from the soul.[61]

It is only natural that, side by side with this emphasis on progress, there should arise an eagerness to encourage the ninth virtue, *attainment of knowledge and scientific skill*. The writers take special pains to point out that reason and science, far from being opposed by Islam, are strongly urged and regarded as essential. As Yusuf Ziya insists:

Islam is a religion based on reason. Of course it is necessary that a great and universal religion should unquestionably be based on reason. Because the religion which does not appeal to reason cannot be the greatest religion. So our Prophet says,

[60] *Ibid.*, III, 12 f.
[61] *Ibid.*, p. 15.

"One's religion is his reason. One who does not have reason cannot have religion." . . . By the help of reason man can overcome
material things and animals. Reason is man's guide in his religion and his daily life. That is why the things which do not
appeal to reason are said to be false, and things which are believed by persons of weak intellect are superstition.

False ideas and superstitions which are rejected by reason are
also repudiated by Islam. Ignorant persons who wish to teach
false ideas as part of Islam are doing the greatest harm to their
religion and restricting the high spirit of Islam.[62]

One of the most remarkable of all the passages which appear in this chapter, because of its frank readiness to face
facts and tell Moslems their shortcomings, is Ali Vahit's
great plea to his fellow-believers to master science:

O you Moslem community! It must be known to you that we
are behind other nations in science, skill, and commerce. They
have gone far ahead of us. It is a heavy shame for us to say it,
but the one who conceals his disease in the world cannot find a
remedy for it. The disease must be understood, and the trouble
must be brought to the surface so that a cure may be found for
it. It is not the proper thing to hide shortcomings. The main
thing is to discover what is lacking and try to find a cure for it.

Now, my brethren and fellow believers, the chief reason of our
backwardness is lack of knowledge—but nothing else. Let others
say what they like, it is science which will raise a man's head to
heaven, and it is the lack of knowledge which will carry man
under the ground. That is the disease which has been the reason
of our troubles for a long time, and whatever damnation has
come to us, it is due to our lack of knowledge. Because the world
is changed, and the time has become different. The nations which
do not have factories, railways, ships and mines are in need. But
to make a factory and construct a machine and to work the
mines, to run railways and ships are not easy. These are all made
possible by science. And it is only possible by science to cut a
hair into forty parts.

What a pity that we are strangers to such sciences. These sci-

[62] *Op. cit.,* pp. 23 ff,

ences to-day are in the hands of other nations, but, as our Prophet informs us, science is essential for a Believer. It is something like his lost property. He must take it wherever he finds it and from whoever may possess it. Again, according to the sayings of our Prophet, those who love life must embrace science, and those who wish to live in both this world and the next must embrace science. You cannot do otherwise. I don't say it. Our Prophet says so. He, who is the joy of two worlds, teaches us the importance of science, and then he commands us, "Get science though it may be in China." . . . Science should be learned even though it may be in any other country. Never should we say it is far or near or it is a country of *ghiaours*. We should have relations with the masters of sciences. We should learn their languages and obtain their sciences.

O God, look at the word of our Prophet! And see the lack of knowledge in our country. We may not notice it, but foreigners do. They laugh at our ignorance and speak of us deprecatingly. We are not aware of our shortcomings or of the way they talk about us. We speak of a "mere religion," and we never see the importance which that religion gives to science. We may see the important thing to which that religion draws our attention, but we say, "That is another science to which our religion refers. It is not a worldly science." We think that the worldly science is a Satanic science, and in such a way we open our hands to foreigners. We open our hands so much that we even import from Europe the paper and ink of the Koran which we read. All things which we need, "from thread to needle," are made and sent to us by those foreigners whom we don't admire, and call *ghiaours*.

To those who realize the significance of this fact it means death. The Koran that we read, does it teach us to be so ignorant and supply our needs from others? Does it teach us not to learn how to manufacture paper and ink? Does it teach us not to do anything but to be mere, dry Moslems? Does our Koran say, "Whatever you do, I will take you to the center of heaven"? No! The Koran praises the gifts of God on earth and in heaven. It puts them before our eyes, and it commands us to appreciate the values of those gifts. But we have to have science to appreciate those commands and to realize the values of those gifts. Praise to those persons who enlighten their country with science and knowledge, and praise to those persons who bring wealth to their country with their art and skill, and save their nation from opening its hands to foreigners.[63]

The great importance which is being given to the tenth virtue, *practicality*, by those leaders who are devoted to making Turkey's Islam up to date and vital, is brought out in another passage from Ali Vahit's sermons, only slightly less striking than the one just completed. Note particularly his combination of practical admonitions with theology.

God has created the air, water, wood with which we build our ships, and iron, and the winds which cause the ships to go, and the coal, in such a way that if we understand their uses, we can make ships like mountains to carry our heavy loads and transport thousands of men. There is great significance in the orderly arrangement of these things. If we could not cut the tree and melt the iron, what could we do? And if the wind did not blow and the water did not carry, what could we do? If coal did not burn and machines did not turn, who could question it? No one! God has been good to us and has granted us different things with qualities. These qualities, which were secrets, now have been discovered by human beings, and it has been found that they have an orderly arrangement. . . . In the word of God there are commands which are open, but there are secret remarks on certain things. For those who understand these secrets, they have a great value.

So we Moslems should obey his commands and understand his remarks and act accordingly. We should appreciate his gifts and become kings of the sea. We should build the greatest docks of the world. We should build sailing vessels and oil- and electrically-driven vessels according to the demands of the time. We should sell our goods throughout the world, and we should declare our independence by large warships.

If we had obeyed the commands of God, we would not have our fields barren, and we would not have our oils, iron, and coal, and thousands of our other mines hidden under the ground. Everybody could find work to do, and a prosperous life would prevail:

[63] *Turkish Sermons,* pp. 65 ff.

No one would dare to disturb our happiness. But we did not do so; as if God had commanded us not to undertake seafaring, we have abstained from it. We did not understand what a great gift the sea is, and the commands of God are being obeyed by others. Our enemies have discovered the values of the gifts which God had granted. They built warships and merchant vessels and they all became rich and lived like Sultans. We were obliged to put in their purses the money we have saved with our teeth and nails.

Men, you know that we do not suffer just because we are Moslems. The present conditions are due to the fact that we are clumsy. In Islam there is no laziness. Our religion does not order us to live like dead men. Our religion commands us to be watchful and strong. It designates distant regions for trade and travel. The Koran does not praise gold and silver, but iron, and wants to turn our attention to the seas and the ships. It requires us to work for our country like lions. What else could religion do? Is there anything like it in the religions and religious writings of other nations? . . .

Also you must pay great attention to the rivers. They are like the veins of a country. In their flow there are great gifts and secrets of God, but of course these are for those who can appreciate and understand them. To those who do not appreciate their significance the rivers are nothing, not only mere things, but the cause of great troubles. . . . To the son of Adam who knows his business, rivers can not break out of control. God knows they become like a lamb. When he orders, they flow in the direction that he indicates. They become the sources not of loss but of interest. The running water is a skilled servant. The river is a wonderful creature; it carries your load, irrigates your field, reaps your harvest, cuts your wood, transports your flour, gives light, cooks your dinner, turns your mill, drills holes in iron, melts the ore. Can you imagine a stronger and more adequate servant than a river? . . .

It is all right to use the rivers, but who is going to buy the machines, and who is going to use them? Who is going to repair them when they are broken? This is the main problem which twists our backbones. No, Moslems, I say that we will buy them, we will use them, and we will repair them. We have had enough of laziness.

How long will we be strange to machinery? It is a shame and

sin. Other men are working day and night to swallow us. On the other hand, we are trying to dig a well with a needle. We cannot accomplish anything with the methods which we have inherited from Adam. When the word machinery is mentioned, we get frightened. We never try to use it. The instrument for drilling holes in iron may be invented, and we see that they are all used by either Jews or Christians. Years pass, but you cannot see the same machine in a Moslem shop. The others do their work by machinery and easily, and earn a great deal. On the other hand, the poor Moslem works hard to make a hole in the iron plates with his hammer, and when he gets tired, he revolts against God and says, "Why hast thou made our lot so difficult?" O you poor creatures of God, why do you not realize that the world is created for you? Why do you not use your mind? Why do you hide your money in a corner or spend it in wedding parties? Is it not good for you to learn the ways of working by machinery like the others?

Do not lag behind the others, and do not blame God for your backwardness. I don't accept any excuse if we cannot manage to use the things I have mentioned above; and if we do not learn the sciences and crafts with a great love, I may say in the name of God that we will never strengthen our backbones though we conquer hundreds of armies, and we will never get rid of our troubles. We fought like lions on the battlefield, and our foreheads are clean, and we will struggle the same way in the field of science and arts. We will find the means by which we will progress. It is our duty to go side by side with the most civilized countries of the world. The word machinery will not frighten us. We will become adepts at machinery, and we will learn the ins and outs of electricity. We will master them all. We will exploit our mines and float ships on the sea. Our rivers will be full of small steamboats like bees. We will generate electricity and in some places we will run our railways by this electricity.

We will spend a little and earn a lot. We will not give our money to foreigners. We will weave and clothe ourselves. We won't become the servants of others. In short, we will show the same activities in the field of science and knowledge as we did on the battlefield.

This is the way to appreciate gifts. This is the way to pay our debts to our country. Appreciation of a river is not given by watering the animals or doing your washing or sitting by the river and hunting flies.[64]

The eleventh virtue which receives attention from republican Moslems is *tolerance*. While this is nothing new in the doctrines of Islam, the spirit behind it seems to be based on genuine respect rather than on contempt. According to Professor Abdulbaki:

> If we respect what other people believe, they also will respect what we believe. We have no right to interfere with the beliefs of others. We respect every thought and belief which does not harm our fatherland and nation. It is certain that God has said that a person will not be held responsible for the conduct of another. For example: a person does not worship; if the person does not neglect his duty, naturally we cannot interfere with his not worshiping. Also, those who do not worship must not interfere with those who do worship. Faith arises in the mind. Every one is free in his thoughts. Every thought is sacred as long as it does not harm the welfare of our nation.[65]

Later in the same book Professor Abdulbaki declares:

> Moslems get along well not only with each other but also with everybody else. What is the cause of quarreling and hurting one another's feelings? You interfere with the idea of somebody, with his religious faith or with his work which he has done without giving trouble to anybody; then if he frowns at you and mumbles to himself at you, hearts are broken and a quarrel begins. But you have seen in the first lessons that Moslems do not interfere with the free ideas or the faith of any one. And since this is so, they get along well with every one.[66]

Yusuf Ziya makes the same point:

> Once our Prophet scolded a soldier for his fanaticism. In the Ķoran it is said, "You are not sent to annoy people." This saying means that the consciences and religions of people are free.

[64] *First Sermon*, pp. 19 ff.
[65] *Op. cit.*, II, 4 f.
[66] *Ibid.*, p. 18.

Do not interfere with the ways of others' religion and conscience. Our Prophet has said, "There is no compulsion in religion," and in the Great Koran it is said, "There is no constraint in religion." [67]

As in the case of education, great emphasis is being placed on the *development of good health*. One of the chief obstacles to be removed by modern preaching is again fatalism, which this time crops up as refusal to adopt health and sanitation measures, the old mentality arguing that disease and filth are part of God's will for his creatures. Ali Vahit's sermon in praise of smallpox vaccination is a classic, in its way, for its use of illustrations and arguments which will appeal to the simple peasant mind:

O Moslem community, I am going to speak to you about disease and its cure, which is in the power of our God, who has created the world. Before speaking to you, I would like to ask you this: it may happen that a dog attacks you, and if it tries to bite you, what will you do? Won't you swing your stick or throw a stone at the dog to drive it away? Won't you try to find means to protect yourself? Of course you will. Of course you will take measures to protect yourself from being bitten.

O you Moslems, I have asked you this in connection with the smallpox vaccination. I use the attack made by the dog to personify smallpox, because they resemble each other. The microbe of the smallpox disease attacks man and kills him or cripples him. Now when a dog attacks, man protects himself with a stick or stone, and when the microbe of the disease attacks, won't the same man run away or protect himself? We carry a stick for the dog and a weapon for our enemies. Why shouldn't we carry a stick and weapon for smallpox disease? The stick and weapon against that disease is vaccination.

When an animal attacks, you don't say, "I have confidence in God; so I don't need to use my stick." When it comes to disease, why do you try to be confident in God? You don't believe in the microbes of that disease because you don't see them. Or you don't pay any attention to them. But they are more harmful

[67] *Op. cit.*, p. 51.

than any other wild animals. God, who has created big camels, elephants, lions, tigers, and dragons, has also created small animals, which are not visible. And some of these small animals are more poisonous than snakes or centipedes. Dragons and other wild animals multiply by twos and threes. But on the other hand, these secret dragons, the microbes of diseases, within a very short time multiply by millions and destroy whatever they meet in their way without pity. The harm that they cause cannot be done by dragons on mountains and valleys.

What do you think? Can not God create animals a hundred thousand times smaller than ants and fleas? Cannot he make them more poisonous than snakes or scorpions? Is it difficult for God to create millions of these animals? These smaller animals are called microbes by doctors. Let doctors call them what they wish, it does not matter to you. Microbes are not created by doctors. They only know them, and they point out their harm and benefits.

O you Moslems, some of those microbes are our friends, while others are our enemies. Those which are friendly to us become our blood and give us strength and fight against harmful microbes. They are like cat and mouse. A smallpox vaccination increases the numbers of these microbes or small animals and strengthens the microbes which are useful to us. It gives them the ability to withstand the smallpox microbes. So vaccination is a gift of God. It is like a sharp sword drawn against this smallpox disease. The microbes of this disease cannot be withstood with cannons and rifles. They can only be withstood by vaccination. We can fight these microbes by other useful microbes. The work of these useful microbes is the work of a sentry.

You Moslem community, see the gift of God. While you sleep, they watch for enemies. If you get any microbes in your body through what you eat and drink, these microbes attack them and kill them. A great many battles take place in your veins that you are not aware of.[68]

It is in connection with such causes as the development of receptive attitudes toward modern innovations that the importance of the Islamic organization is brought out. Since

[68] *Turkish Sermons,* pp. 114 ff.

Turkey's educational system will be unable to reach the entire population for many years, and since the mosque represents the only habitual gathering-place in communities which are not reached by organizations of any other kind, one can appreciate the vital importance to the republican government of using the Moslem meeting places and of spreading progressive ideas in them. It is for this reason that one finds the Presidency of Religious Affairs distributing modern sermons, and the Department of Public Instruction for a time training *hodjas* with modern ideas to function in the mosques. In this same connection there should be mentioned a further venture carried on by Ali Vahit, whose sermons have been frequently quoted. This is the publication of a small, semi-monthly paper called the *Köy Hojasi* ("The Village Teacher"), which goes to various literate individuals in the Turkish countryside and retails advice and hints on how life may be lived more cleanly, progressively, and comfortably.

Implicit in almost every quotation made thus far in connection with religious developments has been the virtue which we have listed thirteenth among those advocated by Islam in Turkey at present: *patriotic loyalty*. Indeed, devotion to the national government seems fairly to have supplanted loyalty to any other individual, creed, or institution as the foremost duty of Moslem Turks. So much does the patriotic note color all the other virtues which have been mentioned that it hardly seems necessary to mention it separately. There are, however, certain features of this alliance between religion and patriotism which must be mentioned. We saw that the first meeting of the Grand National Assembly in Ankara was preceded by a solemn gathering in the Hadji Bairam Mosque of such a character as to give the national defenders a sacred character reminiscent of the crusades. One finds a continuation of this spirit in a news item of March 16, 1930, reported

in *Le milliett*. This date is the anniversary of the Allied
Occupation of Istanbul, when several Turks were slain in
attempting to offer resistance. One of the events of the
program which was arranged to celebrate this "dolorous anniversary" was the pronouncement of a prayer for the repose
of the souls of the slain men by the Mufti. As a matter of
fact, the government continues to provide *hodjas* for the
army, and religious instruction is part of the recognized
military routine.

The jealousy with which the government has protected its
people against the inroads of Christian propaganda in mission
schools, and the failure in practice to grant complete equality
to citizens who profess other religions, are added indications
that no matter how severely Islam may seem to be chastised
by those in control, the Moslem religion continues to rest
close to the Turkish heart and is regarded as an important
element in the country's cultural constitution.

Of course the sermons and schoolbooks are filled with pleas
and commands designed to stimulate the loyalty and patriotism of Turkish Moslems. In Professor Abdulbaki's religious lessons appears the following:

To believe in Allah, the Prophet, and the religion of Islam is
religious faith. We also have a national faith. We are Turks.
Turks are civilized. Our country will always go forward, and
will always conquer our enemies. "When the name 'Turk' is
spoken, my chest swells with pride; my head goes up. I love
people who are useful to my nation and my country; those who
do harm to my beloved country I do not love at all." [69]

Again:

There cannot be a religion without a fatherland. If we had
not struggled in the War of Independence, if we had not saved
our fatherland, to-day neither government nor country would
remain. [70]

[69] *Op. cit.*, I, 8.
[70] *Ibid.*, p. 13.

And it is further insisted that "in Islam only those who serve their country and nation well have a high position." [71]

Ali Vahit stresses in his sermons the importance of such duties as performing military service for the country, paying taxes promptly, co-operating with government schemes for economy and education, and in general of being loyal and obedient citizens. The same spirit is manifested all through the sermons issued by the Diyanet Ichleri, of which the following may be taken as a typical example:

O Moslems, the greatest worship is obedience to God. God in His Koran says . . . obey God and His Prophet and your masters. Our master is the Republican Government.

If there is no obedience to the Government, then the discipline of the world is broken. All of our affairs become mixed; all those who depend on their strength become rulers. Justice, security, and tranquillity will be ended. No one will have surety of his life and property. Then there will not be obedience to God and His Prophet.

That is why God commanded us to obey our government with equal emphasis. Especially the Government which has the authority to-day, since it is not the same government of the old times which merely for the sake of its own pleasures made people work, and decorated its palaces and kiosks with the sweat of Moslems, and wasted for its pleasure the income of every Moslem and Turk, for which they had worked a year, and spent it in an hour. To-day's Government is made up from the hearts of a nation and it is the Government of the nation itself. Let us love our Government, and let us obey it. Because God commands us to obey our Government.

O Moslems, if you want to reach happiness and salvation in this world and the next, obey the commands of God; and to be happy in the world and to have comfort and security, we must obey those who work for us day and night, and who perform their duties. Those who do not obey their masters dig their own graves, and with this behavior they rebel against God and will be punished severely in the next world.

O you creatures of God, I advise you to obey the rules of God

[71] *Ibid.,* III, 11.

and keep away from rebellion. This advice is given to you for your own good in every way.[72]

In Yusuf Ziya's book one finds the statement:

The decisions of the National Assembly have a religious importance. If the responsible persons come together and make a decision regarding some problem, then it becomes *farz* for all Moslems to obey that decision.[73]

This is evidently a continuation of the well-known Moslem principle of *ijma,* which permits alteration in belief and practice through agreement of believers, i.e., *vox populi, vox Dei.*

Another interesting association between religion and patriotism is the current practice of stretching patriotic illuminated mottoes such as "Give to the Red Crescent" or "Patronize Home Industries" between the minarets of mosques at the time of the fast of Ramazan. These mottoes, written in the new Latinized alphabet with electric lights are a great contrast to the old mottoes of a pious nature, written in Arabic with oil lamps suspended by strings.

It is difficult to obtain any accurate information on the actual popularity of the Moslem religion throughout the population of Turkey. As in all countries there are found fundamentalists who regard the innovations introduced by the new régime as utter sacrilege but dare say nothing about it for fear of being regarded as conservatives and enemies of the country. Individuals of this stamp, and they are present in Turkey, predict impending reaction and a return to stricter and more fanatical orthodoxy than ever existed before. Just how such a reaction is to be engineered they do not seem to

[72] *Op. cit.* (1927), pp. 6 ff.
[73] *Op. cit.,* p. 65.

know, inasmuch as the control of the country is firmly in the hands of the younger generation of military and intellectual leaders whose position is apparently impregnable. Nevertheless these scions of the old school insist that God will find a way to punish all the impiety which is extant under the Kemalists.

Then there are the masses of the people, easily led and disciplined, used to taking things as they come. These people, accustomed habitually to perform their religious obligations, continue in large part to carry on a minimum at least of their pious routine, and as long as the government does not antagonize their ritualistic inclinations, they seem rather to welcome the unification of their religious and national allegiances. Although I cannot make comparisons between the numbers attending prayers nowadays with the numbers fifteen or twenty years ago, certainly the mosques which I visited in Istanbul, Kayseri, Ankara, and Izmir (Smyrna) were far from deserted on Fridays and evenings during Ramazan, though there seemed little outward observance of the regular five-times-daily prayers. At Izmir a mosque in the better section of the city which I visited on a Friday during Ramazan was filled to overflowing with devout worshipers.

Turkey boasts, too, her advanced and emancipated thinkers, who have cut loose from organized religion, and whose philosophies and theologies have as much variety as one would meet with in any Western community. While in some emancipation has produced, as it always does, a selfish superficiality, in others it has led to an earnest quest for the essentials of rich and happy living found in loving service to one's fellow-men and in striving to eliminate those things in the world which make for suffering and sorrow.

Two quotations will suffice to indicate the attitudes of two of Turkey's leading philosophers toward religion. First is a piece called *Din* ("Religion") by Zia Geuk Alp, who until his death a few years ago was Turkey's leading sociologist and a thinker much admired by Ataturk:

My religion is neither hope nor fear. I worship God because I love him, and I do my duty without smelling any fumes from heaven or hell. O you preacher, do not speak of the fire of hell which is built up of thousands of *chekis* of wood, but speak of the sun of beauty which is fed with the wood of our love. Speak of the tree *Tuba*, which has its roots in heaven and its branches in our hearts. And my soul is fed with the fruits of that tree. It is not hungry, and my soul has absorbed the honey which is made of love and kindness.

O preacher, explain to me what love is. I do not seek Satan nor angels. Give me the secrets of those who have reached perfection; and tell me who is the lover, who is loved, and what love is. Do not put me off by promising heaven. My soul does not like the vanities of life because it has reached perfection. And do not threaten me with fear of hell, because my soul is foolish: it does not know what fear means.

The second quotation is taken from the writings of the late Abdullah Djevdet Bey, physician, poet, philosopher, and editor of the journal *Idjtihad*. In the issue of his magazine of March 1, 1929, Dr. Djevdet recorded in twenty-five paragraphs his social, economic, political, and religious philosophy. Six of these may be quoted to indicate the trend of his thought:

10. The plausible aim of religions is to develop between men the spirit of concord, love, and compassion; it is preferable to abandon the remedy, when, in place of curing and relieving, it aggravates and perpetuates the evil. . . .

15. The belief in a Supreme Being ruling the universe according to his own fanstasy not only denotes an enormous credulity, but it also ordains a pitiable diminution of the human spirit, which it condemns to an irremediable place of unimportance.

16. Virtue is a disposition which impels us to do good to others: the pleasure which we feel in conforming to it and the moral pain which infraction of that sublime impulse occa-

sions constitute the only motive and sanction of our acts. . . .

17. Man is responsible not only for the evil which he does but also for the good which he does not do.

18. The perfect man is he who is good without aim of recompense and without fear of punishment, not even those of his own pleasure and suffering. . . .

22. There is only one civilization, and that is the patrimony of the great human family. . . .

There is always a temptation at the conclusion of a study of this sort to cast off the shackles of factual evidence and let one's imagination soar into the rarefied atmosphere of fanciful prognostication. Pages could be written upon the future status of religion in Turkey, but their worth would be negligible, merely the expression of a single opinion on the subject. From the material already presented the reader may draw his own conclusions. In so doing he will be reasonably justified if he eliminates as immediate possibilities either a mass conversion to Christianity or a reactionary return to old Islam and the *Sharia* law. And let him bear in mind the preoccupation of Kemalist Turkey with two great tasks: the mastery of Western scientific technique and the building of a nationalistic state. The treatment thus far accorded to Islam has been, on the whole, negative. As one area after another has been removed from the sphere of religious domination, Islam has seen its historic responsibilities limited. With education and legislation established on new bases, Islam has appeared to have less and less to do, and thus to exert less and less attraction to potential young leaders. Islam's chief danger, then, would seem to be neglect. Out-and-out persecution by the government, with a consequent focus of attention upon the dangers facing the faith, might insure its more rapid revitalization. Turkey's religious leaders must examine their position and re-evaluate their task. If this can be done in such terms as to challenge the attention of Turkish youth, there will be assurance that Islam will live and prove to be an asset to the Turkey of the future. Such a religion, more Turkish than Arab in character, would fit in with the picture of the Turkish Fatherland as sketched poetically by Zia Geuk Alp:

A land in which the call to prayer resounds from the mosque in
    the Turkish tongue,
Where the peasant understands the meaning of his prayers,
A land where the schoolboy reads the Quran in his mother tongue,
O Son of the Turk, that is thy Fatherland.[74]

[74] Quoted by Sir Telford Waugh, "Nine Years of Republic in Turkey," *Journal of the Royal Central Asian Society*, XX, Part I (January, 1933), 60.

BIBLIOGRAPHY

I. WORKS CONSULTED AND USED

ABBAS ALI BAIG, SIR. "Peace with Turkey in Its Relation to Anglo-Muslim Goodwill and the Khilafat," *Asiatic Review*, XIX (October, 1923), 577–86.

ABBOTT, G. F. *Turkey in Transition*. London: Arnold, 1909.

ABDULBAKI, PROFESSOR. *Religious Lessons for the Children of the Republic of Turkey—Third, Fourth, and Fifth Grades*. Owner and publisher: Tefeyyuz Bookstore. Translated under auspices of American Bible House, Istanbul. Press of the Compositor's Co., 1929.

ABDULLAH DJEVDET BEY. *Bir filosof un si orteri*. Istanbul: Devlet Matbaasi, 1930.

———. "Les idées directrices de l'*Idjtihad*," *Idjtihad* (Istanbul), March 1, 1929, p. 5134.

ADAMS, C. C. *The Modern Reform Movement in Egypt and the Caliphate*. Chicago: University of Chicago Ph.D. Dissertation, 1928. Pp. 529.

AFLALO, F. G. *Regilding the Crescent*. Philadelphia: Lippincott, 1911. Pp. 310.

AHMED EMIN. *Turkey in the World War*. New Haven: Yale University Press, 1930. Pp. 310.

AHMED IHSAN. "Souvenirs d'un journaliste," *Le milliett* (Istanbul), June 5–July 5, 1930.

AHMED RUSTEM BEY. "Moustapha Kémal Pacha," *Bibliothèque universelle et revue de Genève*, November, 1929, pp. 618–27.

ALI HAYDAR MIDHAT BEY. *The Life of Midhat Pasha*. London: John Murray, 1903. Pp. 292.

ALI VAHIT, OURIANZADE. *First Sermon—from the Pulpit of Hadji Bairam Mosque*. (In Turkish.) Ankara: Hakimiyeti Miliye Press, 1926. Pp. 120.

———. *Turkish Sermons*. 2d ser. (In Turkish.) Istanbul: Press Amedi, 1928. Pp. 368.

229

ALLEN, W. E. D. "The Turkish Mirror," *Asiatic Review,* XXIV (October, 1928), 576–86.

———. *The Turks in Europe.* London: John Murray, 1919. Pp. 256.

ALLPORT, F. H. *Social Psychology.* Boston: Houghton Mifflin, 1924.

AMERICAN BOARD OF COMMISSIONERS FOR FOREIGN MISSIONS. *Annual Reports,* 1931–34.

American Friends of Turkey. (Booklet.) New York, 1931.

AMIR ALI, Maulavi Saiyid. *The Spirit of Islam.* London: Christophers, 1922. Pp. 515.

ANDRÉ, P. J. *L'Islam et les races.* 2 vols. Paris: P. Geuthner, 1922.

ARMSTRONG, H. C. *Gray Wolf—Mustafa Kemal.* New York: Minton, Balch, 1933. Pp. 298.

ARNOLD, T. W. *The Preaching of Islam.* New York: Scribner's, 1913. Pp. 467.

AVNI BEY. Address delivered before the Educational Conference in Copenhagen, summer, 1929. (Typewritten English transcription.)

BAKER, A. G. *Christian Missions and a New World Culture.* Chicago: Willett, Clark, 1934. Pp. 322.

BARTON, J. L. *Daybreak in Turkey.* Boston: Pilgrim Press, 1908. Pp. 294.

BÉRARD, V. *La mort de Stamboul.* Paris: Colin, 1913. Pp. 418.

———. *La révolution turque.* Paris: Colin, 1909. Pp. 352.

BLUNT, W. S. *The Future of Islam.* London: Kegan, Paul, Trench, 1882. Pp. 215.

BRADEN, C. S. *Modern Tendencies in World Religions.* New York: Macmillan, 1933. Pp. 343.

BROWNE, E. G. *The Persian Revolution of 1905–09.* Cambridge: University Press, 1910. Pp. 470.

BRYCE, VISCOUNT. *The Treatment of Armenians in the Ottoman Empire, 1915–16.* Documents presented to Viscount Grey of Fallodon, secretary of state for foreign affairs. Miscellaneous No. 31 (1916). London: H. M. Stationery Office, 1916. Pp. 684.

BURY, G. W. *Pan-Islam.* London: Macmillan, 1919. Pp. 212.

BUXTON, C. R. *Turkey in Revolution.* London: Unwin, 1909. Pp. 285.

CASTAGNÉ, J. *Le mouvement d'émancipation de la femme musul-*

mane en Orient. Paris: P. Geuthner, 1929. Extrait de la *Revue des études islamiques—année 1929,* Cahier II.

CHANTITCH-CHANDAN, K. S. *Le miracle turc.* Paris: La Renaissance Moderne, 1929. Pp. 187.

"Christianity without the Label," *Literary Digest,* June 6, 1925.

"Christianizing Incident, The," editorial translated from *Hayat* (Ankara), February 2, 1928.

COHEN, M. (Tekin Alp, pseud.). *Türkismus und Pan-Türkismus.* Weimar: Kiepenheuer, 1915. Pp. 112.

COLLINS, J. WALTER. "The Political Situation in the Near East," *Contemporary Review,* CXLVI, No. 826 (October, 1934), 405-12.

COLRAT, A. "Turkey Today," *Living Age,* CCCXXXIII (July 15, 1927), 129-34.

CREASY, E. S. *History of the Ottoman Turks.* London: Bentley, 1858.

Croissant-rouge turc: Rapport présenté à la XIIIme Conférence Internationale de la Croix-Rouge sur l'activité du croissant-rouge turc, 1925-1926-1927. Angora: Comité Central du Croissant-Rouge Turc.

Current History: New York, 1930-1934. (Reviews of Near Eastern affairs by A. H. Lybyer and R. L. Baker.)

DAVISON, W. S. "New Lights in Turkey," *Christian Century,* XLIX, No. 46 (November 16, 1932), 1407-10.

DEBUNSEN, V. *The Soul of a Turk.* London: John Lane Co., 1910. Pp. 295.

DEWEY, J. "The New Angora," *New Republic,* XL, No. 515 (October 15, 1924), 169-70.

———. "Secularizing a Theocracy—Young Turkey and the Caliphate," *New Republic,* XL, No. 511 (September 17, 1924), 69-71.

———. "The Turkish Tragedy," *ibid.,* No. 519 (November 12, 1924), 268-69.

DIAMONTOPOULO, HERCULE. *Le réveil de la Turquie.* Alexandria: Typo-lithographie Centrale I. Della Rocca, 1908. Pp. 300.

"Divorce of Islam and Turkey," *Literary Digest,* May 5, 1928.

DJEMAL PASHA. *Memories of a Turkish Statesman.* London: Hutchinson, 1921. Pp. 302.

EARLE, E. M. "American Missions in the Near East," *Foreign Affairs* (N.Y.), VII, No. 3 (April, 1929), 398-417.

ELIOT, SIR CHARLES NORTON EDGECUMBE. *Turkey in Europe.* London: E. Arnold, 1908. Pp. 459.

Etudes pratiques sur la question d'Orient—réformes et capitulations. Paris: Veuve Berger-Levrault et Fils, 1869. Pp. 393.

EVERSLEY, LORD, and CHIROL, SIR V. *The Turkish Empire.* London: Unwin, 1923.

FRANCK, H. A. *The Fringe of the Moslem World.* New York: Century Co., 1928. Pp. 426.

FRASER, D. *Persia and Turkey in Revolt.* London: Blackwood, 1910. Pp. 440.

FUAD BEY, KEUPRULUZADE. "The Conversions to Christianity and the Culture Crisis," *Hayat* (Ankara), No. 63 (February 9, 1928).

GAILLARD, G. *Les turcs et l'Europe.* Paris: Chapelot, 1920. Pp. 384.

GARNETT, L. M. J. *Mysticism and Magic in Turkey.* New York: Scribner's, 1912. Pp. 202.

———. *Turkish Life in Town and Country.* New York: Putnam's, 1904. Pp. 336.

GENTIZON, P. *Mustapha Kemal, ou l'Orient en marche.* Paris: Bossard, 1929.

GEORGES-GAULIS, BERTHE. *Angora, Constantinople, Londres; Moustafa Kémal et la politique anglaise en Orient.* Paris: A. Colin, 1922. Pp. 257.

———. *Le nationalisme turc.* Paris: Plon, 1921. Pp. 145.

———. *La nouvelle Turquie.* Paris: A. Colin, 1924. Pp. 282.

GERMANUS, DR. JULIUS. "The Awakening of Turkish Literature," *Islamic Culture* (Hyderabad, Deccan), VII, No. 2 (April, 1933) and No. 3 (July, 1933), 178–94 and 353–78.

———. "The Rôle of the Turks in Islam," *Islamic Culture,* VII, No. 4 (October, 1933), 519–32; and VIII, No. 1 (January, 1934), 1–14.

GIBB, H. A. R. (ed.). *Whither Islam?* London: Gollancz, 1932. Pp. 384.

GIBBONS, H. A. *The Foundation of the Ottoman Empire.* New York: Century Co., 1916. Pp. 379.

GOODSELL, F. F. *Confronting Moslems with Jesus Christ.* (Envelope Series, Vol. XXIX, Nos. 2 and 3 [July and October, 1926].) Boston: American Board of Commissioners for Foreign Missions. Pp. 30.

GORDON, L. J. *American Relations with Turkey.* Philadelphia: University of Pennsylvania Press, 1932. Pp. 402.

GRAVES, R. *Lawrence and the Arabs.* London: J. Cape, 1928. Pp. 454.

GUERON, E. "Correspondence from the Near East," *Christian Century,* 1933–34.

HALIDÉ ÉDIB. *Memoirs of Halidé Édib.* New York: Century, 1926. Pp. 472.

———. *Turkey Faces West.* New Haven: Yale University Press, 1930. Pp. 273.

———. *The Turkish Ordeal.* New York: Century, 1928. Pp. 407.

HALIL HALID. *The Diary of a Turk.* London: A. and C. Black, 1903. Pp. 269.

HALL, W. H. (ed.) *Reconstruction in Turkey.* New York, 1918. A series of reports compiled for the American Committee of Armenian and Syrian Relief.

HARTMANN, R. *Im neuen Anatolien.* Leipzig: Hinrichs, 1927. Pp. 148.

HAYDON, A. E. (ed.) *Modern Trends in World Religions.* Chicago: University of Chicago Press, 1934. Pp. 250.

HILMI MALIK ADNAN. "Pre-school and Elementary Education in Turkey." (Paper presented to the International Conference in Geneva, Switzerland, summer, 1929; typewritten draft.)

HIMAYEI ETFAL (CHILDREN'S PROTECTIVE SOCIETY). *Report of the General Congress of May 8, 1927.* (In Turkish.) Ankara, 1928.

HOCKING, W. E. *The Spirit of World Politics.* New York: Macmillan, 1932. Pp. 571.

HOGARTH, D. G. *A History of Arabia.* Oxford: Clarendon Press, 1922. Pp. 131.

"How I Gave My Daughter to the American Girls' College," *Resimli Ay* (Istanbul), May, 1929, p. 18.

HUBERT, L. *L'Islam et la guerre.* Paris: A. Challamel, 1918. Pp. 48.

HUGHES, T. P. *A Dictionary of Islam.* London: Allen, 1895. Pp. 750.

HURGRONJE, C. S. *Mohammedanism.* New York: Putnam's, 1916. Pp. 184.

IKBAL ALI SHAH, SIRDAR. "The Religious Revolt of Turkey,"

Review of Religions (London), XXVII, No. 7 (July, 1928), 23–26.

INSABATO, E. *L'Islam et la politique des Alliés.* (Translated from the Italian by Magali-Bossuard.) Paris: Berger-Levrault, 1920. Pp. 237.

ISMAIL HAKKI. "Present-Day Education in Turkey." (Translated by E. T. Perry for *Educational Year Book*, 1928.)

JACOB, G. *Beiträge zur Kenntnis des Derwisch Ordens der Bektaschis.* (Türkische Bibliothek, Vol. IX.) Berlin, Mayer & Müller, 1908. Pp. 100.

JENNINGS, A. K. *The Anatolian Project.* (Typewritten.) Ankara, 1929.

————. "Report of the Executive Vice-President of the American Friends of Turkey." (Mimeographed.) New York, 1932.

JOHNSON, C. R. *Constantinople To-Day, or the Pathfinder Survey of Constantinople.* New York: Macmillan, 1922. Pp. 418.

JUNG, E. *L'Islam et l'Asie devant l'impérialisme.* Paris: Marpon, 1927.

————. *L'Islam sous le joug.* Paris, 1926. Pp. 95.

KADELBACH, DR. H. *Die türkische Landwirtschaft in der Gegenwart und ihre Zukunftsaufgaben.* Leipzig: Dr. Max Jänecke, 1930. Pp. 76.

KAYSER, J. *L'Europe et la Turquie nouvelle.* Paris: Les Presses Universitaires de France, 1922. Pp. 139.

KEANE, T. F. *Six Months in Meccah.* London: Tinsley Bros., 1881. Pp. 212.

KHAIRRALLAH, I. A. "Regeneration of the Turkish People of To-Day," *Current History* (New York), December, 1927, pp. 369–73.

KNIGHT, E. F. *The Awakening of Turkey.* Philadelphia: Lippincott, 1909. Pp. 356.

KOHN, H. *A History of Nationalism in the East.* New York: Harcourt, Brace, 1929. Pp. 476.

————. *Nationalism and Imperialism in the Hither East.* New York: Harcourt, Brace, 1932. Pp. 339.

————. *Orient and Occident.* New York: John Day, 1934. Pp. 140.

————. "Ten Years of the Turkish Republic," *Foreign Affairs*, XII, No. 1 (October, 1933), 141–55.

Koran, The. (Translated by J. M. Rodwell.) New York: Dutton, 1909. Pp. 506.

KRÜGER, KARL. *Kemalist Turkey and the Middle East*. London: Allen & Unwin, 1932. Pp. 223.

LANE-POOLE, S. *The Life of the Right Honourable Stratford Canning, Viscount Stratford de Redcliffe*. 2 vols. London: Longmans, Green, 1888.

LARCHER, M. *La guerre turque dans la Guerre Mondiale*. Paris: E. Chiron, 1926. Pp. 681.

LEVONIAN, L. *Moslem Mentality*. London: Allen & Unwin, 1928. Pp. 245.

————. "Nationalism and Religion," *World Dominion* (London), VII, No. 4 (October, 1929), 383–93.

————. *Turkish Translation Service*. Old Phaleron and Beirut, 1930–34.

LIMAN VON SANDERS. *Five Years in Turkey*. Baltimore: Williams & Wilkins, 1928. Pp. 326.

LYAUTEY, MARSHAL, et al. *L'Islam et la politique contemporaine*. Paris: Ecole Libre des Sciences Politiques; Société des Anciens Elèves et Elèves; Alcan, 1927.

LYBYER, A. H. (ed.) "Modern Turkey" ("Monograph Series of the New Orient Society of America," No. 3), *Open Court*, Vol. XLVI, No. 912 (May, 1932).

M. IHSAN. "Education in Turkey," *Year Book of Education*. (London, 1932), pp. 971–81.

MACDONALD, D. B. *Development of Muslim Theology, Jurisprudence, and Constitutional Theory*. New York: Scribner's, 1903. Pp. 386.

MAHMUT BEY. "Le Ghazi et la révolution," *Le milliett* (Istanbul), November 26, 1929—February 8, 1930.

MARCHAND, R. *Le réveil d'une race*. Paris: Nouvelle Société d'Editions, 1927. Pp. 229.

MARGOLIOUTH, D. S. *The Early Development of Mohammedanism*. New York: Scribner's, 1914. Pp. 265.

————. *Mohammedanism*. London: Williams & Norgate, 1911. Pp. 253.

MARKHAM, R. F. *Adapting Education in Missionary Schools to New Conditions in Turkey*. New York: Columbia University M.A. Thesis, 1928. Pp. 84.

MATHEWS, B. *Young Islam on Trek*. New York: Friendship Press, 1926. Pp. 224.

MEARS, E. G. *Modern Turkey*. New York: Macmillan, 1924. Pp. 779.

MEHMET EMIN. "Is the Conversion to Christianity Incident a Result of a Culture Crisis?" *Hayat* (Ankara), No. 64 (February 16, 1928).

MEHMET ZEKI. *Encyclopédie biographique de Turquie.* (In Turkish and French.) Istanbul: Ekspres Matbaasi, 1929. Pp. 608.

MÉLIA, J. *Mustapha-Kemal, ou la rénovation de la Turquie.* Paris: Bibliothèque Charpentier, 1929. Pp. 240.

MENZIES, S. *Turkey Old and New,* Vol. I. London: Allen, 1880. Pp. 409.

MIKUSCH, D. VON. *Gasi Mustafa Kemal.* Leipzig: Paul List Verlag, 1929. Pp. 335. Also New York: Doubleday, Doran, 1931. Pp. 380.

MILLER, H. A. *The Beginnings of To-Morrow.* New York: Stokes, 1933. Pp. 310.

MILLER, W. *The Ottoman Empire and Its Successors, 1801–1922.* Cambridge: University Press, 1923. Pp. 595.

Milliett, Le (Istanbul). Miscellaneous editorials and articles, September 1, 1929—September 1, 1930.

MITAT SADULLAH. *Yeni Yurt Bilgisi.* (Civics textbooks for third, fourth, and fifth grades of government primary schools.) Istanbul: Orhaniye Matbaasi (third grade), and Tefeyyuz Kitaphanesi (fourth and fifth grades), 1929.

MOHAMMED ASLAM. "Islam and Missionary Christianity," *Review of Religions* (London), XXVII, No. 9 (September, 1928), 39–48.

MOHAMMED IQBAL, SIR. *The Reconstruction of Religious Thought in Islam.* London: Oxford University Press, 1934. Pp. 192.

MONROE, W. S. *Turkey and the Turks.* London: G. Bell, 1908.

MORGENTHAU, H. *Ambassador Morgenthau's Story.* Garden City, N. Y.: Doubleday, Page, 1918. Pp. 407.

MOTT, J. R. (ed.). *The Moslem World of To-Day.* 1925. Pp. 420.

MUFIDE FERID, *Pervaneler* ("Moths"). Istanbul: Amire Matbaasi. 1341 A.H. (1926). Pp. 177.

MUSTAFA KEMAL PASCHA, GASI. *Die neue Türkei, 1919–1927,* Vol. I: *Der Weg zur Freiheit, 1919–1920;* Vol. II: *Die nationale Revolution, 1920–1927.* (German edition of the "Six-Day Speech.") Leipzig: Verlag von K. F. Koehler, 1928.

NAZIM HIKMET. *835 Satir.* (Poems in Turkish.) Istanbul: Muallim Ahmet Halit Kitaphanesi, 1929. Pp. 48.

Near East and India, The. (Editorials, articles, and Turkish correspondence.) Vols. XXXIII and XXXIV (1928).

NIAZ, S. "Changes in the Muslim East," *Review of Religions* (London), XXVIII, No. 3 (March, 1929), 79–86.

OSTROROG, COUNT L. *The Angora Reform.* London: University of London Press, 1927. Pp. 99.

PARKER, BERYL. "Report on Work in Turkey as Educational Adviser to American Friends of Turkey." (Mimeographed.) New York, 1933.

PEARS, SIR E. *The Life of Abdul Hamid.* New York: Holt, 1917. Pp. 365.

———. *Turkey and Its People.* London: Methuen, 1911. Pp. 409.

PEFFER, N. "Hands Off in Turkey," *Asia* (N.Y.), XXIV, No. 4 (April, 1924), 267–71, 316–18.

———. "The Turkish Republic," *Asia* (N.Y.), XXIV, No. 1 (January, 1924), 42–45, 76.

PERCEVAL, A. P. CAUSSIN DE. *Précis historique de la destruction du corps des Janissaries par le Sultan Mahmoud, en 1826.* (Translated from a contemporary Turkish account.) Paris: Firmin Didot Frères, 1833. Pp. 365.

PERNOT, M. *L'inquiétude de l'Orient; en Asie musulmane.* Paris: Hachette, 1927. Pp. 243.

———. "La nouvelle Turquie," *Revue des deux-mondes* (Paris), January 15, February 1, and March 1, 1924.

———. *La question turque.* Paris: Bernard Grasset, 1923. Pp. 322.

PRICE, C. *The Rebirth of Turkey.* New York: Seltzer, 1923. Pp. 234.

PRICE, M. T. *Christian Missions and Oriental Civilizations.* Shanghai: Privately published, 1924. Pp. 578.

PRIME, E. D. G. *Forty Years in the Turkish Empire.* (Memoirs of Rev. William Goodell.) Boston: American Board of Commissioners for Foreign Missions, 1891. Pp. 489.

RAMSAY, W. M. "Geographical Conditions Determining History and Religion in Asia Minor," *Geographical Journal* (London), Vol. XX (1902).

RECHAD NURI. *Yeşil Gece* ("Green Night"). Istanbul: Suhulet Kutuphanesi, 1928. Pp. 312.

REED, C. A. *Problems of American Education in the Near East.* Cambridge: Harvard University School of Education Dissertation, 1921. Pp. 523.

Relation of Missions to National or Governmental Education in Western Asia and Northern Africa, The. (A report typewritten for private purposes.)

RÉPUBLIQUE TURQUE—PRÉSIDENCE DU CONSEIL, OFFICE CENTRAL DE STATISTIQUE. *Annuaire statistique,* Vols. I–VI (1928–33).

RIHBANY, A. M. *Wise Men from the East and from the West.* Boston: Houghton Mifflin, 1922. Pp. 310.

RIZZO EDITIONS. *Code civil turc.* Istanbul: John A. Rizzo, 1928. Pp. 195.

——. *Code pénal turc.* Istanbul: John A. Rizzo, 1927. Pp. 182.

——. *Statut organique de la république de Turquie.* Istanbul: John A. Rizzo, 1929. Pp. 16.

ROSE, H. A. *The Darvishes.* (Revision of J. P. Brown's book of the same title.) Oxford: University Press, 1927. Pp. 496.

ROSS, E. A. *Social Psychology.* New York: Macmillan, 1921. Pp. 372.

ROSS, F. A.; FRY, C. L.; SIBLEY, E. *The Near East and American Philanthropy.* New York: Columbia University Press, 1929. Pp. 308.

SABA, JEAN S. *L'Islam et la nationalité.* Paris: Duchemin, 1931. Pp. 166.

SAID HALIM PASHA, PRINCE. "The Reform of Muslim Society," *Islamic Culture* (Hyderabad), I, No. 1 (January, 1927), 111–35.

SAILER, T. H. P. *The Moslem Faces the Future.* New York: Missionary Education Movement, 1926. Pp. 254.

SANHOURY, A. *Le califat.* Paris: Geuthner, 1926. Pp. 627.

SCHEVILL, F. *The Balkan Peninsula and the Near East.* London: G. Bell, 1922. Pp. 558.

SCHLICKLIN, J. *Angora, l'aube de la Turquie nouvelle (1919–1922).* Paris: Berger-Levrault, 1922. Pp. 350.

SCIPIO, L. A. *Survey of Education in Turkey.* (Privately organized and typewritten.) Istanbul, 1926.

Seçme Yazilar ("Chosen Writings"). (Collected by Yakup

Kadri, Falih Rifki, and Ruchen Echref.) Istanbul: Devlet Matbaasi, 1928. Pp. 254.

SERVIER, A. *Islam and the Psychology of the Musulman.* (Translated into English by A. S. Moss-Blundell.) New York: Scribner's, 1924. Pp. 271.

SOORMA, C. A. "Islam a Great Civilizing Force," *Islamic Review* (Woking), December, 1927, and January, 1928.

STAUFFER, M. (ed.). *Voices from the Near East.* New York: Missionary Education Movement, 1927. Pp. 141.

STODDARD, T. L. *The New World of Islam.* New York: Scribner's, 1921. Pp. 362.

STUERMER, DR. H. *Two War Years in Constantinople.* New York: Doran, 1917.

TCHARYKOW, N. V. "The Political Outlook of Islam," *Contemporary Review* (London), CXXXII (October, 1927), 455–60.

TEWFIK FIKRET. *Tarihi Kadim* ("Ancient History"). Istanbul: Nümune Matbaasi, 1928. Pp. 21.

TOYNBEE, A. J. *Survey of International Affairs, 1925,* Part I: "The Islamic World since the Peace Settlement." New York: Oxford Press, 1927.

————. "Turkey Revisited," *Asia,* XXX, No. 1 (January, 1930), 9–15, 68–70.

————. "The Turkish State of Mind," *Atlantic Monthly,* October. 1925, pp. 548–60.

————. *The Western Question in Greece and Turkey.* London: Constable, 1922. Pp. 420.

TOYNBEE, A. J., and KIRKWOOD, K. P. *Turkey.* New York: Scribner's, 1927. Pp. 329.

Turanians and pan-Turanianism, Manual on. (Prepared by the Geographical Section of the Naval Intelligence Division, Naval Staff Admiralty.) London: H. M. Stationery Office. Pp. 256.

Turkey, the Treaty with. (Statements, resolutions, and reports in favor of ratification of the Treaty of Lausanne.) New York: General Committee of American Institutions and Associations in favor of Ratification of the Treaty with Turkey, 1926.

"Turkey in Transformation," *Literary Digest,* December 12, 1925, pp. 18 f.

"Turkish Religion," *Review of Religions*, XXVII, No. 7 (July, 1928), 1–4.

Turkish Republic. *Laws for Private Schools*. Private English translation, 1922.

Turkish Sermons in the Age of the Republic. (In Turkish.) Istanbul: Prepared and composed by Maarif Kutuphanesi, 1927. Pp. 32.

"Turkish Suspicion of the Y.M.C.A.," *Literary Digest*, November 7, 1925, p. 31.

Türkiye Cümhuriyeti. *Instructions for Primary School Teachers*. (In Turkish.) Istanbul: Devlet Matbaasi, 1929. Pp. 61.

———. *Law for the Selection of Students for Study Abroad*, No. 1416. (In Turkish.) Istanbul: Devlet Matbaasi, 1929. Pp. 14.

———. *Ministry of Public Instruction's Book of Statistics, 1926–7*. (In Turkish.) Istanbul: Devlet Matbaasi, 1929.

———. *Turkish Citizenship Law*, No. 1312. (In Turkish.) Istanbul: Jihan Kutuphanesi, 1928. Pp. 7.

VAKA, DEMETRA. "An Imperial Enemy of Turkish Despotism," *Asia* (N.Y.), XXIV, No. 1 (January, 1924), 32–36, 72–73.

VALYI, F. *Spiritual and Political Revolutions in Islam*. London: Kegan Paul, 1925. Pp. 236.

VROOMAN, L. "The Meaning of the Turkish Revolution," *World Tomorrow* (N.Y.), XII, No. 6 (1929), 263 f.

———. "The Place of Missions in the New Turkey," *International Review of Missions*, XVIII, No. 71 (July, 1929), 401–9.

WAUGH, SIR TELFORD. "A Far-reaching Turkish Plan," *Journal of the Royal Central Asian Society*, XX, Part IV (October, 1933), 578–86.

———. "Nine Years of Republic in Turkey," *ibid.*, Part I (January, 1933), pp. 52–69.

WHITMAN, S. *Turkish Memories*. New York: Scribner's, 1914. Pp. 305.

WILLETT, H. L., JR. "Turkey Has Changed!" *Christian Century*, XLVIII, No. 1 (January 7, 1931), 14–16.

WILLIAMS, T. *Turkey: A World Problem of To-Day*. New York: Doubleday, Page, 1922. Pp. 336.

WILSON, S. G. *Modern Movements among Moslems*. New York: Revell, 1916. Pp. 305.

WOODS, H. C. *The Danger Zone of Europe.* Boston: Little, Brown, 1911. Pp. 324.

————. "Ghazi Mustapha Kemal Pasha: His Career, Power, and Achievements," *Fortnightly Review,* CXXVIII (November, 1927), 637–47.

YOUNG, G. *Constantinople.* London: Methuen, 1926. Pp. 310.

YOUSSOUF FEHMI. *La révolution ottomane (1908–1910).* Paris: V. Giard & E. Brière, 1911. Pp. 282.

YUNUS NADI. "La grande école," *La république* (Istanbul), October 3, 1929.

YUSUF ZIYA. *The Religion of Islam—First Book.* (In Turkish.) Istanbul: Amedî Matbaasi, 1929. Pp. 144.

ZIA BEY, MUFTY-ZADEH. *Speaking of the Turks.* New York: Duffield, 1922. Pp. 271.

ZIEMKE, DR. K. *Die neue Türkei (politische Entwicklung, 1914–1929).* Berlin and Leipzig: Deutsche Verlags—Anstalt Stuttgart, 1930. Pp. 550.

II. ADDITIONAL TITLES FOR REFERENCE

AGHNIDES, N. P. *Mohammedan Theories of Finance.* New York: Columbia University Ph.D. Dissertation, 1916. Pp. 541.

AHMED RUSTEM BEY. "Turkey Taking Her Place among the Nations," *Current History* (N.Y.), XXV, No. 5 (February, 1927), 669–75.

AHMED SABRI BEY. *When I Was a Boy in Turkey.* Boston: Lothrop, Lee, & Shepard, 1924. Pp. 165.

ARMSTRONG, H. *Turkey in Travail.* London, 1925.

BÉRARD, V. *Le sultan, l'Islam, et les puissances.* Paris: A. Colin, 1916. Pp. 443.

BLUNT, MRS. JOHN E. *The People of Turkey,* 2 vols. London: John Murray, 1878.

BRÉMOND, GENERAL. *L'Islam et les questions musulmanes au point de vue français.* Paris: Lavanzelle, 1924.

CHAMBERS, W. N. *Yoljuluk (Random Thoughts on a Life in Imperial Turkey).* London: Simpkin Marshall, 1928.

COBB, S. *The Real Turk*. Boston: Pilgrim Press, 1914. Pp. 301.

CURTIS, W. E. *The Turk and His Lost Provinces*. New York: Revell, 1903. Pp. 396.

CZAPLICKA, M. A. *The Turks of Central Asia*. Oxford: Clarendon Press, 1918. Pp. 242.

DAVEY, R. *The Sultan and His Subjects*. 2 vols. London: Chapman & Hall, 1897.

DRAPER, J. W. *History of the Intellectual Development of Europe*. 2 vols. New York: Harper, 1904.

DWIGHT, H. O. *Turkish Life in War Time*. London: Allen, 1881. Pp. 428.

EKREM, SELMA. *Unveiled*. New York, 1930.

GARNETT, L. *Home Life in Turkey*. New York: Macmillan, 1909. Pp. 296.

————. *The Women of Turkey and Their Folk Lore*. London: D. Nutt, 1893.

GAUDEFROY-DEMOMBYNES, M. *Les institutions musulmanes*. Paris: E. Flammarion, 1921. Pp. 192.

GREENWOOD, SIR G. *The Powers and the Turk*. London: Cecil Palmer, 1923. Pp. 76.

GROTHE, H. *Deutschland, die Türkei und der Islam: zwischen Krieg und Frieden*. Leipzig: S. Hirzel, 1914.

HAMLIN, C. *My Life and Times*. Istanbul: Robert College, 1924. Pp. 540.

HEIDBORN, A. *Manuel de droit public et administratif de l'Empire Ottoman*. Vienna, 1909.

HOWARD, H. N. *The Partition of Turkey*. Norman: University of Oklahoma Press, 1931.

IKBAL ALI SHAH, SIRDAR. *Kamal: Maker of Modern Turkey*. London: Joseph, 1934. Pp. 297.

KRAUSE, P. *Die Türkei*. Leipzig: Teubner, 1918. Pp. 134.

LAMMENS, H. *L'Islam, croyances et institutions*. Beyrouth, 1926. Pp. 288.

McCULLAGH, F. *The Fall of Abd-ul-Hamid*. London: Methuen, 1910. Pp. 316.

MACFARLANE, C. *Kismet, or the Doom of Turkey*. London: Bosworth, 1853. Pp. 452.

————. *Turkey and Its Destiny*. 2 vols. Philadelphia: Lea & Blanchard, 1856.

MARRIOTT, J. A. R. *The Eastern Question*. Oxford, 1917. Pp. 456.

MARVIN, F. S. (ed.). *The Unity of Western Civilization*. Oxford: H. Milford, 1915. Pp. 315.

——. *Western Races and the World*. Oxford: H. Milford, 1922. Pp. 264.

NASIM SOUSA. *The Capitulatory Régime of Turkey: Its History, Origin, and Nature*. Baltimore: Johns Hopkins University Press, 1933. Pp. 378.

OECONOMOS, L. *The Martyrdom of Smyrna and Eastern Christendom*. London: Allen & Unwin, 1922. Pp. 237.

OGILVIE, B. H. "The New Woman of Turkey," *Current History* (N.Y.), 1924, pp. 805–13.

OHSSON, M. D'. *Tableau général de l'Empire Ottoman*. 7 vols. Paris, 1788.

PAILLARÈS, M. *Le kémalisme devant les Alliés*. Constantinople: Editions du "Bosphore," 1922. Pp. 494.

PATRICK, M. M. *A Bosporus Adventure*. Palo Alto: Stanford University Press, 1934. Pp. 293.

——. *Under Five Sultans*. New York, 1930.

POYNTER, M. A. *When Turkey Was Turkey*. London: Routledge, 1921.

RAMSAY, W. M. *Impressions of Turkey during Twelve Years' Wanderings*. London, 1897.

——. *The Revolution in Constantinople and Turkey*. London: Hodder & Stoughton, 1909. Pp. 323.

RIGGS, C. T. "Turkey—Fifty Years Ago and Now," *Missionary Review of the World* (N.Y.), January, 1928, pp. 13–20.

SHERIDAN, C. *A Turkish Kaleidoscope*. London: Duckworth, 1926.

SHERRILL, C. H. *A Year's Embassy to Mustafa Kemal*. New York: Scribner's, 1934.

Stambul und das moderne Türkenthum. Leipzig, 1877. Pp. 324.

TOYNBEE, A. J. *Turkey, a Past and a Future*. New York: Doran, 1917. Pp. 85.

Turkish Empire, The. London: Religious Tract Society, *ca.* 1878. Pp. 316.

VAKA, D. *The Unveiled Ladies of Stamboul*. Boston: Houghton Mifflin, 1923, Pp. 261.

WASHBURN, G. *Fifty Years in Constantinople*. Boston: Houghton Mifflin, 1909. Pp. 317.

WAUGH, SIR TELFORD. *Turkey, Yesterday, To-Day, and To-Morrow*. London, 1930.

INDEX